A MEETING OF HORROR-IBLE MINDS!

Encounter the John Stanley who hosted "Creature Features" :
the John Stanley who covered movie and TV celebrities :
(1960-1993). Together, they take you into the incredible

RAY BRADBURY
Like never before you'll discover Ray's inner feelings and depth-of-thought as Stanley probes
the author's deepest emotions about how he writes his classic short stories and novels . . .

ROBERT ("PSYCHO") BLOCH
This King of Horror bravely plunges into the bottomless depths of how he writes horror tales.

ADAM WEST / BURT WARD
TV's first **BATMAN** and **ROBIN** team carry you into the heights of Gotham City.

KIRK ALYN / CHRISTOPHER REEVE / DEAN CAIN
You'll be "Up, up and away!" meeting **SUPERMAN** from serials, TV, and movies.

NOEL NEILL / PHYLLIS COATES / TERI HATCHER
You'll thrive on three different portrayals of glamorous leggy newswoman Lois Lane.

STEPHEN KING
America's best-selling major horror novelist recounts his younger days . . . and King's killer car
CHRISTINE roars in high gear onto Stanley's "Creature Features" set.

IRWIN ALLEN / RICHARD BASEHART / JUNE LOCKHART
The prolific fantasy TV producer ("Voyage to the Bottom of the Sea," "Lost in Space,"
"Time Tunnel") turned out to be a real-life horror story for interviewer Stanley.

JULIE ADAMS / BEN CHAPMAN
You'll be exposed to Julie's beautiful, expensive legs and Chapman's Black Lagoon Creature.

STAN LEE / NICHOLAS HAMMOND
Learn what made Lee the Marvel of comic-book creators by traveling through time to 1976
followed by an encounter with TV's very first **SPIDERMAN**.

BRUCE LEE / BRANDON LEE
Bruce is Kato on **THE GREEN HORNET** when Stanley meets him in 1966 . . . 25 years later
he meets son Brandon following in his father's footprints . . . and then, DEATH STRIKES!

BUSTER CRABBE / MAX VON SYDOW
Crabbe reflects on 1930s "Flash Gordon" /Von Sydow's Ming the Merciless is strictly 1980 evil.

BOB WILKINS / JOHN STANLEY
Never before told . . . how two former horror hosts are "resurrected" and appear in scores of
special shows in the Bay Area, once again entertaining their forever-loyal audiences.

STANLEY'S FAMILY SECRET ABOUT OSCAR...
Not Wilde! Not Hammerstein! Not the Grouch! About the Academy Award designer!

MORE THAN 780 PHOTOGRAPHS
(SCORES IN PRINT FOR THE FIRST TIME!)

DEDICATIONS

I've been married to my beautiful wife ERICA for 59 years and she has kept me on the straight and narrow. As well as working many years for the Tax Group of San Francisco, she was my producer during the "Creature Features" years. Here you see her with Buddy Ebsen when he guested on the show in 1981. She took care of Leonard Nimoy, Christopher Lee, Ray Bradbury and literally hundreds of others celebs during our six-year run.

In 1990, my son **RUSS STANLEY** (above left) joined the San Francisco Giants and soon was Vice President of Ticket Sales, a position he still holds today. In 2010 he was honored for his 20th year and I was there next to him as he got ready to throw the first pitch of a Giants game. Beside Russ and me are his daughters **SHELBY** and **JORDYN STANLEY**. Both had exciting college educations (Jordyn was in Rome for several semesters) and in their younger years we had great trips to London, L.A. and Montana. Both are now in their early 20s and have full-time jobs. (Above center) **TRISTA STANLEY** is a great daughter who has sired three wonderful children: **HARPER**, who is eleven, **MEGHAN**, who is now 21 and works for Home Depot outside of Davis, and **LILLITH**, 19, who plans to head into the medical field.

Thanks to **DIXIE DELLAMORTO** (left, wife of the horror host **MR. LOBO**) for creating the cover for this book and for her wonderful caricatures in my 2011 book "The Gang That Shot Up Hollywood." And thank you Erik for carrying the torch for me and Bob Wilkins through modern day.

To one of my best friends, **DENNIS WILLIS** (right), my thanks for laying out this book and for tolerating me at a time when my life has had some rough moments. Given the number of photos and pieces of artwork, it wasn't easy but Dennis pulled it off. You can catch his weekly music series, "Soundwaves TV," in the San Francisco-Bay Area at soundwavesTV.com and on KOFY-TV Channel 20.

WAYNE HESS (above left), an Army paratrooper who fought in the Gulf War and served 32 years in law enforcement, retiring as the Emergency Services Lt. For the San Francisco Sheriff's Department, was major in producing my 2007 life biography "I Was a TV Horror Host" and "John Stanley Meets Jack the Ripper." Recently he became a pilot and now flies above the Bay Area.

BOB ANTHONY (above middle) is still a devoted "Creature Features" fan who created and wore wonderful costumes, and who often appeared in my in-studio sketches. Erica and I were very sorry to hear about the passing of Bob's mom a few years ago.

Thanks goes to **ANNE FRANCIS** (above right), whom I interviewed in 1965 when she was starring as a sexy private eye in the TV series "Honey West." That noon, while wearing a provocative mini-skirt, she signed this "Forbidden Planet" photo of her with Robby the Robot.

KENN DAVIS (above) did more than 75 sketches for my "Creature Features Movie Guide" series and most of them are on pages 139-146 in this edition. I met Kenn Davis working at the San Francisco Chronicle in the art department and together we wrote and produced the 1978 feature film "Nightmare in Blood" and co-wrote the 1980 Dell paperback novel "Bogart '48." We also collaborated on "The Dark Side," the 1976 novel about San Francisco private eye Carver Bascombe. Sadly, Kenn passed away in January 2010.

FRANNIE BAXTER (right), portrayer of Princess Leia (see page 241) the day Christopher Lee guested on "Creature Features," currently works for See's Candies and drops off choice nibbles every Christmas and other holidays as well. How sweet she/it is.

Thank you, **TONY VELLA** (left), for driving me to and from dozens of personal appearances during the past decade, and thanks for your wonderful stuntman and stunt rigger work in major movies ("San Andreas") and TV ("Nash Bridges"). Hey, you're also good at make-up.

Best wishes to one-time movie publicist **WALTER VON HAUFFE** (below right), who introduced me to countless stars over three decades. He described the setting in which you see him as "the Fountain of Youth . . . the guy, not the fountain."

Besides kicking off the return of Stanley/Wilkins, **SCOTT MOON** (right with Bob) was there to move the Wilkins family from Reno to Sacramento. In August 2006, a number of us horror movie hosts loaded a moving van and took off with Scott at the wheel. Also helping out was Tom Wyrsch.

The Career That Dripped With Horror

Published by Creatures at Large Press
Copyright © 2021 by John Stanley

ISBN : 9798756674057

THE CAREER THAT DRiPPED WiTH

HORROR

REMEMBERED BY
JOHN STANLEY

A SEQUEL TO I WAS A TV **HORROR** HOST

BOOK LAYOUT BY
DENNIS WILLIS

COVER ART BY
DIXIE DELLAMORTO

HORROR iCON SKETCHES BY
KENN DAVIS
[YOU GOTTA SEE PAGES 139–146]

DAVID EDWARD SMITH
[YOU'LL FIND HIM ON PAGE 224]

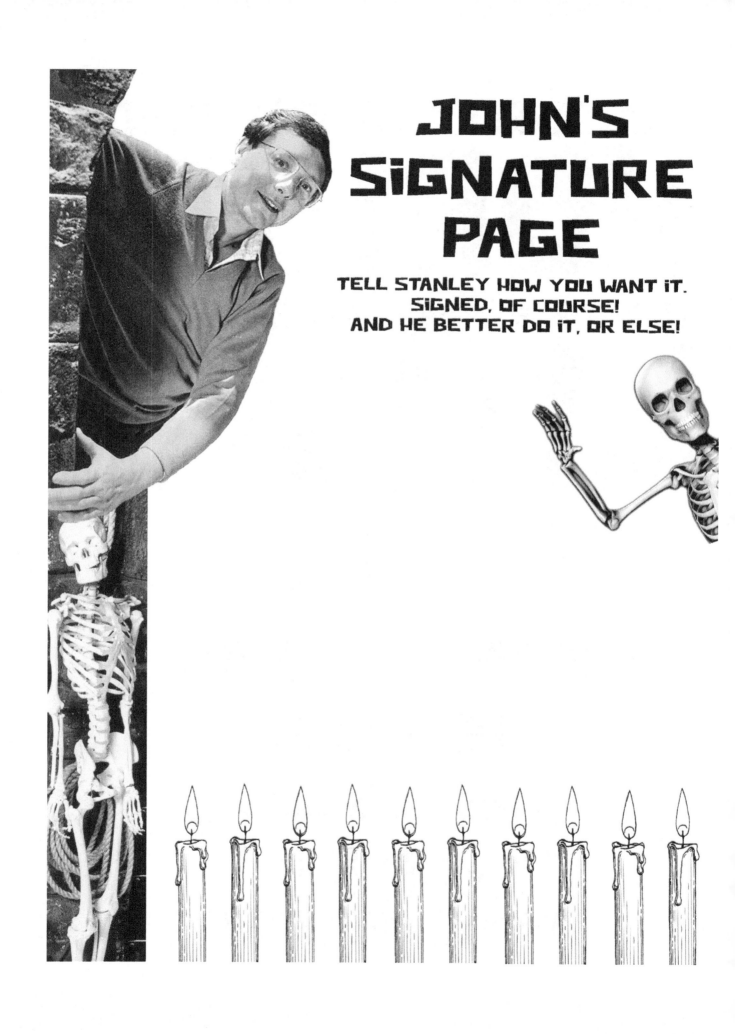

PRE-INTRODUCTION
(THE *REAL* INTRO COMES LATER)

The Clash of Two Mighty Media
Figures Trapped in One Bloodified Body

Excuse me, I'm John Stanley. And it's important I talk to you. Man to man.

What the hell are you talking about? You're not John Stanley. I'm John Stanley!

Hey, bleary-eyed! I've got some hot headline news for you. We're both John Stanley!

Say what? Bullroar! There's no way we can be the same person. You have to be yourself. I'm me. You're you. Neither one of us can be someone else we're not.

I'm not someone else. I'm me. And, don't take it so hard, I'm also you.

Me? I'm me! Not you! That's all bullroar! And you . . . you're a schizophrenic. I'm calling the nearest mental ward. You need more than a good psychiatrist. You need a rugged, rigidly strong straitjacket.

Watch it. Better not call a psycho house. If they come, they'll haul you away. Along with me. Didn't think of that, did you? We'd both end up in that straitjacket, being strapped down together in some fruitcake ward in a house of madness, screaming our hearts out for a beautiful nurse to loosen our straps.

That's John Stanley, newspaperman, standing with movie tough guy Howard Duff, also famed for being the star of radio's private eye show "Adventures of Sam Spade."

What're you trying to do? Drive me nuts?

Listen, jerkola. There are two of us. See, I'm the reporter John Stanley. The guy who worked in the newspaper business for 33 years as an entertainment writer. At the San Francisco Chronicle. Downtown at Fifth and Mission. That's the part of you that's me, whether you like it or not. And to prove it, I'm italicizing myself as I speak, as I try to explain our complexities.

I noticed that. Italic certainly sets you apart from me. I have a normal type-face. It's called Arial Black. It makes me upright and bold. And brave as hell. But you, you're a complete nut job! Totally insane! Utterly psycho bonkers! Lights must be flashing in your eyes! You must be seeing stars!

Exactly. You and me couldn't have said it better. I interviewed hundreds of them. Movies, TV series, night clubs, theatrical plays. Some of the greatest stars of the 20ᵗʰ Century. James Stewart, Mae West, Robert Mitchum, Fred MacMurray, Joseph Cotten, Clint Eastwood five times. Karl Malden four times. Countless others, not forgetting to mention the beauties who exhibited intellectualism when I bowed before them: Carol Channing, Lauren Bacall, Jane Russell, Joan Collins, Noel Neill, Kathryn Grant, Carroll Baker, Ida Lupino, Marie Windsor, Shirley Jones, Carol Burnett . . . and one of the most memorable comedy stars of all time, the one and only, Lucille Ball.

I loved Lucy too. She was the Desilu lady who made "Star Trek" possible. I told her story in my autobiography "I Was a TV Horror Host." You can't scare the pants off me with double talk.

Every word I'm saying is fact. The stories appeared in the Pink Section of the San Francisco Chronicle from 1961 through 1993. Hundreds and hundreds. No, make that thousands and thousands. And I say that with humility. I'm blushing with all the modesty I can administer within my humanity.

And I'm flushing. To get you down the drain, out of my system. I suppose you also met Barbara Stanwyck, Barbara Eden, Mitzi Gaynor, Phyllis Diller! I bet you interviewed them too. Ha!

This is TV horror host John Stanley holding the head of one of his producers, who turned out to be, in his own words, "a basket case."

As a matter of fact, I did. So that's my John Stanley. Try to beat that, bananahead! Oh yeah, bananahead was a demeaning term used by Sam Fuller, the writer-producer-director who became a good friend of mine. Remember "The Steel Helmet" *and* "Naked Kiss"?

I remember Sam's *"Shock Corridor."* Close to pure horror! And that's what I'm about. Listen, Softbrain. My John Stanley achieved more than mere words. Me, I was a TV horror host in the San Francisco-Bay Area, at KTVU Channel 2. The most popular show in the Northern California market! Called "Creature Features." Six years running. I followed in the footsteps of Bob Wilkins, who did the show for eight. Between the two of us, 14 years of Saturday night success. We entertained a generation that has never forgotten us. But you, you were merely a journalist whose stories appeared in the Sunday Datebook of the Chronicle. Just a byline, a name above the story. Big deal! Those readers, if there were any, wouldn't have a clue what you looked like as a human being!

The one and only Bob Wilkins, horror host supreme!

THE CAREER THAT DRIPPED WITH HORROR

But me! My John Stanley, seen by literally millions of Bay Area television viewers, puts your so-called fandom to shame. How does it feel to be unseen? Merely a name. Not a single reader could I.D. you in a police line-up. Did I mention you're a complete, thorough, one hundred percent jerkola? No, one thousand percent!

You think public identity is everything? I wrote with style. Panache. They looked for my byline on Sunday morning before anyone else's. Well, maybe some read Herb Caen's column first. But here's the way I figure it, John who isn't me. I'm the John who is me! Experienced with interviewing techniques, intellectual concepts, brainy movements through the heart of the Universe. Hundreds of times I sat on a sound stage in a Hollywood studio, and I'd talk to Walter Brennan or Lloyd Bridges or Glenn Ford or Anne Francis or Woody Allen, and I'd ask questions designed to probe their psyches.
So they would reveal their deepest, most profane inner workings. So I could translate their feelings and their histories into emotional stories that grabbed the readers by their vital organs and wouldn't let go. And that's what I want to do now. Get you to open up and yatter away about your "Creature Features."

Headline: Kid Reporter Makes Good

What the hell would I do all that for?

Because I wanna do a book that blends together what is best about both of us. A collection of interviews and reviews about horror and sci-fi. And fantasy, too.

Wait! That's my incredible world. Now you're starting, slowly, to get smart.

So, you admit there is "us." Well, here's the deal. The book'll be entitled "The Career That Dripped With Horror." And what I want from you is the best material you came up with during your run as "Creature Features" host.

I'm finally getting the message. My territory: Horror. Science-fiction. Fantasy. The Supernatural. Movies, books, actors, authors. All those who've contributed to the genre of gore. To the pure essence of horror. And to the grotesquely, grossly, grimly, ghastly, ghostly world of the utterly weird.
Or something like that.

You're finally beginning to sound like someone with a profound, incredibly uncommon brain. Someone who knows what you and me are thinking.

I don't need you to ask me questions. I can talk about "Creature Features" on my own. Without help from you. I had this great set at KTVU. A dungeon with a cell, guillotine, special chair with human skulls embedded at the top, a coffin for my guests to sit on, a skeleton for company, a basket for human heads.

Ray Bradbury with John Stanley, 1979.

I interviewed the likes of Arnold Schwarzenegger, Christopher Lee, Vincent Price, Ray Harryhausen, Robert Bloch, Ray Bradbury, Roger Corman. I became the Bay Area's expert about the world of science-fiction, fantasy and horror. It extended from classics such as "Alien" and its director Ridley Scott to "Star Trek" movies with Leonard Nimoy, William Shatner and Jimmy Doohan. I was there in L.A. in 1980 for the World Premiere of "The Empire Strikes Back." Talked exclusively with Luke Skywalker and Princess Leia and Billy Dee Williams. Did I mention George Takei? He used to call and let me know when he was coming to San Francisco so I could book him for my next show. The Disney Studio did the same thing, bringing the star of the studio's latest movie to town on Friday morning, because that's when I taped my shows. Stick that into your journalism meat-grinder and churn it, pal!

What was your philosophical approach?

You mean my ghastly, hideously ugly approach. Monsters, extraterrestrial life-form units and assorted entities of evil don't need philosophies.

Okay, so it was your hideous, slime-covered approach. But dig down deep, Stanley. Don't be shallow like you appear most of the time. Deepen your commentary.

I'll be deep, believe me. I'll sink so much you'll never find the lower depths of my thinking. See, I assumed the point of view of my curious-minded viewers. They were always asking me about the unanswered mysteries of life. What I came to call "The Invisible World Around Us." Wanted to know if UFOs existed. Was there life after death? Do we turn into ectoplasmic goo wearing a bed sheet and go boo to any who? Where did shambling zombies, howling werewolves, muttering mummies, blood-guzzling vampires and other entities of evil, such as the walking dead of George Romero, hail from? And what was this fascination we all had seeing these creatures in movies year after year, never growing tired of being lambasted with the same old cliches and stereotypes?

Two of my favorite followers and longtime fans, who both specialize in monster makeup: (top) Don Bishop and movie stuntman Tony Vella (bottom). You will learn more about these beings a little later.

THE CAREER THAT DRIPPED WITH HORROR

Vampires drinking blood. Werewolves tearing folks apart. Zombies mindlessly coming down the hallway. It's always death at the movies that we love most.

Oh yeah, all that crap was very intellectual. Now please, could you continue to define your job, but in more graphic and colorful images?

I'll give you images. I was trapped in a dungeon of horror, captive to eviscerated evils, a prisoner of putrescent pandemonium. Buried up to my armpits in a gore pool created by a thousand vampiric bites, fanged werewolf attacks, baying hellhound teeth gnashes and man-made monsters gurgling their insanity in a bloodbath filled with chainsawed arms and legs.

Not bad, though not quite as philosophical as I would have told it.

But wait. We are in agreement to do the book.

Yes, but we must first meld our minds together, so they are inseparable.

You're right. We must mentally stand together, side by side.

Just one voice that will describe the events, the individuals. Whether it's journalistic or Creature Featurish. We'll share the pages together and take the reader into a kingdom of horror and science-fiction. Now, get ready to lower your mind. And so that we're on the same track, think of horror hostess icon Elvira. That'll make sure we share an image as we join forces. Now, take a deep breath . . . let out the hot air . . . and join your mind with mine. And please, don't forget to think of Elvira, Mistress of the Dark.

Hey, your brain doesn't seem so awful after all. Hey, I think this is gonna work now that we're joined together.

Call it United Artists. And please, no more italics.

So shall it be. From now on, Garamond typeface is how we will present the real introduction. A genuine presentation of history. About a period of time that has become immortal and a stepping stone in our lives. A touch of "Creature Features" past never before presented to our fan base.

THE NIGHT "CREATURE FEATURES" DIED: A PERSONAL ACCOUNT BY BOTH JOHN STANLEYS

IT WAS EARLY AUGUST, 1984. "Creature Features" had dominated Bay Area television since January 1971, first hosted by Bob Wilkins through March, 1979. I had taken over after that, and now I had to announce to my vast, loyal audience that the show would be leaving the air in just three weeks. Although the series was doing well in the ratings, Channel 2's general manager did not approve of the current types of horror films being produced – too gory for his reserved, sophisticated tastes.

STANLEY AND BOB WILKINS DOING THE FINAL CREATURE FEATURES SHOW ON SEPT. 1, 1984

So, it was time for "Creature Features" to be discarded into the Cauldron of Hell. That night my guest was Bay Area special-effects artist Chris Walas (with me at left), best known at that time for his

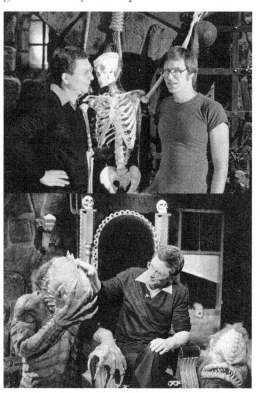

work on "Gremlins." He had brought some of his "monsters" (actors in costumes he had designed) and they began weeping their hearts out when I reluctantly made the announcement. Out of the Walas bedlam rose the head of a crocodile–all because my closing line for the opening segment was about the shedding of what I called "crocodile tears."

Soon, indeed, and sadly, I did my final show in which my special guest was the former host himself, cigar-chomping Bob Wilkins. Bob will always be remembered for creating the motto "Watch Horror Films, Keep America Strong" and for being the only horror TV host who wore an ordinary suit and tie and never tried to portray an inhuman being in a monster's costume.

He sat in a yellow rocking chair (being able to roll back and forth minimized any on-camera fears he may have had) and held a cigar which he never really smoked. He felt it made him appear tougher than he really was. With us that evening were many publicity figures

and close associates who had helped me with the series over the past five-and-a-half years.

After that I continued at the San Francisco Chronicle (where I had started working as a copyboy in 1960) covering movies and TV series produced in Hollywood. And it was time to write more editions in my "Creature Features Movie Guide" series.

THE CAREER THAT DRIPPED WITH HORROR

The first book had emerged in 1981 through my newly founded publishing company, Creatures at Large Press. That was followed in 1984 by a second edition published by Warner Books out of New York. Down the highway of self-publishing, I did editions three ("Revenge of the Creature Features Movie Guide," 1987) and four ("The Creature Features Movie Guide Strikes Again," 1994). A New York publisher, Berkley Boulevard, would publish the final editions five (1996) and six (2000). During this period, I saw at least six or seven horror/sci-fi feature films a week so each edition was loaded with updated material about films old and brand new.

Creatures at Large Press also thrived in the 1980s with the publication of two offbeat books. "Lost in Time and Space with Lefty Feep" (1987, seen at right) was by Robert Bloch, most famed for writing the novel on which Alfred Hitchcock's "Psycho" was based. He agreed to let me reprint his short stories about a race track tout that had first appeared in *Fantastic Adventures*, a popular pulp magazine during the 1940s. We were going to do two more collections of the Feep fantasy yarns but Bob fell ill and died in 1994. If only he had not smoked all those damn cigarettes. I still fondly remember Bob Bloch whom I had first interviewed for Calvin T.

Beck's magazine, *Castle of Frankenstein* (issue #16, 1971). In the fall of 1982 Bloch had appeared on my "Creature Features" show and was one terrific guest with a grand sense of humor (see page 117).

The other book, "Them Ornery Mitchum Boys," was an autobiography by John Mitchum, brother of Robert Mitchum, which I published in 1989 as hardcover and trade paperback. It was a rousing history of the Mitchums with 356 photographs, showcasing John's career as a character actor in TV shows and feature films and Robert's rise to Hollywood stardom as a leading man for many decades. John is best remembered for writing "America, Why I Love Her," a poem read by John Wayne. But alas, John Mitchum was not an easy soul to work with. He was always broke and always drank too much, stepping all over his own future. The hardcover edition signed by both brothers soon sold out, and today is valued at hundreds of dollars if you can find a copy. The paperback, now out of print, has been given much praise by critics.

Meanwhile, Bob Wilkins stayed busy running his own advertising business with Chuck E. Cheese Parlors as his major client. Then, in 1993, Bob closed his Oakland, CA., agency and moved with his wife Sally to Reno, Nevada, where he became an advertising executive for John Ascuaga's Nugget, a major hotel/gambling casino in Sparks, East Reno. The very location where ironically in the 1960s I had interviewed Bertha the Elephant (yes, a major stage star along with her baby Tina), singer-comedian Dennis Day, Liberace and Jimmy Durante. But then Bob was stricken with a heart attack and retired, living a quiet life with his wife Sally on the outskirts of Reno.

Me, I continued to cover movies and television series for the Chronicle until December 7, 1993. No, it wasn't my Pearl Harbor. I had finally reached a point where I needed to focus more on writing my movie guides. And it was time for a new career. In 1995 I became an instructor for Bay Area Classic Learning, an offshoot of Elderhostel, which today is known as Road Scholar. From all over America senior citizens, what I like to call the World War II Generation, came to the Bay Area to hotels where I appeared with special programs about the entertainment world. These covered the careers of Frank Sinatra, Bob Hope, Bing Crosby and many others, as well as classes on Jewish comedians, movies made in San Francisco, the life of jazz artist Louis Armstrong, the beautiful female stars of movies, Hollywood musicals, etc.

David Kleinberg was my Sunday Datebook editor for 13 years (1980-1993) and then invited me to be an Elderhostel instructor, specializing in the world of entertainment. Dave has also been a stand-up comedian and performer of one-man shows.

BUSBY BERKELEY AND BEYOND: THE HOLLYWOOD MUSICAL

AN ELDERHOSTEL OFFERING BY JOHN STANLEY

SHTICKS & STEINS: THE JEWISH CONTRIBUTION TO COMEDY

AN ELDERHOSTEL OFFERING BY JOHN STANLEY

CROSBY & HOPE: ON THE ROAD AGAIN
An Elderhostel Offering By John Stanley

The most popular was about Jewish comedians, mainly those I had personally met. I was able to share their stories and quotations with my audiences, and they loved hearing about Rodney Dangerfield, Shelley Berman, Jack Benny, Sid Caesar, George Burns, Milton Berle, and countless others. I loved meeting the attendees in hotels in Pacifica, Tiburon, San Rafael, Napa Valley and Burlingame. My boss during those years was David Kleinberg, who had also been my boss for 13 years as the editor of the Chronicle's Sunday Datebook. Ultimately, he headed up the most heavily attended Elderhostel offerings in the entire United States. (Above are three of my eight booklets.)

And then, suddenly and totally unexpectedly, something incredible happened in 1998.

Something that was going to change my life, and Bob Wilkins', forever.

HERE IS THE MAN: TOM WYRSCH . . .

. . . WHO WOULD BRING "CREATURE FEATURES" BACK TO LIFE IN THE YEAR 2000 A. D.

THE NIGHT "CREATURE FEATURES" ROSE FROM THE GRAVE
. . . AND A FRANCHISE CAME TO LIFE LIKE NEVER BEFORE

First, you must understand there were "Creature Features" fans who had never forgotten the shows, or the hosts, who were scattered everywhere. In Sacramento was a fan named Scott Moon, a printing and graphic design specialist, who interviewed Bob Wilkins in 1995 for the first issue of his *Planet X* Magazine.

When Scott put out issue #2 in 1998, it was Bob's idea for Scott to hold a publicity party for the magazine at a popular Sacramento night club, Harlow's. "And I'll host the show," Bob told Scott. Among the attendees were special effects artists from Industrial Light and Magic and a newly-rising horror host, Erik Lobo. And wearing a costume from the 1953 sci-fi thriller "Robot Monster" was Scott Moon, a total lover and expert on horror and sci-fi cinema.

Scott Moon, editor of "Planet X Magazine," was among the first to bring Bob Wilkins back before the public with a show in Sacramento, CA.

Here his is, the unforgettable Mr. Lobo, who became a horror host at the suggestion of Bob Wilkins. An expert at tongue in cheek he's hosted "Cinema Insomnia" for 20 years without a single viewer falling asleep. At least that's what he whispered into my ear, waking me up.

Also hanging around the edges was another hardened fan, Bob Ekman, who has gone on to present countless "Psychotronix" film programs at Foothill College (in Los Altos Hills) for many years. These shows have consisted largely of short-subject films of all genres.

It was about a year later that an old "Creature Features" fan stopped at the Tiburon Lodge where I was doing a class on "Jazz in the Movies." He was Tom Wyrsch from nearby Petaluma, and he wanted to know if I would be willing to join ranks with Bob Wilkins and appear before the public in special shows. Tom, a hardened fan of the series for its 14-year duration, said he wanted to keep the tradition alive. I was flattered and told Tom I would love to participate. Then Tom told me he had already published "The Bob Wilkins Scrapbook" and now wanted to bring out "The John Stanley Scrapbook." I agreed and began rounding up photos and other historical material.

THE BOB WILKINS SCRAPBOOK

And then came the event that really opened the door and set Tom's wishes into motion. An old movie theater in Oakland called the Parkway Speakeasy Cinema was where a young entrepreneur named Will "The Thrill" Viharo (son of actor Robert Viharo) and his beautiful wife Monica (known as "The Tiki Goddess") presented thematic movie nights on a regular basis.

Tom had arranged with Will to set up a "Creature Features" evening. That event occurred in October 2000 as Bob and I arrived in a limousine, an idea suggested by Bill Longen, who had been one of my film editors during my "Creature Features" reign. We also walked on a red carpet into the theater lobby.

Waiting for a limo to the Parkway Cinema: (L-R) Bob Shaw, Bob Wilkins, yours truly John Stanley and Tom Wyrsch.

It was Bill Longen (above right) who came up with the idea for the limousine and the red carpet.

The very first "Creature Features" reunion show was hosted by Will "The Thrill" Viharo, a writer of noirish mystery novels, at the original Parkway Theater in Oakland.

Assisting "The Thrill" was another thrill, his wife Monica aka "The Tiki Goddess."

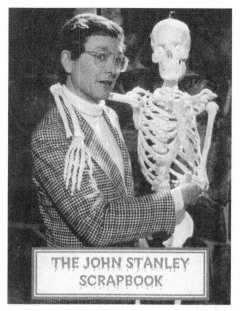

THE JOHN STANLEY
SCRAPBOOK

On the Parkway stage, with Will "The Thrill" hosting and Monica actively visible, Bob and I answered questions from an enthusiastic audience that had grown up watching our programs and still remembered them vividly. With us on stage that evening was Bob Shaw, who had once served as Bob's co-producer and then rose in the ranks at KTVU, Channel 2, to become its long-running movie critic.

Soon after that Marvelous, Super-manly event, Tom published "The John Stanley Scrapbook." It was just in the nick of time for a new, exciting phase of my existence on This Island Earth.

Because I want you to imagine: Bob Wilkins and John Stanley, side by side once again on a regular basis.

In September 2001 Scott Moon was active again with another horror-evening at Harlow's in Sacramento. This time Bob and I co-hosted and presented Vitina Marcus, who had portrayed the Green Girl on "Lost in Space," and Ernie Fosselius, who had made the "Star Wars" comedy spoof "Hardware Wars." Directing the show was Erik Lobo. Bob was so impressed he suggested that Lobo should morph into a TV host, and soon he did, becoming Mr. Lobo with the series "Cinema Insomnia." At every event we attended, Lobo loyally stayed at Bob's side for the next decade.

LEFT: That's me sitting next to Vitina Marcus, the "Green Girl" on "Lost in Space," and Bob Wilkins at Harlow's in Sacramento in 2001. RIGHT: Posing with the Wookiee Monster from "Hardware Wars" are the short film's director Ernie Fosselius, Will "the Thrill" Viharo, and horror host Mr. Lobo.

THE WONDERFUL HUMAN BEINGS AND HORROR HOSTS WHO SURROUNDED ME AND BOB WILKINS FOR A DECADE AND MORE

Now Bob and I would appear annually at the WonderCon (which moved from its original Oakland location to the Moscone Convention Center in downtown San Francisco in 2003) and at least once a year at the Parkway with Will the Thrill and tantalizing Monica. In San Francisco, we did specialty programs at the Castro and Balboa movie theaters that were part of Bob Johnson's Bay Area Film Events. (That's Johnson, still busy today, to the right).

THE CAREER THAT DRIPPED WITH HORROR

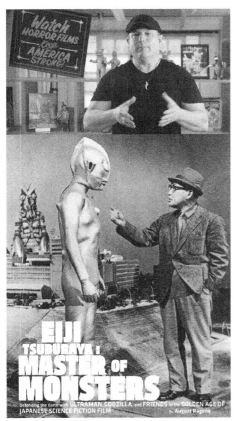

Helping with some of these shows was Japanese movie-monster expert August Ragone (top left), author of the biography "Eiji Tsuburaya: Master of Monsters." Guests included Julie Adams for a weekend of "The Creature from the Black Lagoon." Also at the Castro was the beautiful Veronica Carlson, a star of many Hammer horror films and one of the sweetest ladies imaginable. (She would return to our CreatureCon in 2018.)

A major event in 2003, and one I still remember fondly, was when Bob and I were honored by Broadcast Legends, a Bay Area organization dedicated to radio and TV personalities active and retired. In a hotel at the foot of the San Francisco Bay Bridge, we met some of the finest media personalities of our time. I had the opportunity to read a poem I had written about Bob Wilkins – a comedy "ode" you will find on pages 127-134. Also, Bob and I were interviewed and photographed that same afternoon by documentary film-maker John E. Hudges, who was making "American Scary," a historical account of horror hosts that would finally be released in 2007 and shown at the Roxie Theater in San Francisco.

In 2003, Scott Moon set up a bobwilkins.net website, using rare photos and memorabilia, and that site is still going today with new redesigns every few years. There is also a John Stanley website (stanleybooks.net), which you can access today thanks to Mr. Moon.

TOP: Julie Adams had dinner with me and wife Erica when she appeared at the Castro Theater. There I was, sitting beside the most memorable member of the cast - besides the Black Lagoon Creature himself, of course! BOTTOM: Veronica Carlson, star of many Hammer horror classics.

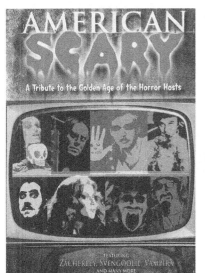

The fans were continually coming up to me and Bob to tell us of their love for our shows, and the circumstances of watching. It was on Saturday night and, because the VCR had not yet arrived, they had to stay home to see the show. They would watch it, if not alone, with brother and sister, mother and father, boyfriend or girlfriend. And our shows became indelibly embedded in their memories. It was a part of growing up they would never forget.

A highlight was the appearance of Cassandra Peterson, although she did not wear her costume of Elvira, Mistress of the Dark. I had first interviewed Cassandra in 1986 at her home in Los Angeles, and in 1991 she and I had recorded shows with Joe Bob Briggs at the Magic Castle in Hollywood. (We would have one more meeting at the 2012 WonderCon held in Anaheim.)

The only disappointment when Bob and I met Cassandra Peterson: she wasn't wearing her Elvira costume. She was screening "Elvira's Haunted Hills," which she co-wrote.

During these years some currently-popular horror hosts and other horror-related personalities joined our ranks and appeared with us at major events. Prominent was Mr. Lobo, whose "Cinema Insomnia" continues to this day out of Pennsylvania, where he and his wife-artist Dixie Dellamorto now live. Dixie is an artist who did several caricatures for my book "The Gang That Shot Up Hollywood" (2011).

Although he appeared for several years with us, it's been a while since I've seen Ernie Fosselius, maker of the "Star Wars" parody "Hardware Wars."

His close companion, Karen Lewis, was a stage actress who once did a play with "The Munsters" star Al "Grandpa" Lewis, and eventually married him. She asked for help in editing her detailed autobiography "I Married a Munster," and it was a memorable read which can be ordered online.

Also within our ranks was Miss Misery aka Reyna Young, whose original horror hostess show was "The Last Doorway" (2008-2011) and who staged and hosted several special shows over the years. Today she has another series, "Movie Massacre,"

Miss Misery aka Reyna Young, one of San Francisco's finest horror mistresses: of the dark and of the shadows.

and is married to her co-producer John Gillette with whom she had a son, Logan.

And I want to bow to Gail and Ray Orwig, who put out the monthly Big Eye Newsletter, highlighting sci-fi and horror events in the Bay Area, and who always managed to mention appearances Bob and I made. Their book "Where Monsters Walked" describes the locations where horror and sci-fi movies were produced, and is filled with location photos.

Then there was the wonderful Gary Meyer, a movie lover who ran the UC Berkeley Theater for years and is the co-founder of the Telluride Film Festival. For years, he managed the Balboa Theater in San Francisco where Bob, Tom and I attended annual shows. One included an appearance by Sara Jane Karloff, the one and only daughter of Boris Karloff. She gave me a signed copy of "Boris Karloff: A Gentleman's Life – The Authorized Biography," co-authored with Scott Allen Nollen.

Karen Lewis (upper right), who became Ernie Fosselius' lady friend, wrote a compelling history of her marriage to Al Lewis, who portrayed Grandpa on "The Munsters" (1964-66). I had the pleasure of helping Karen edit "I Married a Munster." It's a rich, fulfilling read.

BORIS KARLOFF'S ONLY DAUGHTER SARA . . . "READ THAT BOOK OR ELSE, MR. STANLEY"

Sara Karloff attended a double-bill of movies starring her father Boris Karloff at the Balboa Theater in San Francisco. We struck up a friendship that took us to her cabin in North Lake Tahoe, and she attended the 2007 WonderCon with us.

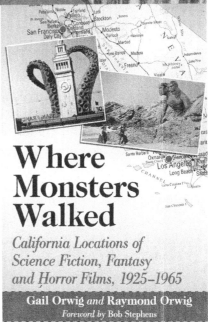

Two of Wilkins' most dedicated fans have been Gail and Ray Orwig (above right) who publish the monthly Big Eye Newsletter that covers major events and obits within the sci-fi/horror world. Their recent book "Where Monsters Walked" is a fabulous read about the shooting locations for many genre movies.

Bay Area personalities Steven Kirk, Chasta, and Dennis Willis (lower left) host "Soundwaves TV," a music and entertainment show that annually produces a Christmas special, to which I am always invited.

Willis has also written a series of "Flick Nation" movie guides including "American Popcorn: Hollywood and the War on Common Sense" (left) and the crime thriller "Barca's Jackpot."

Where Monsters Walked

California Locations of Science Fiction, Fantasy and Horror Films, 1925–1965

Gail Orwig *and* Raymond Orwig
Foreword by Bob Stephens

Gary Meyer (below), co-creator of the Telluride Film Festival, managed S.F.'s Balboa Theater on the night Bob and I appeared at the Boris Karloff show.

Part of the mix became Dennis Willis, a neighbor of mine in Pacifica who has written the movie-review book series "Flick Nation" and who has reviewed countless movies on San Francisco radio station KGO. But more importantly, he is the creator of "Soundwaves," a popular music show that dates back decades and originated at Pacifica Community Television. In July of 2018, he began producing a rebooted "Soundwaves TV" series that moved to KOFY two years later. My thanks goes to Dennis' partner-in-crime, Steven Kirk, who flies in from L.A. to take part in many Soundwaves events and who has been a bearded joy to watch week after week alongside the beautiful Chasta, host of the "Rock Your Life" podcast and heard daily on 107.7 The Bone.

THE BEGINNING OF THE END...

Make a note that Bob Wilkins' family were busy participants of the shows we attended. His two children, Rob and Nancy, who had sometimes appeared on his "Creature Features" shows, were now adults who sometimes sat beside us along with their mom Sally. Things slowed a bit in 2004 when we were told by Sally that Bob had been diagnosed with Alzheimer's disease. Nevertheless, Bob continued to appear with us until 2005. He would still make an appearance but only in the audience.

In the summer of 2006 several of us, at the command of Tom Wyrsch, traveled to Reno, Nevada, to Bob Wilkins' residence. He and Sally had

"Where's my cigar?" Bob Wilkins asked when he and his wife Sally were visited by Tom Wyrsch and his wife Lisa. Tom paid many visits to the Wilkins family once they had moved from Reno to Sacramento.

purchased a new home in Sacramento and it was time to move. Scott Moon and I helped to fill one of two vans and then climbed in. "I'm driving," Scott told me, like a military commander. "You're co-pilot." I gave him a salute and we drove to Sacramento and helped Bob settle into his new residence. I would only go back to Bob's once – a year later for a Fourth of July party. I went into

Bob's den and asked some questions, but Bob was not able to complete a sentence. Alzheimer's was in full play.

March 30, 2007, was a memorable moment when "the Creature Features Gang" drove to Sacramento's Crest Theater for a show called "Creature Features Forever: A Tribute to Bob Wilkins." Among those who talked about Bob (who was seated in the audience) was yours truly, KCRA-TV personality Harry Martin, horror host Geoff Wong, Ernie Fosselius, Sally Wilkins, Mr. Lobo and Scott Moon. And Tom Wyrsch, of course. An evening to remember. To step back for a moment: In early 2007 my publishing company, Creatures at Large, brought out my autobiography "I Was a TV Horror Host," featuring a history of the TV series as well as my interviews with such great horror/sci-fi figures as Ray Bradbury, Leonard Nimoy, William Shatner, Robert Bloch, Christopher Lee, Arnold Schwarzenegger, on and on.

BELOW: MICHAEL MONAHAN AS DOKTOR GOULFINGER

NEXT TO ME: MR. LOBO AND, THE ONE AND ONLY, BOB WILKINS

I sold the very first copies at the WonderCon show that year, with Sara Jane Karloff and her late husband "Sparky" seated nearby.

Tom Wyrsch, meanwhile, had begun making a documentary in early 2008, "Watch Horror Films, Keep America Strong," which had been Wilkins' motto and which was embedded on a sign that hung on the wall of his set. (It was Wilkins who first suggested to Tom that he make the documentary himself.) Helping Tom as co-producer was Robert Napton, a comic-book writer, editor and publisher at Legendary Comics in Los Angeles. Born in Berkeley, Napton had begun watching Bob Wilkins at the age of four and stayed tuned for the duration of the series. Later, he read my movie guides and eventually came in contact with Tom Wyrsch.

For production help, Tom turned to Napton, who in turn asked Hollywood film editor Anthony Cava to assist in the cutting. Michael Monahan, a one-time Bay Area horror host who portrayed Doktor Goulfinger for a short time, and who had been part of our gang for a few years, was also a co-producer in the beginning but suddenly left the project due to creative differences. (Napton has gone on to write hundreds of comic books. Among his credits are the graphic novel "Shannara,'""Godzilla Awakening," and "Warlord of Mars." Monahan officially gave up his character of Doktor Goulfinger and was no longer involved in our shows. (In 2011, he co-wrote "Shock It to Me: Golden Ghouls of the Golden Gate" with Lon Huber.)

"Watch Horror Films" was first screened at the Grand Lake Theater in Oakland in May of 2008 and proved to be absolutely

2 - DISC COLLECTOR'S EDITION

Watch HORROR FILMS Keep AMERICA STRONG!

A JOURNEY INTO CREATURE FEATURES

STARRING
BOB WILKINS · JOHN STANLEY · BOB SHAW

popular with our fans. We later took the documentary to Quentin Tarantino's L.A. movie theater, the New Beverly Cinema. Also shown that evening, with actor Clu Gulager sitting in the front row, was my horror film "Nightmare in Blood."

Napton, who at the age of 10 had met Bob Wilkins at Space-Con 6, also helped to produce the documentary "Back to Space-Con" (2011), an account of how "Star Trek" conventions of the 1970s, of which Bob Wilkins was a part of, came to life and opened the door to new kind of gatherings for fans. (These exciting events eventually led Paramount, which had inherited the series when Lucille Ball sold Desilu, to reactivate the TV franchise with a series of "Star Trek" motion pictures.)

Comic book writer-editor Robert Napton, relaxing on one of the re-creations of Bob Wilkins' "Creature Features" set, loving the atmosphere he grew up with from the age of ten.

THE CAREER THAT DRIPPED WITH HORROR

Next up for Tom: "Remembering Playland at the Beach," a colorful history of an amusement park next to San Francisco's Ocean Beach until 1972, which ran for many weeks at the Balboa Theater. This was followed by histories of other San Francisco landmarks: "Sutro's: The Palace at Land's End" (2011) and "The Cliff House and Sutro Heights" (2013). Contributing to these three documentaries was Tom's new co-producer Strephon Taylor, famous for portraying a costumed character named Slob on a long-running San Francisco horror series, "Creepy KOFY Movie Time." Tom and Strephon also covered the history of horror historian Forrest J.

Strephon Taylor (left), Tom Wyrsch's co-producer for several years, portraying his character of Slob during production of "Creepy KOFY Movie Time," a "Creature Features"-like series that ran for a decade in the San Francisco Bay Area and on which I appeared almost yearly. In the center is co-host Balrok Del Cavo.

Ackerman in "Uncle Forry's Ackermansions," a 2014 detailed account of Ackerman's three historic residences in the Hollywood Hills.

Taylor, back in 2012, had produced "The Complete Bob Wilkins' Creature Features," which detailed Bob's 16 years on three stations showing 1,800 films on 1,200 individual programs. He also made a compelling documentary about Universal Studio's historic make-up artist: "Jack Pierce, the Maker of Monsters" (2015).

Singly, Tom went on to make a documentary about the annual Harry Houdini Seances held in Sonoma County and followed that up with two outstanding feature-length documentaries about special haunted sites in Northern California: "Haunted Sonoma County" (2016) and "Haunted Wine Country" (2018). Appearing on camera to introduce segments was Laurie Jacobson, wife of Jon Provost, star of TV's "Lassie" series of the 1950s. (Laurie has also written "Hollywood Haunted," a history covering ghostly events of movieland for a hundred years.)

Check out the website garfieldlaneproductions.com for ordering and learning more about Tom's excellent filmmaking. (And stand by for Tom's personal essay included in this introduction.) Strephon Taylor's website is novemberfire.com.

LAURIE JACOBSON, HOSTESS OF "HAUNTED WINE COUNTRY" AND "HAUNTED SONOMA COUNTY"

Flashback to 2008. I had begun work on "I Was a TV Horror Host," my own DVD documentary about the highlights of my life and my years as "Creature Features" host. Helping me as editor, cameraman and co-producer was a fellow Pacifican, Wayne Hess, a one-time paratrooper during the Gulf War and a San Francisco police officer now retired. Mr. Lobo opens my story standing on the stage of the Castro Theater in San Francisco. We filmed other sequences at the theater with the help of my one-time KTVU film editor Bill Longen, who was then programmer at the theater. Our documentary did well on DVD and Hess and I would end up working together on several

Director of Photography Wayne Hess

other DVDs covering the history of "Creature Features." Topping the list: "John Stanley Meets Jack the Ripper," which featured mini-movies I made while hosting "Creature Features," and "Czar of Noir," a documentary on film noir expert Eddie Muller, who is now the "Noir Alley" commentator on Turner Classic Movies. Also

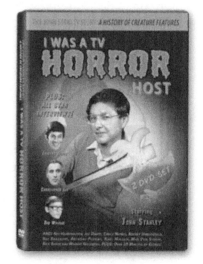

featuring Wayne Hess' photography and editing skills is "Homecoming II: The Devil's Payback," our 2018 DVD which covers the history of Devil's Slide (a deadly part of Highway #1 near Pacifica) and the background to the making of my horror film "Nightmare in Blood" (see pages 219-223).

Meanwhile, we made occasional appearances at the Niles Essanay Silent Film Museum in Fremont, which is devoted to the silent era of motion pictures. Bob Johnson, who put on those shows at the Castro Theater over the years, also programmed some appearances at the San Francisco Giants' ballpark. One evening in 2011, I had the pleasure of interviewing the star of "Night of the Living Dead," Judith O'Dea, immortalized by her role as Barbra. Remember the line "They're coming to get you, Barbra"? They being, of course, the walking dead. We did our talk on the pitching mound and the film was shown on the scoreboard screen. It was a hit! We scored!

I also want to thank some of the most devoted fans who came repeatedly to our personal appearances and were always adding character to what was happening. I consider Don Bishop one of the finest of fans, often joining us in a "Planet of the Apes" costume.

There is also Eric Yee (cameraman on "Watch Horror Films, Keep America Strong") who has attended our events almost always dressed in a Japanese monster costume.

Another superb fan is Tony Vella, a movie-TV stuntman who lives in Pacifica just a few blocks away from yours truly.

I hit a homer the night at the San Francisco Giants' ballpark when I interviewed Judy O'Dea on the field surrounded by a few hundred horror fans. O'Dea portrayed Barbra in "The Night of the Living Dead," which was then projected on a huge screen.

Movie publicist Walt Von Hauffe, who helped me more than any other publicist during my Chronicle years, is a lifelong fan of Frank Sinatra (above left). Bob's children (Nancy and Rob, above right) at one of the Halloween shows.

Don Bishop (left) of Vallejo, CA., proved to be one of the most devoted and loyal fans. He rarely missed one of our events and often came wearing horror make-up and costumes. Thanks, Don, for always being there for Bob and I, and for the fans.

Stunt specialist Tony Vella (right), famed for working in feature films and TV episodes, is wearing bloody make-up for one of his less sophisticated roles. No one I know can fly through the sky faster and better than Tony …even when he's flying feet first.

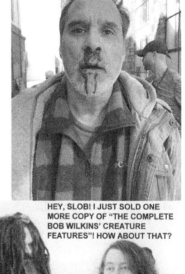

HEY, SLOB! I JUST SOLD ONE MORE COPY OF "THE COMPLETE BOB WILKINS' CREATURE FEATURES"! HOW ABOUT THAT?

Thanks goes to my son Russ (Vice President of Ticket Sales for the SF Giants) and daughter Trista (above left) for supporting me during my years with Bob Wilkins. Russ always called me whenever Stan Lee was appearing at the Giants' ballpark so I could meet him personally. Heather Taylor (above right), wife of Strephon Taylor, was always faithfully there for hubby (featured here as Slob) selling his DVD collection. Forever friendly, and always greeting me when I showed up, she deserves a warm thank you.

Steven Roark, who has travelled with me to more of my "Creature Features" shows than any other single fan, is pictured here with Lord Blood-Rah (left) and Jeff Wyrsch (right), son of Tom Wyrsch. I want to thank Roark for wearing that "Creature" shirt, designed by Strephon Taylor.

And there is Steven Roark, a dedicated fan and musician. I've picked him up countless times and thrown him into my backseat before driving to a Stanley-Wilkins event.

Among fans most famous: Walter Von Hauffe, who rose up in the movie industry to become one of its busiest film publicists, working for MGM, United Artists and other major production companies over the years out of San Francisco. He was also traveling the world as the head publicist for the James Bond film "Moonraker" (1979) and also worked with Steven Spielberg on "1941."

For years Walt was part of a Frank Sinatra fan club. We'd been pals for decades and I will always consider him one of my best friends. Happy days, to be sure . . . and then, tragedy.

AS IT DOES TO ALL THINGS, AND TO ALL MEN, SO DID DEATH COME ONCE AGAIN TO "CREATURE FEATURES"

It was January 7, 2009. My phone rang. It was Tom Wyrsch to tell me Bob Wilkins had passed away from Alzheimer's Disease. He had reached the age of 76 with a flamboyant life experience of bringing joyous memories to a generation of fans.

First at the Sacramento station KCRA from the mid-1960s, then at KTVU in the San Francisco-Bay Area from 1971 through 1979. From 1977-1980 Bob portrayed a costumed character, Captain Cosmic (right), on a weekday afternoon series on KTVU that played Japanese serials. Bob had also done a show at another Sacramento TV station, KTXL, Channel 40, called "Bob Wilkins' Double Horror Show," which had lasted a good decade.

While attending his funeral in Oakland, I had the opportunity, along with many others, to speak about his legacy, and how we had appeared together

during the final decade of his life. During that overwhelming funeral service Bob's son Rob and daughter Nancy together sang "Unforgettable," a song once made popular by Nat King Cole. It remains an unforgettable moment for me. Seeing the look on the face of Sally, Bob's wife, told me she was feeling the same emotion.

A few weeks later, in March, Tom Wyrsch, myself and those who had been close to Bob throughout the 2000s staged a tribute at the Maison Theater, once part of the Alameda Naval Air Station. The theater reached full capacity and on stage we paid thorough homage to Bob's memory.

THE CAREER THAT DRIPPED WITH HORROR

THAT'S ME WITH BOB SHAW, WHO HELPED BOB WILKINS PRODUCE HIS EARLY SHOWS . . . EVENTUALLY HE BECAME KTVU'S FILM CRITIC

Helping us prepare the show was the theater's operator, Allan Michaan, a long-time personal friend. Allan also runs the Grand Lake Theater in Oakland, deemed one of the top-ten movie palaces in America, and where "Watch Horror Films" had premiered. I had appeared for several nights in 2008 at the Grand Lake as part of one of Bob Johnson's Bay Area programs. Rory Calhoun in "Motel Hell" was the highlight. (Ironically, Allan had been my guest when I auditioned for "Creature Features" and we pretended that he owned a theater showing horror and sci-fi films daily.)

Ironically, only three months after Bob's death, his one-time assistant/movie reviewer Bob Shaw passed away in a San Francisco hospital from Crohn's Disease. He was only 56. Fortunately, just days before his death, I paid him a visit in hospital and although he couldn't speak, he was able to hear me compliment him on his contribution to Bob's horror series and his on-camera strengths as a movie reviewer at Channel 2, KTVU. Tom Wyrsch luckily visited Bob the very next day.

It had been one helluva wonderful experience, but it didn't stop there. For several years Tom Wyrsch and Frank Wallace-Ailsworth produced CreatureCon at the Bal Theater in San Leandro, an East Bay town. Then the CreatureCons moved to San Jose as part of the Big WOW shows created by Steve Wyatt, a comic-book show planner from Bakersfield. That franchise was bought up by Apple in 2015 and became The Silicon Valley Comic Con at which we appeared for a few years.

Then Tom hosted two major CreatureCons at hotels in the East Bay before the franchise was taken over by Wallace-Ailsworth, better known as Lord Blood-Rah, a now-popular horror host on "Nerve Wrackin' Theatre."

In 2016, Tom became the director for a new creation of "Creature Features" with horror host Vincent Van Dahl. Vincent lives in a Victorian mansion in Bodega Bay, California, and is assisted by Tangella, a lovely lady who never speaks, only pantomimes, and an extra-tall manservant, Livingston, who never agrees with what Vincent tells him. The show runs Saturday nights on KOFY, a Bay Area-based station, as well as on YouTube.

To everyone's delight, the series has made an impact in many parts of the world. And it is a wonderful tribute to Bob and my "Creature Features" shows. I've guested several times and it's always a delight to set next to Vincent with Tangella close by, giving me a wink.

It was when my book "I Was a TV Horror Host" finally sold out in July of 2019 that I realized I possessed heaps of sci-fi/horror-related material I had yet to publish. And I wanted to detail my life with Bob Wilkins. And so, I decided it was time for this sequel. So, stand by for a leap into the past, highlighted by interviews with some of the major figures in the world of fantasy and horror entertainment. So, after Tom Wyrsch's upcoming four-page memoir, prepare yourself for bloody horror A to Z, from aliens to zombies. Drop by drop by bloody drop . . . and please, don't call me a drip. After all, there will be a few subtleties along the way . . . really? . . . Hmmm.

PHOTOS THAT GOT LEFT OUT

BOB WILKINS WITH ERNIE FOSSELIUS, CREATOR OF "HARDWARE WARS"

Left: Me and Bob Wilkins at an early WonderCon at San Francisco's Moscone Center.

Right: Me and cameraman Wayne Hess at the Niles Essanay Silent Film Museum in Fremont.

Lower Left: Also at the Niles Essaney museum, Ernie Fosselius and Tom Wyrsch giving me the finger.

Lower Right: Stuntman Tony Vella with *Famous Monsters* legend Forrest J, Ackerman at a sci-fi convention held many years ago in San Diego.

NILES ESSANAY SILENT FILM MUSEUM

THE CAREER THAT DRIPPED WITH HORROR

I WANTED Tom Wyrsch, who was responsible for bringing "Creature Features" to life again, to share his personal feelings about why he got so involved. After all, it changed his life forever and put him on a pathway to making documentary films on a non-stop basis. And in turn, he has promoted Bob Wilkins in a way that has kept him alive and living in our imaginations.

MY 20 YEARS AND NOW MORE OF BOB WILKINS AND 'CREATURE FEATURES'

BY TOM WYRSCH

LOCAL San Francisco-Bay Area television was full of horror and science-fiction movies through the 1960s and '70's, most days after school and Saturdays. I loved the genres right from an early age. Add in *Famous Monsters of Filmland* magazine and one felt like you had it all. Then in early 1971 Bob Wilkins and "Creature Features" came to KTVU Channel 2 in Oakland, CA. He started in prime time at 9 p.m. on Saturday nights, which was unusual for that kind of show. But it was great to have such an early start. And Bob was definitely the main draw.

I watched the show faithfully throughout Bob's run from 1971 until 1979 and continued when John Stanley took over. The show went off the air in 1984. The show died and so did that enthusiasm he had created within me.

Then, in the early 1990s, I talked to John Stanley about releasing some of the best segments of his "Creature Features" shows on VHS tape. He was interested but was unsure of how much demand there would be. When I wrote "The Bob Wilkins Scrapbook," Bob was thrilled, but, like John, not sure of the demand. A "John Stanley Scrapbook" did follow.

Bob Wilkins with Monica and Will "The Thrill" Viharo at the Parkway Cinema in Oakland on the evening of the first of many "Thrillville" shows dedicated to "Creature Features."

Will Viharo was hosting his "Thrillville" shows at the Parkway Theater in Oakland, CA. He had asked Bob if he would appear. Bob was living in Reno and wanted me to meet with Will and get the details. A show came together in 2000 called "The Return of Bob Wilkins." It was a fast sellout, and it started a resurgence of interest in the Bay Area. Bob, John and I went on to do nearly 50 other shows and conventions together from 2000 to 2006.

Fans loved seeing Bob & John again. I found both to be exactly the same as you saw on TV. Bob loved joking around and always had that dry sense of humor. I remember how he would use it on my kids at the dinner table. Because they hadn't see him on TV while growing up, they didn't know what to make of it.

A rare photo of the Parkway Four: Monica (aka "The Tiki Goddess"), Will "The Thrill" Viharo, yours truly, and Bob Wilkins.

John, of course, is a walking encyclopedia on film. And not just horror and science fiction, but all types of film. After Bob passed away in 2009 John and I continued on with more than another 50 plus shows by now.

Writing and publishing the scrapbooks and creating nine different "Creature Features" DVDs led to a desire to tell Bob and John's story. Fans of the show had so many questions and there were so many different answers. What better way to get the story correct than with a video documentary? So I made "Watch Horror Films, Keep America Strong: The Story of Creature

THE DYNAMIC TRIO: STANLEY, WYRSCH AND WILKINS

Features" in 2008 and it became a hit. As time went by the creative bug bit me. Could I do it again? Could I make another film and achieve the same level of popularity? So I decided to try, and my first

pick was to do a documentary about the first "Star Trek" conventions in the Bay Area: called Space-Cons.

Space-Con conventions were really major events in the San Francisco-Bay Area back in the mid 1970's. Each show drew well over 10,000 people. Bob Wilkins was the emcee for every show. Members of the original "Star Trek" series were among the guests. There were huge dealers' rooms, and plenty of film rooms so that you could see rare science-fiction movies on the screen. These were the days before VHS home video, so it was still very rare to see movies other than waiting for them to come on the TV. During these two- to three-day convention events, there were more than enough things to do. Of course, nowadays conventions like these are much more common.

Strephon Taylor, of November Fire Recordings, and I did three San Francisco historical documentaries that were very popular and had great success: "Remembering Playland at the Beach," "Sutro's: The Palace at Land's End" and "The Cliff House Story." We also did "Back to Space-Con," featuring much of Bob's footage.

For five years, we appeared onstage at the Parkway, with Will the Thrill.

All three had excellent Bay Area theatrical runs and sold well on DVD. Our next full-length documentary was a tour of Forrest J. Ackerman's house/museums. It's called "Uncle Forry's Ackermansions" and it's probably the most detailed video tour produced to date. It's loaded with video footage, HQ photographs, Uncle Forry narration and interviews of Forry done by Bob Wilkins.

In 2013, I published "Bob Wilkins in TV Guide." Back in the 1960's and early '70's fans were very limited in monster items to collect. Monster magazines, Aurora models, Castle film shorts, a few monsters masks, toys . . . and that was about it.

TV GUIDE

Bob Wilkins in TV Guide
Compiled by Tom Wyrsch

Bob Wilkins

So I used to cut out the monster/sci-fi ads from *TV Guide* magazine and newspapers and put them in a scrapbook. It was great! Little did I know that kids around the country were doing the same. Just like making audio recordings of movies from TV. I thought I was the only one doing that. I had saved a few ads from Bob Wilkins "Creature Features." For years I thought it would be great to find a place to see them all again. But how? You would have to locate every *TV Guide* issue from January 1971 through February 1979 in San Francisco Metropolitan editions. Over 400 issues. Forget it, right?

Well, by chance we had our "Creature Features" booth at a local convention in San Jose, CA, some years ago and not too far from us was a dealer I'd known since SpaceCon. Go figure. They told me there was a chance they might have most of the *TV Guides* I wanted and would check their storage units to find out.

Some months later I got a list and sure enough – they had 90%. We made a deal and I ended up with almost 400 *TV Guides*. Wow! After a few weeks going page by page, finding photos & art ads, I had enough to lay out "Bob Wilkins in TV Guide." HQ scans of each entire *TV Guide* page, laid out in chronological order and just slightly larger than the original *TV Guide*. Add a retro cover and off to printing. People that have purchased a copy love looking at all the ads again and seeing the programs on other channels around "Creature Features." A real fun return to the 1970s.

Top Left: Wilkins and yours truly selling their wares. Bottom Left: On stage with Bob Wilkins and the original Creature chair. If only that had been the real Elvira . . .

Top Right: three horror hosts: Mister Lobo, Miss Misery and yours truly. Bottom Right: Horror host Zomboo (Frank Leto) of Reno's KOLO-TV.

"LOOK, OUT THERE ON THE OCEAN! IT'S A SEAGULL . . . IT'S A GHOST SHIP! AND SUPERMAN IS ONBOARD!"

The Man of Steel signed this photo on the day of our meeting at the Fairmont Hotel. "To John – Thank You and best always! Christopher Reeve"

IT IS APRIL, 1993, and it's a sunny day in downtown San Francisco. I have to get over to the Fairmont Hotel atop Nob Hill and I decide to walk from the Chronicle building at Fifth and Mission Streets to the cable car turnaround at Powell and Market, just a block away. As the railed unit starts up the hill, I take a moment to check my list of questions I've prepared for Christopher Reeve, who is hopefully awaiting my arrival. Suddenly, I stiffen and experience a totally new experience as a newspaperman-former TV horror host. Shock rips through my sublime body, and I feel ennobled.

Holy Moly! I'm on my way to meet Superman!

Wait! Not only Superman but Clark Kent, valued newspaper reporter for the Daily Planet in the city of Metropolis. Two guys in one, just like me!

Suddenly I'm filled with superstrength. I'm shining in the city's bright sunlight, exclusively fulfilling a role few others have ever undertaken. How many sitting with me aboard the cable car have faced such a challenging realization? I'm meeting Superman. But not just any Man of Steel. Christopher Reeve, with four major "Superman" films to his credit, who has since 1978 enjoyed super success. It's only moments later that we reach the top of the hill at Powell and California Street. Still shining, I jump off the cable car and walk briskly up California. I'm suddenly, for the first time, thinking of the other Superman moments in my life: My meetings with Kirk Alyn (serial Superman of the '40s), Phyllis Coates (TV's first Lois Lane), Noel Neill (serial and TV's second Lois Lane), and Teri Hatcher and Dean Cain of "Lois & Clark: The New Adventures of Superman" TV fame. (You're going to meet all of them soon, so relax.)

How lucky can a mere human be in dealing with a classic-of-all-time superhero who flies into space?

It's only a few minutes later, high noon, when I join Reeve in his expensive Fairmont suite. He speaks as casually as he is dressed–in burgundy turtleneck, beige trousers and brown loafers. Reeve is pleased to reflect candidly on his career, so I start throwing out question after question.

I couldn't go home to my wife Erica without at least one photo signed to her. Flying above the city of Metropolis, Reeve is holding tight to his beautiful co-star Margot Kidder, who played Lois Lane in all four of their "Superman" films.

"Thank God, I never experienced such a cursed legacy!"

"Portraying Superman was the greatest, and it couldn't have done more to open up the sky to an incredible career," begins Reeve. "Other Supermen weren't so super. Kirk Alyn, he never rose up out of the ranks of B-picture players. George Reeves of the '50s TV series? That turned into pure hell.

This "Superman" photo Reeve signed, at my request, to my son Russ' then-girlfriend Corey Driscoll. They would be married in 1993 and have two daughters, Shelby and Jordyn Stanley.

"He became typecast so severely he fell into a depression and died all too early in 1959 from what appeared to be a self-inflicted gunshot wound. At least that's one theory. Another is that he was murdered by an angry lover. Maybe we'll never know. Thank God, I never experienced such a cursed legacy."

I have to interrupt Reeve to tell him that I still recall the night I saw the first film at a screening for reviewers in December 1978 and fell in love with the music themes by John Williams. Especially when Superman flies through the sky carrying Lois Lane (Margot Kidder). Only two days later, with that tune rolling through my mind, I did my audition for the role of "Creature Features" . . . and ended up being chosen to replace Bob Wilkins, that popular host of the 1970s.

"Good for you," says Reeve. "Of course, that was my wonderful beginning. Just holding on to shapely Margot Kidder made it worthwhile. After finishing my fourth flight through the heavens in 'Superman IV: The Quest for Peace,' I enjoyed a total freedom of movement within the business, picking movie and TV roles based on the challenges of the parts."

And what could his fans expect in the near future? "I'm an ex-con handyman who falls for widow Deborah Raffin in 'Morning Glory.' In 'The Remains of the Day' I'm the only American actor in a collection of British and German celebrities that include Anthony Hopkins and Emma Thompson."

"Wait a minute," I tell Reeve. "What about the reason I'm here? I mean, I love talking Superman, but you have a brand-new TV movie coming up. Right?"

"It's an unusual adaptation of 'The Sea Wolf,' based on Jack London's turn-of-the-century novel set aboard a doomed sailing ship, the Ghost. It'll be on the TNT network soon with Charles Bronson co-starring with me as the infamous, brutish Captain Wolf Larsen. I play Van Weyden, who is trapped on Larsen's ship."

"I've done some research," I tell Reeve. "Did you know 'Sea Wolf' is one of the most photographed stories? Two silent versions were made in 1913 and 1920. There was a sound version in 1930 but that got knocked out of the water in 1941 by the powerful adaptation with Edward G. Robinson as the not-so-lovable Captain Larsen.

"And, here's something not many people know: It was lightly disguised as a noir Western made by Warner Brothers in 1950. Retitled 'Barricade,' it starred

One of Hollywood's great seafaring thrillers was "The Sea Wolf" (1941) with Edward G. Robinson at his villainous best as Captain Wolf Larsen (above left). Playing the same role opposite Reeve in the 1993 TV movie was Charles Bronson, who often was cast as an anti-hero in scores of films, including the "Death Wish" series.

Raymond Massey as Larsen and Dane Clark in the Van Weyden role. More faithful was a stark 1957 rendering under the title 'Wolf Larsen,' with Barry Sullivan and Peter Graves. Finally, it was redone in Europe in 1974 as 'Wolf of the Seven Seas' with Chuck Connors as the captain."

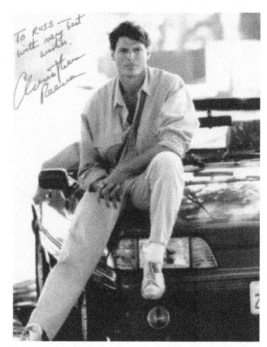

Reeve signed this one to my son Russ, who was then (and still is) Vice-President of Ticket Sales for the San Francisco Giants – a position he has held since the 1990s. When Reeve finished signing, he asked, "Is that all you brought me?" And he swooped his pen through the air as if doing a flyover of Metropolis.

Reeve praises me. "You know your stuff. That's more history than I was aware of. Ask yourself, though, what is there about the novel that's stimulated so many variations? Well, 'Sea Wolf' is a brutal tale of life at sea in the time of whaling ships. This version depicts how my character Van Weyden and a woman [Catherine Mary Stewart] survive a ferry boat accident in San Francisco Bay and are rescued by crew members of The Ghost. Rescued yes, but they are virtual captors in Larsen's prison-like seafaring world.

"My character is forced to work in the ship's galley and fight for survival in an animalistic way while Larsen watches from the sidelines, bemused that an intellectual human–that would be me–must revert to brute force. Van Weyden also sees Larsen carrying out acts of sadism against his vulnerable crew. I think Marc Singer gives an excellent performance as seaman Johnson, whose violence matches Larsen's. There's a great line by Larsen: 'Might is right and weakness is wrong. Better to reign in Hell than serve in Heaven.'

Reeve had two reasons for choosing the role.

"The allegorical battle between Van Weyden and Larsen reflects the enlightenment and darkness in man. I read the novel version which was written not long after Darwin's theory of evolution became a major topic of the day. What is man? Why is there the animal in man? How far have we really evolved from the primate on all four paws? It's still a relevant issue today."

And the second reason? He replies, "We shot in Vancouver, a very pleasant location, ideal for me to bring along the family. We filmed at sea aboard the 120-foot schooner Zodiac, just off the coast of Vancouver. Myself, I own my own 46-foot cutter which is docked in Maine, so I've done my share of playing a yachtsman over many years."

And what about working with Charles Bronson? "That," exclaims Reeve, "proved to be an unusual experience because Charles is reserved at first, and daunted by the volume of words exchanged. He's used to playing characters who don't talk much. He came to the set with every move already worked out. Not a lot of flexibility. Frankly, I tried to be as invisible around him as possible. I took the attitude I was a reactor, cast adrift in a new world. A fish out-of-water with no control over events."

Elements of Reeve becoming an actor are fascinating. Born in 1952 in New York City, Reeve eventually studied at Cornell University, where he was selected (along with Robin Williams) to attend the Juilliard School, learning about the art of acting under the apprenticeship of John Houseman.

He had few credits to his name when suddenly he was selected to portray Superman. His trainer for the role turned out to be David Prowse, who had portrayed Darth Vader in the "Star Wars" series (more about him on page 86).

Reeve, dressed as newspaperman Clark Kent, pays a visit to Margot Kidder's Lois Lane. Kidder, who also scored well in 1979's "The Amityville Horror," stayed busy in TV and films for years before the onset of mental problems. She would die in 2018 (at the age of 69) from suicide by drug overdose.

I just had to ask him about the popularity of his "Superman" feature films. "The first and second," he responds quickly, "were classics and I have wonderful memories of making them. The less said about the third and fourth, the better. I think where we succeeded with 'Superman–The Motion Picture' (1978) and 'Superman II' (1981) was with a light, romantic touch, combined with the advanced technology to make the flying sequences convincing. When we were making those two films there was a sense that we were doing something new and original and experimental with the best minds applied to the problems. Cinematography, special effects, 70mm, Dolby stereo–they were big-screen entertainments. It was a fun, fascinating, creative time for movies."

Superman, he continues, "had a more generous attitude and was relaxed in a woman's company for the first time. He could share and do things with Lois Lane [Kidder] that had not been explored before. But it was the lightheartedness of it all that worked for me. Playing Superman was definitely a highpoint in my life, but now it's like looking back into the pages of a yearbook. That was then, this is now. The next project is what I'm thinking about."

Reeve still returns annually to a theater in Williamstown, Massachusetts (he started there as a stage apprentice at the age of 15), because of his need to perform before live audiences and because he considers theater "a polished form," while film is "raw input that a director has to make jell."

On the stage "you've boiled down the input and everyone has agreed on the brew being served. You can strive for a form of perfection that I don't think you can find working in film, which is usually made under somewhat chaotic conditions."

"I'M THE LUCKIEST GUY ON PLANET EARTH!"

Diversity, he maintains, "has been something I've always chosen. The Superman role gave me more impetus to do the things I wanted to do. 'Deathtrap,' 'The Bostonians,' 'Somewhere in Time,' 'Street Smart,' 'Noises Off.' It's like eating out. I never have liked going back to the same old restaurant all the time. Why miss the opportunity of eating so many rich foods?"

When the interview with Christopher Reeve is finished, I walk down Powell Street, always pleased to see a cable car passing me by as a reminder of how rich San Francisco can be with its unique features. I cross over to Market Street and curve onto Fifth Street, reaching the front of the Chronicle without incident. Suddenly, as I'm about to enter the main door, I stop and look around.

My God, I think to myself. *I JUST INTERVIEWED SUPERMAN! I'M THE LUCKIEST GUY ON PLANET EARTH!*

And I have managed to keep my feet on planet Earth the whole time. I laugh out loud, glancing across the street to the old Mint Building . . . swinging around to look at the Chronicle entrance. My God, how many people on this planet can tell their family and friends that they had a sit-down visit with Superman, and talked about what it's like to be the Man of Steel?!

AFTERWORDS

Meeting Christopher Reeve was a moment I will never forget. But I am also reminded of what happened to the wonderful man who had portrayed Superman. Just two years later, on May 27, 1995, he was riding a horse in Culpeper, Virginia, when he fell from the saddle and hit the ground with incredible impact, which paralyzed him.

From then on, he was forced to live in a wheelchair.

So much damage had been done to his body, there was no alternative.

The next nine years were tough ones, although he managed to perform in a TV version of "Rear Window" in 1998 and played Dr. Virgil Swann on "Smallville" before his death of a heart attack in October 2004. It was the final time he cried "Up! Up! And away!"

Sadly, he was only 52 years old.

After his accident, Reeve became a kind of philosopher who, in looking back on playing Superman, said…

"The American hero is an ordinary individual finding strength to persevere and endure in facing overwhelming obstacles. So many of our dreams at first seem impossible, then improbable. And when we summon the will, they soon become inevitable."

Superman Meets a Super-Shaped Supervillainess . . . And You Meet a Super-Shaped British Life-Form Unit, A Lass With Class Named Sarah Douglas

SARAH DOUGLAS had never flown before, but she knew she could do it, even though she had no wings or propellers capable of spinning. All she had to do was put her mind to it. She remembers that it was four years ago on a lovely morning and she was all "prim and proper" as she climbed 40 feet into the air to show the Salkind brothers that she had the evil makings to portray Ursa, villainess from the planet Krypton, who corrupted children, destroyed men, and leaped tall buildings in the style of . . . why, Superman, of course.

"I was fitly dressed," Douglas recalls, when we meet for lunch at the Beverly Hills Hotel in May of 1981. "Clad in my black leotards and Plimsoill pumps. My long hair, straight down my back. I got up on the platform, about 40 feet off the ground, and I flew superbly, I must say. As I was flitting about, one of the ground crew shouted up to me: 'Sorry, love, but you don't stand a chance of getting the role. The pretty young thing who tried out before you flew without any knickers on.' Of course, at that altitude, any woman in a dress without her panties on, floating horizontally on a wire rig, would have been a popular tourist attraction."

Before Sarah Douglas signed this photo, she suddenly found out I was also a TV horror host. Immediately, she asked to be a guest on my show to promote her second "Superman" movie. I welcomed her with open arms (figuratively). But unfortunately, her schedule did not allow her time to come to the Bay Area. Sarah, I want you to know how sorry I was we didn't do a show together.

By the time Sarah got back down to earth, however, it was clear that the pantyless actress before her hadn't made that big of an impression on the producing Salkind brothers, after all. Sarah was immediately cast to portray one of three Krypton heavies for "Superman–The Movie" (first released in December 1978) and "Superman II," set to open across America in June 1981.

Another girl who did not get the part was Dana Gillespie, with whom Sarah had worked in the 1977 science-fiction thriller, "People That Time Forgot." Says Sarah, "Dana is a girl with very large, splendid breasts. She tested for the role of Ursa but they couldn't lift her off the ground."

Talk about a heavy role taking a new curve into space.

"YOU ARE SUCH A BITCH!"

Because Ursa's part in that first '78 film was minuscule, the sequel will give American audiences their first close-up look at this unusual British actress who apparently projects such superb wickedness that one matron in Washington, D.C., after seeing the film, looked Sarah straight in the eye and exclaimed, *You are such a bitch!*

"Bitch" only begins to describe the image of this outer-space menace who–in the company of two other humanoid villains, Non and General Zod–escapes the Phantom Zone (a timeless, spaceless prison for extraterrestrials) to fly to Earth and engage in a battle royale, in the sky above Metropolis, with the Man of Steel himself.

Ursa, who possesses superpowers equivalent to Superman's, is a sexual presence in black see-through organza with slits in strategic areas, upraised eyebrows, black lipstick, false fingernails, and a stark white make-up that banishes Sarah's freckles.

"Even when I'm sitting down, I stand for nothing but evil," she says through mock-clenched teeth. "Usually in British telly I play a nice girl who's a little naughty on the side. Now I'm directly naughty, not the least bit on the side. Totally from the front.

"I'm just a good old downright bad creature. I do a bit of gooching around, kicking men off the surface of Earth, and placing my thigh-length black leather boots in tricky spots. Crucial spots, actually. People ask me how I can be so evil, when the real me is so different, so civilized. In England, we simply call it superb acting. If I may be so bold. After all, I am a superhuman."

And England is where she's been acting since the age of eight when she was "third fairy" in "A Midsummer Night's Dream" on stage. After winning an opening in the National Youth Theater, and

Jack O'Halloran as Non, Terrence Stamp as General Zod, and Sarah as Ursa in "Superman II."

touring with that company all across Europe, she was cast in a science-fiction movie, "The Final Programme," which led to almost invisible parts in "Rollerball" and "Tommy" (both 1975).

It was her role two years later in "The Brute" as a victimized wife that originally brought her to the attention of the Salkind producing team, which has been using her off and on for four years. Sarah now vacillates back and forth between BBC-TV and feature films, a few in America, a few in England.

She promises me that "Superman II" has greater visual delights. "In the first film, Superman had to be born, grow up, and all that exposition stuff. In the new film, there's more time for pure action. Ursa has superheat vision. I can't begin to describe it. Somewhere between my withering looks and the film process, they managed to implant a red heat emanating from my eyeball sockets."

Another sequence has Ursa and her villainous buddies (Terence Stamp and Jack O'Halloran) sending a combined Super Breath through the city, tumbling everything and everyone into a mighty tornado. "Super Breath? Hardly," quips Sarah. "It took us five days, standing on a set, blowing with all our might with puffy cheeks. It's not exactly acting, is it? It isn't the kind of thing they teach you in drama school. It's really a lot of hot air."

With that sense of humor of hers always active, Sarah has been traveling the world since October 1980, preparing assorted races and cultures for the release of the Salkind brothers' comic strip blockbuster (which some insiders say cost as much as $40 million).

Just before our meeting, she had finished a long walk along one of Los Angeles' beaches. Filled with energy, Sarah could barely sit still during lunch in her white jumpsuit which she describes (in her thick British accent) as a "housekeeper's frock." She defines her remarks as being "cruelly witty."

"The Australians are a bit raunchy and I was able to say 'Ursa kicks men in the balls.' In South Africa I had to be more gentile and say: 'Ursa kicks men in the groin.' In America? Oh, they don't have any balls at all in America."

Streaking from Sarah's eyeball sockets (in black and white) are the red-colored killer rays for which Ursa is feared. Not to mention her thigh-length black leather boots, which are often aimed at . . . well, you know.

"At night, I practiced by hanging from a chandelier."

Frequently tossing her head, she recalls the ordeal of doing the flying sequences for "Superman II." "For the original we were simply hung on wires and pulled to and fro on tracks. We even filmed scenes for Part II in that style. But by the time we went back to make the sequel, two years had passed and the effects people had perfected the flying technique with new standards. And what I call higher ideals."

This new technique consisted of body molds and removed the last vestiges of glamour Sarah savored about film-making. "First, I stripped down, then a little man with a big bucket of plaster came in and started slapping it on me, whistling all the while. From this he made a body mold from my chest down to my knees. Then the thin little fiberglass mold was attached to a 40-foot pole. The pole would be elevated into the sky—and guess who would be strapped into the mold, wearing only underwear?" And yes, that included panties.

And that's where Sarah, Christopher Reeve (aka Superman), and the others hung out for the next 28 weeks, 40 feet above the studio floor, filming new sequences and redoing most of the ones originally directed by Richard Donner (who had been fired and replaced by Richard Lester.)

"At night," says Sarah, "I practiced by hanging from a chandelier. In the day, I was sprawled face down in the body mold. Now, I'm extremely British. I'm a trooper, but when I get pushed around by jolly men, that's when I explode and that's when the old withering look begins. It became an effort to keep my sense of humor, hanging there all those days."

There was nothing funny about the case of bronchitis that struck Sarah in mid-production. Yet she kept her head in the air. "Supervillains don't carry hankies or tissues, so they gave me a man named Fred with a 40-foot pole with a tissue on the end. My nose would begin to stream and Fred would gently poke me from below. And I'd reach down and take the blowrag."

There were many pains, plus bumps, bruises, scrapes, and nicks, month after month, Sarah recalls. "You have to fly slightly on an angle so the camera can get a good look at your face. My spine shifted. I swear it did." Then there was the day that Sarah lifted a motorbus off the street.

So there's Chris Reeve's Superman giving a lift to bad guy Lex Luthor (Gene Hackman at the wheel) ... but imagine what Sarah Douglas had to endure lifting a motor bus off the street as she did in "Superman II." Hanging 40 feet above the studio floor off and on for 28 weeks.

The vehicle contained 40 passengers, some of them hanging from the windows of the bus. "The bus was on a chain which was on a crane, but as I lifted the bus, it shifted slightly and for a moment the weight came down on my arms and I suffered new injuries.

"Director Lester ran over and asked me why I hadn't relaxed my arms. Well, there were 150 people watching, and at that moment I really did believe I had superpowers. That I was a mighty lady as well as a naughty lady. It was an unforgettable moment."

The changing of directors in mid-airstream has resulted in a different kind of Ursa. "Originally," explains Sarah, "Donner wanted Ursa to be asexual, no sex appeal at all. I thought that was ridiculous; I felt she should appeal to kids and dads, even goats for that matter." After Donner's departure, replacement Richard Lester had Ursa's costume redesigned. Which mainly gave her back her remarkable cleavage and those lower areas of special concern.

"Lester never messes around," explains Sarah. "One day he asked me to pick up a manhole cover and throw it like a Frisbee. I'd never even rehearsed it or prepared for it, yet I was too terrified to disobey. 'You will do it,' Lester told me. You're damn right I did it. And it was perfect."

Sarah sighs, knowing our time together is almost up. "Perhaps I work better under the threat of death. When I threw that manhole cover, the crew applauded me. I have to give Lester credit: From that nervous man has come a much funnier movie. He knew what he wanted. By golly, he got it."

AFTERWORDS

If you remember that Christopher Reeve said something unpleasant about "Superman II," he was right, given the critical reaction. But for Sarah, it helped to catapult her to stardom in American TV series, especially "Falcon Crest," in which she portrayed Pamela Lynch for 51 episodes (move over, Joan Collins, to make room for another British beauty). She also co-starred in "Conan the Barbarian" (1982) as Queen Taramis. She really has flown on to greater fame. (See pages 162-165 about Arnold Schwarzenegger's experience portraying Conan the Barbarian.)

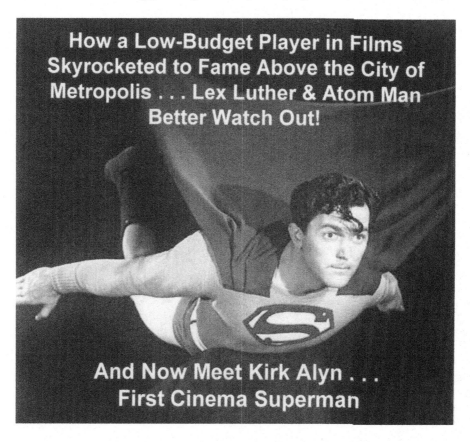

How a Low-Budget Player in Films Skyrocketed to Fame Above the City of Metropolis . . . Lex Luther & Atom Man Better Watch Out!

And Now Meet Kirk Alyn . . . First Cinema Superman

The history of Superman as a comic-strip superhero begins in 1938 in Action Comics #1, with stories by Jerry Siegel and artwork by Joe Shuster. The character is an instant phenomenon and will make history through hundreds of comic books to follow. The Man of Steel begins showing up in cinemas across America in 1948 and 1950 in two multi-chapter serials from Columbia Studios. I want you to meet the first actor to portray him, Kirk Alyn. We'll dive into the never-solved mystery of George Reeves' untimely death, followed by Lois Lane portrayers Phyllis Coates and Noel Neill, and then the "Lois and Clark" team of Teri Hatcher and Dean Cain.

I n **"Superman–The Movie,"** released in the closing days of 1978, there is a sequence in which a young version of the Last Son of Krypton (Christopher Reeve) runs 60 miles per hour on nothing more than his two feet, keeping pace with a streamlined passenger train. Two of the incredulous faces pressed against the windows, watching this superhuman feat with wonderment, belong to Kirk Alyn and Noel Neill.

For the knowledgeable Superman crowd, the presence of Alyn and Neill was a nostalgic "in" joke. They starred together in two serials made by Columbia ("Superman," 1948, and "Atom Man vs. Superman," 1950). Alyn was Superman/news reporter Clark Kent while Neill portrayed the strait-laced Daily Planet reporter Lois Lane.

When I meet Alyn in 1979 during the Fantasy Symposium at the San Jose Convention Center, he is still flying high, a popular face wherever science-fiction fans gather, and is still enjoying some literary popularity through his autobiography, "A Job for Superman," published in 1971.

Before my very eyes, Alyn turns out to be a charming, gregarious fellow now experiencing his 68th year on planet Earth. And he still loves to talk about Superman, given he has instant recall and is full of anecdotes and trivia about what Hollywood was like in the Forties.

"When the producers of the new 'Superman' movie first contacted me," Alyn tells me as hundreds of horror and sci-fi fans swarm around him in the huge convention center, "they were considering me to portray Superman's father, Jor-El. But then, blast it, they decided they needed a bigger star like Marlon Brando to ensure box-office success. After that disappointment, I was considered anew for the Pa Kent role. But that, blast it, went to Glenn Ford. So I finally had to reluctantly settle for the train-window cameo. At least I was somewhere in that film."

And what, I have to ask Alyn, does he think of the new $55-million version of "Superman" with Christopher Reeve playing the leading role and Margot Kidder as Lois Lane?

Kirk Alyn was appearing at fantasy conventions across America in the late 1970s and here he poses with a poster of his second Superman film serial produced by Columbia in 1950. He loved meeting fans and we had a great chat... but curses! I didn't come back with a signed photo.

"They tried to make Superman more human, so people could better relate to him. But I say if you have him making love to Lois Lane, you really haven't got Superman. He's just a normal human being in a hero's suit. I don't think it's faithful to the original comic-book concept, or the style in which I played Superman back in the late Forties. Technically, the film is entertaining and you certainly get your money's worth. But I wish they hadn't made a spoof of Lex Luthor [Gene Hackman] and his sidekick Otis [Ned Beatty]. Those two should have been more sinister. In short, more threatening and dangerous for Superman to battle.

"They spent more than $50 million, while back in those good old days a Columbia serial was made for just $285,000 and we had to innovate and improvise because that was the first time anyone had put Superman on film as a live-action hero. Also, we wanted it to look as close to the comic strip as possible. We wanted Superman to feel like a soul from another planet."

The two serials Alyn made were both directed by Spencer Bennett, whom Alyn still believes was "a master of the cliffhanger. In our first Superman effort, Carol Forman was Spider Lady and she spun a devious web. And in the second serial, Lyle Talbot portrayed Lex Luthor, who was plotting to disintegrate mankind with an atomic device."

I ask Alyn to explain how he emotionally felt the first time he "flew" through a scene. "The special effects department hung me from wires attached to a special breastplate and I spent hours, I mean literally hours, of my life dangling 16 feet off the studio floor, with no support for my legs. When we looked at the footage the next day, we could see every wire. So we scrapped the whole thing, and the technical crew was fired for incompetence. A new team came in and shot close ups of me leaping on and off various platforms, and those scenes worked out okay. As for the actual flying sequences . . . well, they were all animated, as in a cartoon. That's quite obvious when you see the serials today."

"Thank God I've always been athletic."

As for landing the role, Alyn clearly recalls the day he met with producer Sam Katzman for the first time. "Truth is, I was the 125th possible choice for the role, and at first I didn't fare so well. I was sporting a mustache and goatee, because I was in the middle of making another project . . . but ultimately Sam was able to see me unshaved and came through for me. Mainly because without all that hair I looked exactly like the comic book version of Clark Kent. I'll always be thankful for that.

"They asked me to take off my pants . . . (gulp) and I hesitated!"

"We wanted Superman to feel like a soul from another planet!"

"Well, they also asked me to take off my shirt. No problem. Then they asked me to take off my pants. I hesitated. I thought that only happened with female ingénues. It was important, I was told, so the wardrobe department could see how well I'd fit into tight-fitting tights, a major part of the Superman physique. Within 15 minutes of revealing my upper torso, and some of the lower half, I was signed to a contract. You see, I was in great physical shape after all those years of ballroom and adagio dancing, and I had been working out with weights every day. Thank God I've always been athletic."

In this scene from the first Superman movie serial, Kirk Alyn is with his newspaper co-worker Lois Lane, played by Noel Neill, who went on to star in the 1950s TV series "Adventures of Superman."

Columbia was apparently not all that pleased with the final result, because it decided to sell the 15 chapters to RKO Radio Pictures. RKO accepted the deal and began playing the serial every day of the week in its theater chain, on a first-run basis, and made a fortune for the time. This was unprecedented for a multi-chapter serial which normally was shown only as part of a Saturday matinee, one episode per week.

Angry at having made a major blunder, Columbia boss Harry Cohn bought back the rights and released it again, this time as part of the usual Saturday matinees. Incredibly, "Superman" the 1948 serial ran for eight years without let-up. The sequel was just as successful.

Alyn was born John Feggo Jr. in New Jersey to Hungarian immigrants. After attending Columbia University, he worked his way into the world of Broadway as a member of the chorus. He appeared in such memorable fare as "Hellzapoppin'" and "Girl Crazy." "Yeah," confesses Alyn, "I was a hoofer on Broadway. I did musical comedy, adagio dancing, everything they needed when you were a newcomer working the stage. I danced alongside Bill 'Bojangles' Robinson, Billy De Wolfe and a few others. I was really burning the candle at both ends when a girlfriend invited me to travel with her to California.

"Suddenly I was in Hollywood doing my first picture, 'My Sister Eileen,' with Rosalind Russell. It was a bit part, as was my role in 'You Were Never Lovelier' with Rita Hayworth. I decided to marry that girlfriend of mine, an actress named Virginia O'Brien. We stayed together for 14 years and have three children.

"In retrospect I realize it would have been the perfect capper to my career."

"Then I landed my first Western at Republic Studios, 'Overland Mail Robbery,' with Wild Bill Elliott. Republic wanted to turn me into a cowboy star but my agent said no deal. I still did six or seven Westerns with Roy Rogers [including "The Cowboy and the Senorita"] and Sunset Carson ["Call of the Rockies"] and I was in one of the worst musicals ever made, 'Pistol Packin' Mama.'" His credits throughout the 1940s seem endless, for he worked freelance at most of the studios making low-budget features in parts big and small.

Kirk Alyn also played the leading role in the 1952 serial "Blackhawk," which was produced by Columbia Pictures' Sam Katzman.

The Superman serials kept him afloat for several years but he became so strongly identified as the Man of Tomorrow that he couldn't nail down other major acting roles. Foolishly he turned down the TV role of Superman that was eventually played for several seasons by George Reeves. "Big mistake. I thought it would only further stereotype me. In retrospect I realize it would have been the perfect capper to my career."

Alyn did do other serials: "Federal Agents vs Underworld USA" and "Radar Patrol vs Spy King," (left) both released in 1949. Another major effort was Columbia's 1952 serial "Blackhawk: Freedom's Champion," based on a comic strip that had been popular throughout the World War II years. "Afterward I bought up the TV rights, but none of the networks wanted to show the serial because our black flying uniforms reminded everyone of the Nazis, and finally I lost the rights and made no money at all. I fell on really hard times and left Hollywood to live in Arizona."

Alyn received no residuals from the phenomenal success of the Superman Columbia serials ("in those days you worked for a flat salary") and he is puzzled why Columbia had not re-released either serial. "They haven't been shown for more than 20 years now." (They would be released on VHS by Warner Home Video in 1987 and DVD in 2006).

Jobless by the mid-1950s, Alyn began a new, distinguished career on Broadway. He performed in three shows with Imogene Coca and did many revues and melodramas. He was opposite Ilona Massey in "Angel in Paris," June Havoc in "Strike a Match" and Veronica Lake in "Personal Appearance."

Alyn still lives in Arizona, surrounded by the mementoes of a colorful career. "The nostalgia craze started around 1971 and I've been having fun with it ever since. I enjoy meeting the fans and recalling those old, wonderful days. It's still a lot of fun and I have no regrets. Superman will always be a part of me."

AFTERWORDS

After our meeting in 1979, Alyn played the role of an old man on "Battlestar Galactica" and appeared opposite Adam West in the TV movie "Time Warp." And he continued to appear at comic-book and sci-fi conventions as well as on the college circuit. He was living in Houston when he died from Alzheimer's disease in 1999 at the age of 88. He lived long enough to see his two Superman serials and the Blackhawk adventure released on VHS and DVD.

IT'S NOW TIME to shift focus from the movie versions of "Superman" to an earlier time when the Man of Steel was popularized off the pages of comic books onto the television screens of America. Ironically, the star almost had the same name as Christopher Reeve. What George Reeves had was an extra ess to set him apart. Although I never met George, I do want to cover his unusual death. And please stand by for two of my encounters with the beautiful Lois Lane . . . aka Phyllis Coates . . . aka Noel Neill.

THE CAREER THAT DRIPPED WITH HORROR

THE TRAGEDY AND MYSTERY BEHIND THE GREATEST SUPERMAN OF ALL – AND THE IRONY OF HIS DEATH

ONE OF THE phenomena of Superman's success–when you consider all the phenomena that the Man of Steel has generated in films, TV, radio and comic books–is the continued exposure of a low-budget, live-action syndicated TV series produced from 1950-58, beginning on RKO's 40-acre backlot.

Originally sponsored by Kellogg's Frosted Flakes, a cereal that had spoon-fed the nation on the earlier radio version starring Bud Collyer, "Adventures of Superman" showcased George Reeves as ace reporter Clark Kent, who continually entered empty storage rooms and phone booths in street clothing and then emerged clad in the blue tights of the greatest of superheroes, with that giant letter "S" adorning his chest. "Superman" for TV was always tinged with an old-fashioned patriotism (mother, country, apple pie and the American flag) and embraced opposition to crime and intolerance, for "truth and justice for all." It was honored over the years with awards from the United Parents Association of New York, Youth Builders and the National Conference of Christians and Jews. Not to mention the award of continued good ratings, even if it was cheaply produced with limited special effects.

George Reeves as the Man of Steel, the Protector of Metropolis.

A rewarding moment for George Reeves as he portrays Stuart Tarleton, the beau of Scarlett O'Hara (Vivien Leigh), in "Gone with the Wind," one of his early film roles. But then along came Rhett Butler . . . you know, Clark Gable . . . and Tarleton was done.

George Reeves–even if he did not totally immerse himself in the dual role–became totally identified as Superman after he was chosen from 200 "leading men" in what was then one of the greatest talent hunts in Hollywood history. The series became among the first to be photographed in color after the first season, and for three episodes in 1957 Reeves directed as well as starred. In all, there would be 104 episodes.

Reeves was a tall, solidly-built man who looked right for the part and for his portrayal of Clark Kent, "seemingly mild-mannered reporter for the Daily Planet." Then there was that stiffened jaw, which was in keeping with the series' squareness. If Reeves was adept at using his fists to lower the boom on such villains as Knuckles Nelson, Babyface Stevens and Rausch the Henchman, so was he adept with his fists in real life. Born George Bessolo in Ashland, Kentuck, he was brought up in Pasadena, where he won the light heavyweight championship of the Pasadena Golden Gloves for three straight years.

In "So Proudly We Hail!" (1943), Reeves portrayed Lt. Summers, a lover of Lt. Davidson (Claudette Colbert) and his first leading role – but his connection with Warner Bros. ended when he signed up that same year to serve in World War II.

Reeves joined the famous Community Playhouse in Pasadena, rubbing elbows with Robert Preston and Victor Mature. But while they went on to instant stardom, Reeves lingered for six years, working part time in a broker's office. It was a frustrating time but his patience was rewarded with his first major break: by affecting a Southern accent, he won the role as one of the Tarleton twins in "Gone with the Wind."

His career, after that stroke of luck, seemed assured. He was signed by Warner Brothers and made a long series of movies, among them "Strawberry Blonde" (1941), "Blood and Sand" (1941) and "So Proudly We Hail" (1943). After his service in the U.S. Air Corps (1943-46) during World War II he had difficulty making a comeback. He seemed destined for cheapjack films such as "Jungle Jim" (1948), "Special Agent" (1949) and "The Good Humor Man" (1950). Small, second banana roles continued in his next four features: "Rancho Notorious" (1952), "Bugles in the Afternoon" (1952), "Forever Female" (1952), and "From Here to Eternity" (1953).

With "Superman" came newfound fame in 1952. The kids couldn't get enough autographs. But Reeves, always a sensitive type, did not find fulfillment as an actor being the Man of Tomorrow. He had accepted the role, he told friends, "because I was hungry."

His fear of being stigmatized by Clark Kent proved all too true when, at the end of 1957, the series suspended production and he tried, without success, to line up film or TV work. (However, he was able to have a cameo appearance as Superman on Lucy Ball's TV comedy classic "I Love Lucy.")

Producers were synonymous in agreeing that Reeves was too strongly identified as Superman to be taken seriously as an actor. The best Reeves could do after two and a half years of unemployment was acquire one booking as a professional wrestler and a pending exhibition with then-lightweight champion Archie Moore.

To Reeves, his career seemed finished.

I LOVE LUCY: "Lucy and Superman" (1/14/1957)

One of Reeves' most memorable appearances was when he showed up in costume on "I Love Lucy," helping Lucy Ricardo (Lucille Ball) pull off a surprise party for little Ricky. "Lucy and Superman" was the 166th episode of the series.

And so, in the early morning hours of June 16, 1959, in a state of seeming despondency (and intoxication, according to coroner Theodore Curphey), George Reeves retired to the bedroom of his Benedict Canyon home and shot himself with a .30 caliber Luger pistol.

He was 45.

THE CAREER THAT DRIPPED WITH HORROR

THE ONLY MORTAL SUPERMAN

TO THIS DAY HIS SUDDEN DEATH REMAINS UNSOLVED

New York café socialite Leonore Lemmon, who was to have married Reeves in Mexico a few days after his death, sobbingly said he had killed himself "because he was known as Superman to nine million children but he couldn't get a job." There had been rumors that the actor, shortly before dying, had tried to sever his relationship with Lemmon.

Still another theory: Reeves was despondent about being typecast in the Superman role, and had been unable to get classier acting parts. Another theory is that Reeves, who had sustained injuries to his forehead in an automobile crash two months earlier, was suffering from brain damage and killed himself in a fit of depression, or might have shot himself accidentally.

But these are unresolved theories that continue to surround the actor's death.

Reeves' grief-stricken mother, Helen Bessolo, hired Hollywood attorney Jerry Giesler to investigate her son's death, for she was totally unsatisfied with the suicide ruling.

For one thing, there was the mystery of the gun, which was found at the scene of death without fingerprints. Reeves had not been wearing gloves—in fact, his body had been discovered totally nude. Also, police dug a bullet out of the bedroom carpet—a bullet that Miss Lemmon admitted she had fired when the Luger "accidentally discharged" when she was examining it a "few days" before the alleged suicide. Another slug was found buried in the living room wall downstairs, although no living being ever came forward to admit having fired it.

There was speculation about Reeves' car accident. Two months earlier he had suffered a five-inch, 25-stitch gash in his forehead when his auto had crashed on Benedict Canyon Drive. Miss Lemmon claimed he had been "lethargic" after the accident, and his mother Helen suspected he might have suffered brain damage—enough to throw him mentally off-balance.

Coroner Curphey remained satisfied, without the help of any unearthly strength or skill, that Reeves' death was a suicide. Period. End of case.

And so, the case of the death of the most popular Superman of all time was closed.

But there's one final fact to give all of us pause. "Adventures of Superman" was scheduled to resume shooting in the fall of 1959, just weeks later. Another reason not to accept the suicide story. One more chance for Reeves to be seen by millions. Would that have been enough to keep him from any thoughts of suicide? If only Krypton could give us the power to know!

THE CAREER THAT DRIPPED WITH HORROR

AFTERWORDS

In 2006 the motion picture "Hollywoodland" was released and told elements of Reeves' mysterious death through the eyes of a private investigator played by Adrien Brody. Reeves was portrayed by Ben Affleck. While Brody was a totally fictional character, director Allen Coulter and screenwriter Paul Bernbaum claimed that the clues he pursued were based on factual data. One major element that emerges is that Reeves had had a long-time affair with Toni Mannix (played by Diane Lane), wife of MGM executive Eddie Mannix (played like a villain by Bob Hoskins), who knew of his wife's affair. (In fact, Mannix openly admitted he had a woman of his own on the side.)

This element plays strongly in the screenplay, but ultimately it has to be left behind as just another theory of what might have happened. Portraying Leonore Lemmon, Reeves' wife-to-be, was Robin Tunney, who gives a fine performance. Ultimately, the film focuses on Brody's strange-mannered private eye Louis Simo and his own personal problems with his wife and young son, who has grown to hate him.

A strange film, yes, but the only one to deal with the mystery of Reeves' death.

And there it remains, unsolved to this day.

BEN AFFLECK AS GEORGE REEVES WITH DIANE LANE IN THE BIO-MYSTERY "HOLLYWOOD-LAND" (2006)

Left: The real Leonore Lemmon
Right: Robin Tunney as Leonore

WEARING the 1954 equivalent of a mini-dress, one fashioned from buckskin, Phyllis Coates fearlessly stalked through the African jungle in "Panther Girl of the Kongo," a 12-chapter serial, searching for a mad doctor (none other than Arthur Space) who was creating giant crayfish beasts in his ill-lit laboratory.

Although Republic Studios championed her screen image as "the serial queen of the 1950s," Phyllis was following in the footprints of Kay Aldridge (the cliff-hanging star of 1942's "Perils of Nyoka") and Frances Gifford (the star of 1941's "Perils of Nyoka"). However, no matter how short her dress, Coates would not play that Panther Girl again.

It turned out to be the studio's last gasp to keep alive the chapter genre in a time when theater attendance was waning and the Saturday matinee was all but a relic of Hollywood's past.

Originally serials were shown in 15-minute increments on Saturday afternoons, each chapter ending with a life-threatening cliffhanger. They were fashioned solely for visual thrills, action piece after action piece. Throughout its history (1935-1959), Republic showcased its female stars as stolid, resourceful women, heroic to the extreme and often outperforming their male counterparts.

These heroines, who cannot be stopped by the most diabolical forms of villainy and who ultimately achieve their far-flung goals in Chapter 15, now seem to forecast the expanded roles of modern women with the most positive of images.

It isn't until "Panther Girl" is brought to home video in the early 1990s that one can relive Coates' exciting three-hour adventure. So, in 1992 I take the opportunity to contact Phyllis Coates to hear her side of the cliffhanger experience.

Coates, who also starred in Republic's serial "Jungle Drums of Africa" in 1953, is almost a forgotten portion of Hollywood history. She played Lois Lane in the 1951 feature "Superman and the Mole Men," which led to her doing the first season of "Adventures of Superman" (1952).

She was in the first 24 episodes as Lois Lane opposite George Reeves' Superman. She now lives in Monterey, California, having retired there after giving up a lucrative career for marriage and family.

"Back in the 1950s," she tells me, "none of us thought of the Panther Girl in a feminist light. The heroine had become a serial tradition by then that required a lot of strenuous work to uphold. It was very trying to keep up to the impossibly fast production schedule imposed on us by [studio boss] Herbert Yates. You were lucky to get one take, let alone ask for a second. We were shooting so quickly, and in as few days as possible."

"I was a fast study and I always hit my marks. That's a lot when you have 40 setups a day."

Before serials, Coates was primarily a leading actress in B films. "In those days we worked six days a week, and I'd often make two Westerns back-to-back. The studio system was a well-oiled operation, and it made a comfortable career possible. It kept you working, it protected you, and there was often a family feeling, being part of a studio. Certainly that was true at Republic. We all knew we had to pull together to complete these projects. We tried to make our work fun; everybody was good to each other. There was no room for bruised egos."

She remembers Franklin Adreon, director of "The Panther Girl of the Kongo," as "an old-timer who really knew how to churn out a serial. He'd been working on them as far back as 'The Adventures of Captain Marvel.' He hired me, I think, because I could memorize lines quickly. I was a fast study and I always hit my marks. That means a lot when you have 40 setups a day."

Also being released with "Panther Girl" is a companion serial of 1953 starring Coates, "Jungle Drums of Africa." "In that one I portrayed a missionary's daughter turned doctor who helps geologist Clayton Moore. You remember him as the Lone Ranger on TV.

"Well, I help Moore prevent a uranium mine from falling into the hands of foreign agents (hinted to be communists) and a voodoo-happy witch doctor, played by Roy Glenn. And he's angry that my medical abilities are more powerful than his."

I ask Coates about Clayton Moore. "He was the king of the serials in a way," she answered. "He'd been making them for years. Of course, he went on to become the definitive Lone Ranger on TV.

Phyllis Coates became the serial queen of the cliffhangers in the early 1950s, starting with "Jungle Drums of Africa," playing the daughter of a medical missionary in Africa, who finds herself the target of a witch doctor and uranium thieves. Helping her fight these villains is Clayton Moore, who had already established himself as a masked hero on TV's "The Lone Ranger." Hi-Yo-Silver, Away!

THE CAREER THAT DRIPPED WITH HORROR

"But as dedicated as we were, and as much as we worked well together, we still depended on stuntmen and stuntwomen to pull off those dangerous cliff-hangers. I'll say this: Republic had the best-trained stunt people in the business. They could line up a difficult stunt and get it right in the first take. I recall 'Camera! Action! Print!'"

The Panther Girl was required to ride an elephant in one chapter and Coates still hasn't forgotten that experience. "Emma was a wonderful creature but I told the director, 'Once I'm up there shoot everything you can because when I climb down, that's it.' I had on this short costume and elephants have long, bristly hair. Well, my legs were absolutely raw afterward. When I slid down, I couldn't get my legs together. They had to take me to a steam bath in Studio City before I could start moving normally."

Coates is surprised to learn that her Republic serials were becoming very popular among video collectors of the day. "I never dreamed at the time that any of these things would last beyond their day. Frankly, we considered them the bottom of the barrel. We had the lowest budgets on the lot. But we still gave them everything we had."

Coates was born Gypsie Ann Evarts Stell and came from a broken Texas family. She grew up in convents and Catholic schools all over Texas. "We were a very dysfunctional family, and Texas, with all its oil fields and honky-tonks, was very depressing–a great place to be *from*. My mother and I came to Hollywood in 1943 and I got a job working in 'Ken Murray's Blackouts' as a chorus girl. I remember Ken asking me to pull up my skirt so he could see my legs and then he poked my breasts to see if they were real. It was dark and dingy backstage and the whole thing looked so decadent. I was shaking so much that first night, standing onstage in my sexy gown, that Ken finally put me behind a couch so nobody could see that I was trembling."

Eventually her Hollywood exposure as a chorus girl (including a stint with Earl Carroll) brought her to the attention of MGM, where her name was changed to Phyllis Coates. (Her new surname was borrowed from "Confidential U.S.A." writer Paul Coates.) She began making a string of Westerns, her "bread and butter" at the low-budget studio Monogram.

In all, she worked with Wild Bill Elliott, Johnny Mack Brown, Scott Brady and Joel McCrea. She made three oaters with Whip Wilson in just a year. And she was also fed to the crocodiles by Whit Bissell in the B-favorite "I Was a Teenage Frankenstein."

In her own mind, "Adventures of Superman" remains a high point in her career. "Producer Bob Maxwell was looking at hundreds of gals to play Lois for the feature, 'Superman and the Mole Men.'

For Phyllis Coates, the "Superman" franchise began in 1951 with the release of a full-length feature, "Superman and the Mole Men," in which she co-starred for the first time with George Reeves as Superman/Clark Kent.

"When I auditioned, he told me, 'Your attitude is just right.' And I got the role. We did the movie first, then we started the TV series at the old Selznick Studios. It was like making a serial–24 pages of dialogue each day. Unlike Margot Kidder in the 'Superman' movies, Lois wasn't able to have any kind of flirtations with Clark Kent or Superman. It was like working with a bit in my mouth. She emerged a straight-on, one-dimensional character, but I still enjoyed doing it because there was an atmosphere of fun that surrounded the set."

And George Reeves? "I'm afraid I got into this crowd that was drinking a lot. It became a merry-go-round that wasn't very good for me. Maxwell wanted me to stay on as Lois after the first season and they offered me five times more money. But I decided that when my contract ran out, I'd leave. I've never regretted it. Some kind of ESP was warning me to get away from the situation."

After her five-year marriage to film director Norman Taurog collapsed, she married a doctor and got involved in lucrative real-estate deals. Divorced a second time, she now lives alone in Monterey and occasionally accepts acting jobs. More recent work has included the Whoopi Goldberg TV movie "Kiss Shot (1989)," the mother of Marilyn Monroe in "Goodnight Sweet Marilyn" (1984) and assorted TV commercials. "I think there's still a lot to be enjoyed from my career, but I'll never go back to Los Angeles," she vows. "I ran away from there a long time ago."

Coates appears with "daughter" Lois Lane (Teri Hatcher) on "Lois and Clark: The New Adventures of Superman."

AFTERWORDS

Since our conversation in 1992, Phyllis Coates only returned to Hollywood on rare occasion. She was lured back in 1994 to portray Lois Lane's mother Ellen Lane in "Lois and Clark: The New Adventures of Superman." The episode was "The House of Luthor," and the casting suggestion was made by none other than then-current Lois Lane (Teri Hatcher). She also did two episodes of "Dr. Quinn, Medicine Woman." She has since remained in her world of anonymity.

Next Up: She Followed in Coates' High Heels as Lois Lane and Was Raised to New Heights . . .

But She'd Already Played Lois in Two Serials . . .
Yeah, It's the Wonderful Pin-Up Queen Noel Neill

NOEL NEILL'S once-fiery red hair, which radiated excessively during World War II when she was a favorite pin-up of Hollywood, has lost some of its flame. But hey, she's still a spunky, good-looking woman in her mid-60s as she opens the door to her suite in the Fairmont Tower and instantly starts bubbling about Lois Lane.

And I'm off into another Universe, flying as high as one can achieve with both feet on solid earth.

It is now August, in the year 1986, and it's all coming back to her with the velocity of a speeding bullet . . . The history of TV's "Adventures of Superman" comes spinning out from between her lips as she recalls the 78 episodes (1953-58) in which she starred as the Daily Planet reporter who always wore the same working suit with the "Lois Lane" lapels. Come on, you remember Lois: the she-demon of journalism scoops in the city of Metropolis.

Yet she could never figure out that the Man of Steel, who kept rescuing her from fates worse than death, was really fellow newspaperman Clark Kent, that mild-mannered, sometimes-shy gentleman back in the City Room who always seemed to be looking for a phone booth so he could make an emergency phone call – or was there some other reason?

Neill, whose hair is now whitish gray and swept back in a tight bun, is remembering the sudden death of her co-star George Reeves; her experiences hanging in a body harness for the flying sequences; the cheap sets and the fast shooting schedules at the old Ziv Studio (which specialized producing syndicated shows in the early years of TV before all the major studios began filming TV series); her friendship with Jack Larson, who played the irrepressible copy boy Jimmy Olson. . . it all comes flowing out as she flies headfirst down television's Memory Lane.

Betty Grable was said to be the leading pin-up gal in the early days of World War II. So here's a little known fact: Noel Neill was rated as the second leading pin-up gal in the early days of World War II. One GI at the Hollywood Canteen remarked she was "the unsecret weapon."

Noel arrives at the Fairmont hotel only hours before I meet her in her grand suite to discuss the history of becoming the first Earthling to portray reporter Lois Lane in two Columbia serials. She was in town to serve as hostess for a 30-hour TV Marathon replaying episodes from her series "Adventures of Superman."

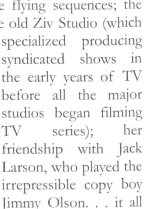

Neill's enthusiasm has been unleashed anew because a Bay Area TV station is televising a 30-hour marathon of "Adventures of Superman," and she will serve as hostess, recalling anecdotes about a piece of Americana entertainment that refuses to stop soaring.

Those 30 hours will contain 60 half-hour episodes of the 104 produced in the years 1952 through 1958, which have been recycled countless times in syndication.

"Who would believe Superman would still be flying after three decades?"

Noel signed this photo of her and George Reeves clad as Superman when we bumped into each other during one of the WonderCons held in San Francisco. Always with her was her friend Larry Thomas Ward, author of two fabulous books about Neill's career. (They're coming up soon!)

By modern standards, the series might seem cheaply scripted, cornily acted and shot on the barest of sets, with special effects of minimal impact, but it continues to play and enhance generations of viewers.

Is it the patriotic squareness? The campy characters?

Is it the way it embraces "truth, justice and the American way?"

Neill, on what she considers a very special morning, is wearing a black knee-length skirt and a blouse of large, multicolored polka dots, enhanced by a large black bow and a ruffled collar. And is she happy to be back in the limelight, talking like an old pro, even though she hasn't done any serious acting since 1959, when the "Superman" series was cancelled following the death (officially a suicide) of George Reeves and she voluntarily went into retirement to enjoy married life.

"Boy oh boy," she gasps excitedly. "Who would believe Superman would still be flying after three decades? I guess it's because there's always a new audience for the series. It's not like the adult TV shows that come and go like the wind. Kids grow up watching 'Superman.' Gosh, it's the American way. Talk about truth and justice.

"People always ask me why. Simple: It's about the fantasy. Young and old enjoy seeing the good guys win. We had plenty of physical action but very little violence back in the '50s. Superman used to knock together the heads of the dumb crooks, or shove them against the wall with one hand after watching their puny bullets bounce off his chest. Real comic book stuff. I can remember we even had to reshoot some scenes because Kellogg's, our sponsor, felt they were too violent. Too much snap, crackle and pop." (For the record, Kellogg's, a maker of breakfast cereals, had first spoon-fed America on Superman by sponsoring the radio series of the 1940s that starred Bud Collyer.)

"Phyllis bowed out playing Lois Lane to do another series she thought was going to be more important ... but I don't remember the title now."

The Man of Steel first entered Neill's life in 1948 when she played Lois Lane in the 15-chapter Columbia serial "Superman" opposite Kirk Alyn. That was followed two years later by a second Sam Katzman-produced cliff-hanger, "Atom Man Vs. Superman," in which she was again teamed with Alyn. Neill seemed washed up as Lois Lane when Phyllis Coates was signed to do the television role opposite George Reeves. (Coates and Reeves had first worked together a year earlier playing Lois Lane and Superman in the 1951 feature "Superman and the Mole Men," the popularity of which would lead to the TV series.)

"Suddenly," blurts Neill, "after doing 24 episodes, Phyllis bowed out playing Lois Lane to do another series she thought was going to be more important . . . but I don't remember the title now." (A check of Coates' credits reveals a number of other movie serials and TV series. Coates worked steadily until 1960.)

"So, because I had portrayed Lois in the Sam Katzman serials, I stepped in and we did 26 episodes in just 13 weeks, shooting all the newspaper office scenes back-to-back, all the flying sequences back-to-back, and so on. We worked fast, six days a week. While we filmed on one set, carpenters were building the next set on the other side of the wall. Then we were finished, and we didn't work on 'Superman' again for a year and a half."

Her first time on the set led to a confrontation with old serial director Thomas Carr. "Phyllis Coates had played the role very brusquely, in the ballsy way Margot Kidder played her in the film series with Christopher Reeve. Phyllis had none of the softness that I visualized in Lois Lane. Carr wanted me to emulate Coates, but I didn't feel comfortable with that. We argued; pretty soon I was in tears. George Reeves came over and, realizing what a tough job it is to replace someone who has already established a part, told Carr to ease up and give me a chance. Carr softened up, and after that I was allowed to play Lois my way. George was really wonderful, a true Southern gentleman who would stand up for you."

Neill further remembers Reeves as "always a little embarrassed about wearing his Superman suit. He was basically a good actor who had appeared in 'Gone with the Wind,' portraying one of Scarlet O'Hara's suitors. He was also in 'So Proudly We Hail!' and 'From Here to Eternity.' He really did take acting seriously. But his eyes would glaze over when he put on that Superman suit."

Neill feels Reeves was a better actor than Kirk Alyn, but Alyn

George Reeves as Clark Kent and Noel as Lois in one of the TV episodes involving a phone call. What Clark needs now is a phone booth for a little privacy.

probably made a superior superhero because "he had a better build and could do more athletically. George just didn't have the shoulders." On the other hand, "Kirk was hammy. I hate to say it, but I had less than love for Kirk. He was on a total ego trip; he really believed he was Superman. He also thought he was God's gift to women and was always on the make. What a cornball. He had this spit curl, like in the comic books, and even off the set he would go around with this spit curl across his forehead."

"I firmly believe that George died at hands other than his own. There is nothing worse than a woman scorned."

In 1955, the third season, the episodes were shot in color, and continued in color through 1958, when the series entered its usual 1 1/2-year hiatus. "It was in June of 1959 when we all met in the office of director George Blair to discuss the seventh season; 26 new scripts were waiting to be produced. I remember George [Reeves], Blair and producer Whitney Ellsworth were playing gin rummy, and George looked absolutely great. He was in top spirits. In fact, he was getting ready to do a feature film too."

That's why she was totally shocked two days later when she received a phone call informing her that Reeves had "committed suicide by blowing out his brains with a .30-caliber Luger pistol in his Benedict Canyon home. He was only 45." I ask Neill to tell me her personal thoughts about Reeves' death, given the theory that he might have been murdered. "I won't go into details," she answers, "but I firmly believe that George died at hands other than his own. There is nothing worse than a woman scorned."

Whatever really happened, "Adventures of Superman" was not to continue without George Reeves. Recalls Neill: "National [the company that publishes the *Superman* comic books under the DC label] decided they had 102 episodes for syndication and that was enough."

Later, she tells me, "Jack Larson, who played Jimmy Olson, was approached about a Jimmy Olson TV series that would have used scenes of Reeves lifted out of the old episodes. But Jack hated the idea. He thought it would be demeaning to George's memory, and he turned it down." Also, attempts to make a "Superboy" pilot never clicked.

For Noel Neill, it was the end of her acting career. "I was never the gung-ho type about movies or working in Hollywood. Maybe it's basic laziness or a lack of ego drive, but I really didn't want to work anymore. I was happily married to a man in the aircraft plating business."

Neill received only $225 per episode and never was paid a penny in residuals. She has spent the intervening years leading a very private life, working for a long stretch at United Artists as a secretary in the public relations department.

In the early 1970s she made personal appearances at colleges to discuss her Lois Lane experiences. Many young students applauded her as one of the first working women on TV, and in more recent years she has been described by some critics as "an inspiration to the ERA movement."

Neill was born in Minneapolis, the daughter of a newspaperman. She and her mother visited Los Angeles after her high school graduation and Noel found herself auditioning for a job as singer at the Del Mar race track, where Bing Crosby was appearing.

Crooning star Bing Crosby discovered Noel Neill in 1938 and gave her work as a singer at the turf club, part of the race track in Del Mar, California. It was the moment that opened her door to success.

Crosby liked her voice (and, no doubt, her figure) and suggested she look for film work at Paramount. She was under contract to that studio for four years, working in several low-budget Henry Aldrich movies and other B flicks. Except for a 1944 Crosby film, "Here Come the Waves," she never graduated to bigger things. When her contract expired, she began her serial career in "Adventures of Frank and Jesse James" (1948) and "The James Brothers of Missouri" (1949). She also played a jungle girl, Lula, in the 1947 serial "Brick Bradford."

Neill filmed a brief cameo role in the 1978 "Superman" film starring Christopher Reeve but her scene aboard a speeding train, with a young Clark Kent racing outside her window, was cut from the release print.

"I was playing Lois Lane's mother, and I turned to my daughter and said, 'You have such a vivid imagination; someday you'll probably be a writer.' Later, that scene was restored and shown in the network TV version."

One of the stories Lane is planning to tell as part of the marathon she is about to do involved Reeves crashing through a wall and rescuing Lois Lane.

"All I saw come through the wall was one foot and one arm. Someone had forgotten to rig that wall so George could knock it down.

"The things that can go wrong when you're supposed to be a superhero!"

Noel thought this was one of her best outfits from the 1956 episode "The Tomb of Zaharan," which ran on "Adventures of Superman."

AFTERWORDS

That memorable encounter with Noel Neill would not be my last. We would meet several times in years to come at the WonderCon, an annual sci-fi/comic book convention held at the Moscone Convention Center in San Francisco. It was in 2003 during the WonderCon that I rushed to her nearby table to say hello. She presented me with a copy of her brand-new book, "Truth, Justice and the American Way: The Life and Times of Noel Neill, the Original Lois Lane." Remarkably large (9" x 12"), this biography, flowing with photographs of Noel from all periods in her life, was by Larry Thomas Ward, her "close friend and companion" who was also at the convention. Both signed my copy that unforgettable day.

And then in 2007 emerged her second book (also by Ward, also 9" x 12") entitled "Beyond Lois Lane," an amazing display of 142 color photographs and descriptive captions detailing her entire life. I don't think I've ever seen a book as thrilling, with photos of Noel in her movies, her personal appearances and a few in her private life. Yes, many of them are of a pin-up nature, as if asking Ava Gardner, Betty Grable and a few other Hollywood beauties to please move over and make a little more room for her.

Eventually Noel fell into bad health and no longer attended special events. She died on July 3, 2016, after a prolonged illness at the age of 95 at her home in Tucson, Arizona.

According to Ward: "Few of her fans actually knew her real name, almost always simply calling her 'Lois' to which she would unfailingly answer with a bright smile and a kind word. It was more than a role to her. 'Lois' was someone she believed in and a character she happily and warmly embraced. Noel Neill maintained that bright, perky and engaging personality up until her death."

CAN A TAP-DANCING, would-be mathematician from Sunnyvale, just south of San Francisco, find happiness in the arms of newspaperman Clark Kent while trying to win the Pulitzer Prize as a reporter working at the Daily Planet in the city of Metropolis? Currently that's the big question on the mind of Teri Hatcher, a one-time Bay Arean who could have had a news-reporting job at KPIX-TV, Channel 5, but forsook the opportunity to move to Hollywood, where soon she was appearing in 19 episodes of "The Love Boat," making a splash as a singer-dancer nicknamed Amy the Mermaid.

After that minimal wave of success Hatcher appeared in meatier roles in "The Big Picture" (1989), "Tango and Cash" (1989) and "Soapdish" (1991). It was then she was chosen to portray the legendary lady reporter of the Daily Planet, Lois Lane, in "Lois and Clark: The New Adventures of Superman," another incarnation of the famous comic-book superhero. Hatcher, during our interview in a Warner Brothers studio in the year 1993, is quick to point out that this is not quite the same Lois Lane as depicted in the DC comic books, nor is it a copy of Margot Kidder's version from the big-screen series that starred Christopher Reeve.

The New Age Lois Lane: More Love Moments With Clark Kent –But Where's Superman?

Meet Teri Hatcher and Dean Cain

"My Lois breaks down a lot of the old stereotypes," she says, "and sets up a more modern version of a newspaperwoman. She's feisty, aggressive, funny, vulnerable and sensual as she makes her way through masculinity in a Superman's world." It's no accident, Hatcher adds, that the credit for Lois appears before the credit for Clark Kent aka Superman (Dean Cain).

"Lois and Clark" was created by producer / writer Debra Joy LeVine, who left after the first season. She did go on to produce the popular TV series "Early Edition" (1996-2000) and "Dawson's Creek" (1998-2003).

Continues Hatcher: "The series was set up to emphasize the romantic relationship Lois has with Clark/Superman, and not so much Superman involved in some fantastic plot with a supervillain."

Hatcher is called to the set and I am quickly joined by Deborah Joy LeVine, the series' creator and co-executive producer. "I knew that on a TV budget those blockbuster movies with Reeve were impossible to follow," LeVine confesses to me, "so I decided a new tactic was needed. Usually the Superman/Lane/Kent love affair gets short shrift and has become one of the most unrequited love stories of all time. But why not expand on it? It's natural for Superman to be attracted to Lois, and Lois to Superman, and Clark to Lois, but not Lois to Clark. What a great triangle, involving just two human beings."

An attorney for ten years before she turned to writing TV, LeVine tells me that the new, improved Clark Kent/Superman "is a more sophisticated man, not a nerd who bumps into tables, or pretends to be near-sighted, or goes away to meditate in his Fortress of Solitude. He knows ballroom dancing, he could serve tea at the London Savoy, he can be romantic and charming. And he wants to fit into the real world, and not just look for a place to change his costume on the way to a rescue."

THE CAREER THAT DRIPPED WITH HORROR

LeVine claims to have read 300 comic books in order to become an expert on the Superman legend and that she had little trouble in choosing Hatcher to play Lois. "Teri's comedy instincts are brilliant, and her vulnerability was perfect for the role." On the other hand, "Casting Superman was a nightmare experience because a lot of good actors would instantly shy away from the role, afraid that it might be a career killer." (Certainly Kirk Alyn, the serial Superman of the 1940s, and George Reeves, the superman of 1950s television, had their share of problems getting jobs after portraying the Man of Steel.)

LeVine's final choice for the role was Dean Cain, a one-time Princeton student who became an All-American football star and still holds the NCAA record for the most interceptions in one season. Before Superman, Cain's only acting claim-to-fame was playing a hunk named Rick in four episodes of "Beverly Hills 90210." Recalls LeVine: "I knew there was something unusual about Dean the first time I met him. The hallway outside was full of young women, fans who had followed him to the audition. His popularity is amazing."

"At first, I thought Dean was too young, that he was more suited to play Superboy. But I finally realized, when I saw him up close in the proper lighting, that he was the perfect Clark Kent, man about Metropolis."

Dean Cain just happens to be on the set and I am

Just the fact that Lois Lane's name comes before Clark Kent's in the series title ("Lois and Clark: The New Adventures of Superman") reveals that the super-popular ABC series (1993-1997) was searching for new portrayals of both now-famous personalities. Avoiding past clichés, the re-imagined Super show attracted a vast audience that averaged 18 million viewers. Up, up and away!!!!

able to pin him down for a few minutes. I ask him if he has gone back through time to see some of the old TV episodes or the serials. "I didn't need to look at all that stuff. This 1990's Clark Kent is

In the Season 3 episode "Ultra Woman," Clark Kent marries Lois Lane, unaware that Lex Luther has replaced Lois with a clone after kidnapping the real thing.

completely different, a guy with a sense of humor struggling to fit into society as a normal person. Superman is his alter ego, not the other way around. In his mind, Clark comes before Superman. So, in that sense, Deborah has reversed the roles around."

One aspect of the movies that the new series is retaining is the flying element. "We've been hanging around a lot of wires these days," jokes Cain. "Not that I mind it so much. And Teri . . . let me tell you, Teri is the sexiest, prettiest Lois Lane I've ever personally met." (Too bad he never got to meet Noel Neill, a plenty sexy-pretty gal.) Before I leave the Warner Brothers set, I catch up to "Hatch" (as she is called by crew members) for one final question.

How does she feel about doing all those flying sequences? "Hah," she replies. "I have to concur with Dean. Despite all the bruises, strained muscles and backaches the flying sequences give me, hanging in those harnesses 30 feet off the ground is an unbelievable experience. The moment that Dean scoops me up and carries me away into another dimension, I feel as if it's the most romantic thing that's ever happened to me."

AFTERWORDS

"Lois and Clark: The New Adventures of Superman" would last for four seasons with Cain and Hatcher completing 87 episodes. Each performer has gone on to great success.

Hatcher portrayed Susan Mayer in 180 episodes of "Desperate Housewives" (2004-2012), for which she won the Golden Globe Award for Best Actress in a Musical or Comedy, three Screen Actors Guild Awards, and a Primetime Emmy nomination for Outstanding Lead Actress in a Comedy Series. She continues to fly high through the Universe, also having played Paris Carver in the Pierce Brosnan James Bond flick "Tomorrow Never Dies."

Meanwhile, Cain continues to have parts in TV shows and feature films. Highlights: He was Dr. Jeremiah Danvers in "Supergirl" (2015-17) and he played Pete Davenport in 34 episodes of "Hit the Floor" (2013-18).

SHOCKING FAMILY SECRET AND STUNNING REVELATION FROM HORROR HOST JOHN STANLEY

REVEALED NOW FOR FIRST TIME . . . IT'S ALL ABOUT A GREAT UNCLE . . . WHO WAS GREATER THAN GREAT!

BRACE YOURSELVES, loyal fans. I have a family secret I am finally revealing, mainly because it's directly connected to the history of Hollywood and its movies. How ironic I should develop a love for cinema, following in the footprints of my father, Myron Stanley. He took me to movies almost every week, until I became a teen-ager and left home to join the U.S. Army in 1957.

It started in 1944 when we lived in Oakland and numerous times the two of us rode a streetcar across the Bay Bridge to San Francisco. (This form of Bay Area travel no longer exists.) From there we walked to Market and Fifth Streets, to the Telenews Theater that specialized in exclusively playing newsreels. Most of the footage then dealt with the wars going on in the Pacific and Europe. Then we'd go next door to the Esquire Theater that played double bills of B-movies. It was there I saw my first Western (a Cisco Kid oater) and began to develop that love for cinema, especially for westerns, musicals and horror flicks.

Dad loved watching all the warfare footage at the Telenews and wanted to serve but he had volunteered to lay hardwood floors in new army bases being built in California. At the end of 1944 he finally joined the U.S. Army and went through basic training at Camp Roberts, where ironically he had laid the floors in the very barracks where he slept. (That's my dad at right, standing in front of his Camp Roberts barracks.)

In the summer of 1945 dad's outfit landed in Manila, on the island of Luzon in the Philippine Islands. He was soon on patrol in the jungle.

In Uncle George's garage, my dad found an Oscar, which he proudly posed with. Anything to "win" an Academy Award!

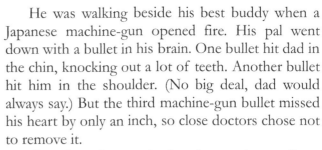

He was walking beside his best buddy when a Japanese machine-gun opened fire. His pal went down with a bullet in his brain. One bullet hit dad in the chin, knocking out a lot of teeth. Another bullet hit him in the shoulder. (No big deal, dad would always say.) But the third machine-gun bullet missed his heart by only an inch, so close doctors chose not to remove it.

Somehow, he survived and came home. Soon after we moved to Napa Valley where cinema engulfed me like never before. To this day I remember the night in 1946 when we saw "The Best Years of Our Lives." One year later, when I was all of seven, "Gone with the Wind" was re-released for the first time since its opening in 1938. I came home from school and told my mother Frances I wanted to see the film. It was only playing for two nights. But it was a school night, and she said I couldn't go on a school night. Rigid family rule.

Nevertheless, I left the house and began a long walk down Soda Canyon Road toward downtown Napa's Fox Theater, which, sadly, was torn down in 1954. Soon my dad pulled up in his Ford pickup and told me to get into the truck. I said no, I was going to see "Gone with the Wind."

His reply: "Get into the truck. We're both going to see 'Gone with the Wind.'" It was a grand evening and we consumed several bags of popcorn. Another moment I still remember: on a Sunday night in 1949 we saw John Wayne's "Sands of Iwo Jima" at the Uptown Theater and on Monday night we saw "Twelve O'Clock High" with Gregory Peck at the Fox. (Mom never said a word about it being a school night– it was dad's idea.) What a great way to start off the week.

Another memorable moment: A U.S. Army band was playing music in front of the Uptown Theater in Napa in 1951 for the opening of Samuel Fuller's "The Steel Helmet." My dad and I were there that night and Fuller's imagery of war left unique impressions that still clobber my mind to this day. (I would meet Fuller in Hollywood several times in 1963 . . . my accounts can be found in "The Gang That Shot Up Hollywood," a book I published in 2011.)

From this love came the magic of becoming the host of a TV series that introduced movie after movie after movie after movie after . . .

Okay, steady yourself! Here comes my Stanley family secret:

My father's uncle, George Maitland Stanley, was the man who took a sketch on a napkin drawn by MGM studio art director Cedric Gibbons and went home that night to physically create the very first Academy Award, officially known as the Academy Award of Merit. It took him a year to design and sculpt the Oscar.

SIDE BY SIDE: MY GREAT-UNCLE GEORGE STANLEY AND THE ACADEMY AWARD WHICH HE CREATED BACK IN 1929 . . . LET'S LOVE MOVIES FOREVER

Designed the Academy Award!

Sculpted it too!

No wonder movies were in the blood of my father!

And me!

How many other TV horror hosts, present or past, could make this same claim?

In retrospect it now seems strange that it wasn't until I was 26 years old that I finally met George. My father always had a close relationship with his immediate family and we often traveled to Santa Maria, Ventura and Bakersfield to visit with them. Yet dad had never gone to the trouble to visit George and his wife Peggy, who lived in Los Angeles.

Left to right: My father Myron, my mother Frances, my wife Erica, yours truly, George's wife, and George Stanley, taken at his Los Angeles home.

That's me with my Great Uncle George Stanley in the summer of 1966 at his home in Los Angeles. It was the one and only time I spent a day with him.

So, it was in the summer of 1966 that my mom Frances and dad Myron picked me and my wife Erica up in a brand-new 1966 Ford station wagon and we traveled to L. A. to George's home. I cannot remember actually which part of L.A. but George greeted us with enthusiasm even though he did not look well and his hands shook, like one suffering from Parkinson's Disease.

In his backyard he explained some of his history. He had attended the Otis Art Institute in his 20s and had learned the art of molding clay into images. He went on to create a statue of Isaac Newton in Griffith Park and did additional statue art for schools in Glendale and Long Beach.

By 1927 George had developed incredible skills for molding images from clay. So it was, he was invited to dinner with MGM's art director Cedric Gibbons. As they finished eating, Gibbons did a rough sketch on a napkin of a man standing on a reel of film while clutching a sword. On a napkin yet? It was Gibbons' way of telling George that he wanted him to design what was going to be called the Academy Award. A prize to be given by the Academy of Motion Picture Arts and Sciences to Hollywood artists who had created the best cinematic work during a given year. Immediately George designed a three-dimensional object based on Gibbons' crude sketch. What would eventually be nicknamed The Oscar, the Academy Award. They were first presented in 1929 at the Hollywood Roosevelt Hotel and the annual ceremony continues to this day.

But that's not all George achieved. He was to be responsible for one of Hollywood's finest landmarks. In 1937 he began work on what would become known as the Streamline Modern-style fountain (right) at the entrance to the Hollywood Bowl.

THE CAREER THAT DRIPPED WITH HORROR

This was a 200-foot long, 22-feet high sculpture.

The Bowl represented drama, music and dance so the fountain featured human figures representing the world of entertainment. As one critic described it, "Its combined Hollywood set design and construction." It took three years for George to complete, and officially opened in 1940. In later years it was renovated and today looks like new.

George died four years after I met him, in 1970, at the age of 67.

Ironically, one year later, my father was stricken with a heart attack, but had been saved at the last minute by my mom, who saw he wasn't looking well and immediately drove him to the Queen of the Valley Hospital in Napa. Literally the attack occurred as he was being wheeled into the emergency room.

Here is George Maitland Stanley in his younger days, posing with the Academy Award he designed and sculpted.

He survived to live another twelve years before a stroke claimed him in 1982. And we got to see a lot of movies during those years.

And that Japanese bullet, an inch from his heart, was still in him. Even modern doctors had decided it was too dangerous to try and remove it.

Thanks, George, for opening up the world of cinema to me and my dad.

AFTERWORDS

One other member of the Stanley clan whom I would meet later in my life was (below left) Maitland Cotton Stanley, the son of Oscar-designer George Stanley.

He and his lovely wife lived in Greenbrae in nearby Marin County but I did not meet them until around 2005. We enjoyed a few dinners together and I learned of his career as a sketch artist and painter (talents similar to some of his father's) and his 35 years working for Swissair as a cargo specialist.

In 2009, the same year he would pass away at the age of 81, he sent me a brand-new second-edition copy of his book "A

Guide to Gold Hill, Nevada," a detailed and fascinating history of a once-famous mining town located near Carson City. The town thrived from 1864 through 1877. The book is loaded with historic photographs and maps of the region, and describes how it

eventually became abandoned. I had no sooner received the book than Maitland began descent into bad health.

Isn't it wonderful how son follows father and elements are passed on to another generation?

Thanks, Maitland. Thanks, George.

And thanks, dad.

The three of you will live with me forever.

BATMAN BEGINS!
THE ORIGINS OF A SUPERHERO AND YOUTHFUL SIDEKICK ENCOUNTERING FACES OF EVIL IN DOWNTOWN GOTHAM CITY!

MAY 1939 is an unforgettable date in the annals of crime fighting. It was that month that the greatest combatant of arch-criminals was born: Bruce Wayne, bachelor-millionaire, alias The Batman. He and his youthful ward, Dick Grayson, alias Robin the Boy Wonder, came to life in *Detective Comics* No. 27 in the drawings of Bob Kane.

In what is now nostalgically alluded to as The Golden Age of Comics, Batman matched his free-wheeling prowess against the diabolical cunning that was conveniently headquartered in Gotham City, undoubtedly the most crime-infested metropolis in our Nation. Not common-face villains but unique criminals with names like

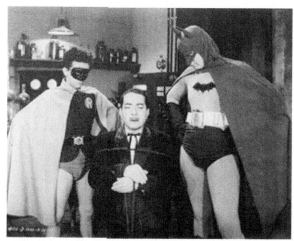

"The Batman" (1943) starred Lewis Wilson as the Caped Crusader and Douglas Croft as sidekick Robin.

the Riddler, the Penguin, the Mad Hatter . . . And the indefatigable justice-seekers have thrived ever since in an aura of hero worship that few other comic-book characters have sustained.

Dr. Frederic Wertham would go down, down, down, down, down in comic book history.

For while Batman, Robin and the Batmobile have undergone some noticeable alterations as editorships have changed, the same basic theme of good triumphing over evil has maintained its virtuous attraction to generations of readers. Also instrumental in inducing fresh readership and interest were two Columbia series made in the 1940s, which were devoted to depicting Batman's dedicated fight to preserve democracy. The 1943 version (above right), titled simply "The Batman," is considered so inept and bigoted by modern standards as to be moderately amusing.

The singular appeal of these crimefighters began to be endangered when a doctor of

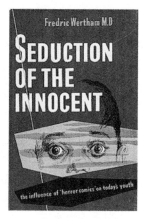

psychology, Dr. Frederic Wertham, labeled Batman and his young companion as "dream world" homosexuals in his book "Seduction of the Innocent." Many consider that book to be laughable, a mostly naive attack on the comic-book industry when it was first released in 1954. However, it was taken seriously by Senator Estes Kefauver who formed an investigating committee that erupted when E.C. Comics editor-publisher William Gaines voluntarily appeared alone before the committee to defend his horror, science-fiction and crime comic books (and his best seller of all, *Mad Comics*). It wasn't enough and soon a Comic Code Authority created a self-imposed form of censorship on comics that would change them for the next ten years.

So strong has been devotion to the caped crime-crushers Batman and Robin that there existed a core of young and old who studied with unprecedented fervor what became known as "The Batman Credo." It consisted of an "Academy" (begun by a Michigan college professor), amateur fanzines, tons of correspondence and the buying, selling and trading of old comics.

THE CAREER THAT DRIPPED WITH HORROR

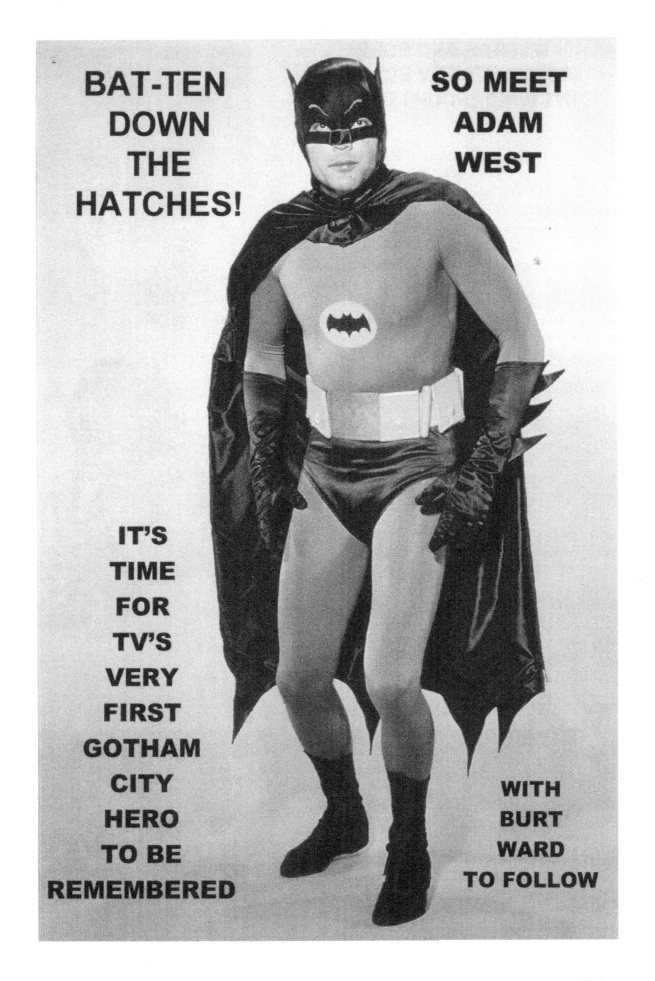

BAT-TEN DOWN THE HATCHES!

SO MEET ADAM WEST

IT'S TIME FOR TV'S VERY FIRST GOTHAM CITY HERO TO BE REMEMBERED

WITH BURT WARD TO FOLLOW

BATMAN AND ROBIN BURST ONTO TV SCREENS IN LIVING (ROOM) COLOR!

In late 1965, a ripple of intense excitement swept through the world of fandom: Word leaked out that there was an ABC series, "Batman," in the making, even though the television network had kept tight wraps on its new vehicle, treating it with unusual secrecy.

At last, I was able to learn the series is scheduled to begin running in January 1966 with Adam West portraying Batman and Burt Ward portraying Robin. I immediately contact a publicist I know at ABC and arrange for a meeting with West at 20th Century Fox. Ward I know nothing about but I recall that West had been one of the plainclothesmen playing second banana to Robert Taylor in the series "The Detective" (1959-62). West had portrayed Sgt. Steve Nelson in 30 episodes.

"Thanks for remembering things that quickly fade away into the past," says West when we sit down to talk things over. "Now, about Batman. I was recalled suddenly from Europe where I'd been living and making a series of pictures, including the spaghetti western 'The Relentless Four.' The caller was producer Bill Dozier, who had decided it was time to broaden Batman's exposure on the home screen. That was at least six weeks ago – that's how long I feel like I've been locked away in a closet of pure fantasy, comedy and action."

On this afternoon, West is shooting a laboratory sequence with George Sanders, who is portraying the glacial villain Mr. Freeze. "The order came through so unexpectedly and urgently that we've been pushing against a very tight schedule to meet the January airdates. It's hard work, yes, but I've never before enjoyed a part as much as

Holy Secret Identity! That's Adam West under the Bat cowl!

this part. A man . . . well, maybe not quite made of steel, but still as tough as they come. And I have the good fortune to portray him."

Left: Adam West as Batman and Burt Ward as Robin. Right: Just three of the unique criminal rulers of Gotham City: The Penguin (Burgess Meredith), The Riddler (Frank Gorshin) and the Catwoman (Julie Newmar)

West grabs me by the shoulder and I wonder, for a split second, if I am about to fly through the air and crash against one of the walls of the laboratory in which I stand. "I say this in all sincerity. I think 'Batman' will appeal to one of the largest audiences in TV history—adults as well as the younger set. For another, I've always loved comic books. Batman and Submariner are two of my favorite characters. And still another reason: I love cliffhangers. And believe me, we're featuring some bizarre ones at the end of each Wednesday night episode. The Thursday night installment will resolve Wednesday's cliffhanger and round out the story for that particular week. So, you get two lightning bolts per week. Tell me that's not a superb deal."

Looking down on Robin (Burt Ward) and Batman (Adam West) in the Batmobile, a takeoff on the 1955 Lincoln Futura, built in Italy by the Ford Motor Company.

West points out that Bob Kane was still drawing the Batman comic strip. "We're definitely trying to keep alive the classic criminals he created. You know, Kane never killed off a villain because he realized that if the readers especially liked a character, he could revive him or her. Listen to this: Frank Gorshin is playing the Riddler (see page 75). Cesar Romero is the Joker. Anne Baxter, holy cow, is Zilda the Great. And Burgess Meredith is The Penguin, who else?"

How exactly is Batman being played? "Certainly not in the way of the old George Reeves 'Superman' series. It's satirical as far as tendency toward style. And certainly, satirical as far as exaggeration and overstatement are concerned. But the rudiment here is to play it with truth. You might say my job is to make the overstatement as subtle as possible. I like to think of myself as nature's nobleman, with a sole desire to stamp out crime, by stomping on each villain in the end."

And what was his attitude toward the infamous Dr. Wertham, who helped to destroy comic books? West cleared his throat with pseudo-indignation, paused for only a moment, and replied: "The only ones who ever believed that chapter in his book were homosexuals—and Dr. Wertham."

Stand by! That day with Adam West on set at 20th Century-Fox is only the first time I will be covering the series. Next up is an afternoon at Fox in the summer of 1966. Not inside a studio but outside on the studio grounds, standing next to the Batmobile. This time I will be meeting for the first time Burt Ward, portrayer of Robin the Boy Wonder. And all historically preserved in screenplay format!

"RENDEZVOUS WITH
A GOTHAM CITY GIANT"
(WHO STILL HAS SOME GROWING TO DO)

Screenplay by
JOHN STANLEY

Produced by
DENNIS WILLIS

Unauthorized by
ADAM WEST

A CREATURES AT LARGE
PRODUCTION
REVISION DATE: 7/15/66

Holy Moly!!! There's the Boy Wonder And Over There Sits the Batmobile . . . Smack in the World of 20th Century Fox

EXT. FOX MOVIE STUDIO - DAY (STOCK FOOTAGE) - HIGH ANGLE

Looking down through a thick cloud of smog onto a huge complex of sound stages, bustling commissaries and long lines extending out from casting offices.

NARRATOR'S VOICE
(greatly excited)
It's a super muggy summer afternoon in Los Angeles, sprawling metropolis of sprawling metropolises. A most fitting site for a duel between the forces of stardom and the power of fandom. Did I forget to mention the duel between good and evil?

NARRATOR'S VOICE (CONT.)
Not far from stately Beverly Hills stands stately 20th Century Fox Studios, home of the Seaview submarine, the lost Jupiter II rocketship, Peyton Place Plaza and that Dynamo Duo of derring-do and dash, Batman and Robin.

DISSOLVE TO:

EXT. GOTHAM CITY SQUARE - DAY - WIDE ANGLE

We see a huge crowd of camera technicians, actors and curious on-lookers milling around a mall area especially constructed for this fall's "Batman" episodes. The Batmobile, now covered by a mucky layer of dirt, is parked off to one side, seemingly abandoned.

CENTERED IN FRAME as CAMERA DOLLIES IN for TIGHTER ANGLE is a red-and-green Costumed Crusader, seated in a typical Hollywood star's canvas-folding chair with the name stenciled across the back: BURT WARD.

The sparkling Costumed Crusader stares profoundly at the Court Jester-style booties he wears.

NARRATOR'S VOICE
(extra enthusiastically)
Holy Celebrity! It's none other than Burt Ward, portrayer of that robust, rascally revenger of wrongs, Robin the Boy Wonder, or RTBW for short. He's buddy of that brave, bold, brazen battler of the blameworthy, Batman.

Ward suddenly bounces up, searching his immediate area as if it is an emergency.

BURT WARD
Makeup man! Where the hell are you? I need you now!

There is no noticeable response so Ward sits back down in canvas chair. ANGLE TO INCLUDE a sprightly-stepping YOUNG LAD as he makes his way through the crowd, preceded by a fair-haired ABC PUBLICITY MAN.

NARRATOR'S VOICE
(hysterically enthusiastic)
Hang on, Bat Fans. The most devastating is yet to come!

DIRECT CUT TO:

YOUNG LAD, PUBLICITY MAN and BURT WARD as PR man introduces YL to RTBW.

PR MAN
Burt, I want you to meet Willie Pringletittle from Pahrump Flats, Nevada. Willie is in town on vacation and just happens to be president of the Robin Nest Fan Club, which has a total membership of 1000 fans, all of whom idolize and adore you. Well, you fellas chat while I go hand out some publicity releases.

PR MAN EXITS FRAME.

WILLIE
Hiya, Burt. This is a great moment for –

BURT WARD
The girls are the ones who love me most, Willie.

WILLIE
(Shocked and taken aback)
Girls?

BURT WARD
My fan mail. I get 12 to 15 thousand letters a week. Give or take a few hundred.

WILLIE
Yes, we write a lot of those letters --

BURT WARD
Eighty-five per cent from 12-13 year olds. Fifteen per cent from 15-16 year olds. All girls! Not a single guy anywhere!

WILLIE
I bet most of those letters say-

BURT WARD
(finishing for Willie)
"I love you, Burt. Come to New Jersey (or wherever the place is) and marry me. I'm all yours for the taking."

WILLIE
Gee, Burt, I just read in a fan mag that you finished a "Batman" film. Not for TV, for movie houses.

BURT WARD
(pushing finger into his puffy cheek)
Yes, Adam West and I made a movie during our hiatus from the TV series. "Batman: The Movie." That's what it's called, strangely enough.

WILLIE
Geez, a hiatus. That's utterly incredible. Will the movie be just like the TV series?

BURT WARD
No, no, no, Willie. It'll be one hundred per cent better than the series. We weren't so pushed. We had five weeks to make it. I'm excellent in it. I stole so many scenes, Batman almost called the police. He still wants to put me under arrest.

WILLIE
Wow, Burt! What are some of the new things in it?

Ward glances up and down the busy studio boulevard, and begins to look angry.

THE CAREER THAT DRIPPED WITH HORROR

BURT WARD
(screaming)
Where is that blasted make-up man, anyway?

WILLIE
The new things in the movie version you described . . .

BURT WARD
Huh? Oh, yeah. Well, we got ourselves a Batboat. We got a Batcopter. We got all the villains together. We got Joker, Penguin, Mad Hatter, Riddler. All of 'em. We hit theaters this coming July.

WILLIE
Hey, ha ha. I'd sure like to know how you reach the bottom of the Batpole dressed as Batman and Robin when you started at the top dressed as Bruce Wayne and Dick Grayson.

BURT WARD
(frowning at Willie)
That'll be shown in the film. Also, how we got up the Batpole.

WILLIE
Backwards? Geeeezzzz . . .

BURT WARD
(to a nearby stand-in)
Hey, have you seen my make-up guy?

THE STAND-IN shakes his head.

WILLIE
You know, Burt, I read a lot about how big roles change actors. Would you say that Robin the Boy Wonder has changed you any?

BURT WARD
Willie, this is the first time I've acted in my life and it hasn't changed me one little bit. I've got more money than I had before but otherwise I'm the same guy-
(Interrupting himself)
Makeup Man! Where the hell are you? I need you now!

WILLIE
Tell me a little about yourself, Burt. Where you're from --

BURT WARD
I was born here in L. A. I'm 21. My father is a real estate agent who . . . say, my personal agent Gene Shefrin, he has all that stuff in my biog. Call [phone number censored] and tell him to send you the Robin PR Personality Packet.
(close-up photographs)
My life story, autograph, everything you need. Even photos of me as a baby, rocking in a cradle.

WILLIE
Gosh, Burt, I bet you've been meeting lots of fan club presidents just like me since "Batman" went on the air.

Ward turns and for the first time looks Willie squarely in the eye, as if to say: Brother, you summed it up in a Batshell.

BURT WARD
(through clenched teeth)
Yeah. Lots of fan club presidents. At least a thousand. Maybe more.

WILLIE
(taking the hint)
Well, guess I better be moving on. Mom is out front waiting in her station wagon. The fellas back in Pahrump are gonna flip out when they hear I talked with Robin the Boy Wonder.

BURT WARD
Yeah, sure, Willie. It was my pleasure too.

CAMERA PULLS BACK as Willie starts somewhat dejectedly across the bustling Gotham City Square, almost entering the range of the current TV camera set-up. The DIRECTOR'S YES MAN chases Willie out of the area. Ward, meanwhile, stands up with his hands on his hips, glancing to the left, glancing to the right, his face filled with anger.

BURT WARD
(determinedly)
I want that makeup man. I want him right now!

CUT TO:

CLOSE UP - WILLIE

Willie stops for just a moment, to muse to himself.

WILLIE
Holy six-pack! And to think that only a year ago that Ward fella was taking Coke bottles back to the market for the three-cent deposit.

Willie walks on hurriedly, though with slumped shoulders.

HIGH ANGLE - FOCUSING DOWN

as Willie MOVES OUT OF FRAME and Ward is still searching left and right for his vanished never-to-be-seen makeup man, still screaming at the top of his lungs as we:

FADE OUT.

A MAJOR EVENT: "SARGE" BRINGS ME AND ADAM WEST TOGETHER OFFSCREEN, AND THEN COMES THE EXPLOSION OF WORLD WAR III!

THE CAREER THAT DRIPPED WITH HORROR

MY RELATIONSHIP with Adam West was not over yet – by any means. For the next few years, we communicated by phone calls and letters and during one of those calls (months after "Batman" had left the air in March 1968) he mentioned he was not happy with the roles being offered to him–everything hinged on his "Batman" presence and he wanted to escape that stereotype and have a wider range of choices.

That was the moment when I told him about "Sarge," a screenplay I had written in the late 1960s which dealt with a futuristic war between the armed forces of China and the United States. Plot: American dogfaces (troops) were sloshing across China with "Sarge" in command. "Sarge" personified the history-making soldiers who had fought in the Revolutionary War, the Civil War, World War I and World War II. During pauses in action, he would relate to his men a seemingly personal narrative about one of those wars in vivid detail. Also involved, since this was in part a satirical war story, was a squad of chimpanzees well-trained for battle with the names Bonzo, Son of Kong and King Kong.

"Sarge" was everything American military – a character that had been inspired by writer-producer-director Samuel Fuller (seen above chomping his eternal cigar). I saw his "Steel Helmet" (1951) when I was just 11 and considered it one of the best movies I had ever seen. It actually had the courage to show an American sergeant (played by Gene Evans) cold-bloodedly shoot to death a Chinese prisoner-of-war. That explosive film was soon followed by "Fixed Bayonets!" - a Korean war saga which Fuller wrote and directed for Fox.

Sam had a way of depicting war and its effect on soldiers unlike anything I had seen before. "Helmet" was so unusual and successful at the box office it opened the door to Sam making many films for Fox and a life-long career that climaxed in 1980 with "The Big Red One," a history of his own experiences with the 16th Infantry Regiment from Omaha Beach on D-Day through the liberation of the Birkenau concentration camp in Czechoslovakia in 1945. I was to rub elbows with Sammy in 1963 when he invited me to spend two days on the set of his film noir "The Naked Kiss." (More up close and personal about Sam in my 2011 book "The Gang That Shot Up Hollywood." For more, see page 247.)

Adam West was intrigued with my description over the phone and asked me to send him a copy of the screenplay "Sarge." Soon after I received a letter from Adam:

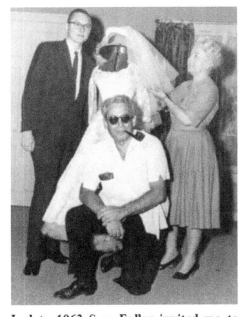

In late 1963 Sam Fuller invited me to spend two days at Samuel Goldwyn Studios on the set of "The Naked Kiss," one of his last film noirs. At my request he posed with me and Betty Bronson on a set first used in Dean Martin's film "Toys in the Attic."

Dear John – At the moment I am about to go to dinner with a Robert Wise associate to try to interest him in "Sarge." Your screenplay is great as far as I'm concerned. I mean it's the best thing for my money I've read in a long time. It has remarkable potential and I am quite excited about it. I'm doing my damnedest to get the right people interested in it.

As hard as he tried for a full year, Adam couldn't sell "Sarge" and he finally called me to say he was moving on. I decided to turn "Sarge" into a novel which I retitled "Napalm Sunday." It was purchased by the first publishing house I sent the manuscript to, Avon Paperbacks. It was retitled "World War III" by the Avon editors because "Napalm Sunday" sounded too anti-religious.

The book cover ads prepared by Avon were great and I'm sharing them with you now.

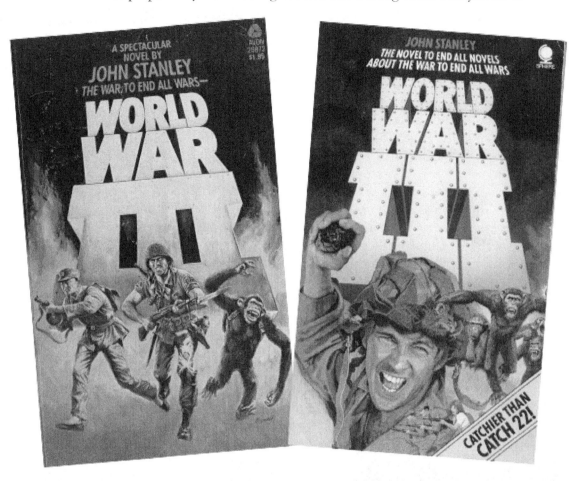

Upper left: This is the American paperback cover for "World War III," my 1976 novel published by Avon. Upper right: This was the British edition I discovered in a train station bookstore when traveling through London in 1977. I hadn't seen it before and was totally shocked, but in a most positive way. Eventually, the paperback sold very well.

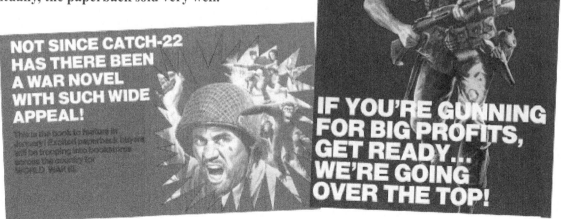

Despite the failure of "Sarge," and the fact I did not see Adam West for many years, he finally called in 1986 to let me know he was starring in a new crime-comedy series, "The Last Precinct." I immediately connected with NBC-TV public-relations contact, and Adam West and I soon met in Hollywood for a final one-on-one interview.

THE YEARS have been kind to Adam West since he starred in "Batman," one of television's most phenomenal successes in the years 1966-68. It's now 1986 and his face is glowing healthy and his eyes retain that twinkle when he and Robin the Boy Wonder set out to defy the forces of evil. And if the light falls just right, there is a sparkle off his upper front tooth when he smiles.

WHERE'S BATMAN WHEN I NEED HIM?

NOW I HAVE TO SEARCH FOR INSPECTOR CLOUSEAU!

West's laugh is hearty, his stride brisk and his self-effacing humor a sign that he has remained happy in an industry that typecast him beyond the norm and defied him to crash out. More importantly, 18 years after the fact, Adam West can still fit into his Utility Belt and discuss how much fun it was to portray Gotham City's crimefighter.

Yet, the years have not been so kind to West since "Batman" slipped into syndicated reruns. Despite his talent for comedy and dramatics, which he has shown in such films as 1971's "Marriage of a Young Stockbroker," he has never fully escaped the cowl-and-cape image that established new TV trends in 1966 and that made comic-book heroes and superheroes a respectable commodity for the viewing masses. (With young Robin at his side, he did do the voice work on the animated 1977 series "The New Adventures of Batman.")

While he and Burt Ward (aka Robin) were in demand for personal appearances as the crime-fighting team after the series left the air, it is amazing to learn that they are still making those appearances today. And the series is still seen in reruns by an estimated 400 million throughout the world.

Despite all that, West's career as a serious, dedicated actor suffered. As he is the first to reveal, good roles became nonexistent. What he was offered and accepted were science-

Adam West's first attempt at playing a cop was in "The Detectives" (1961-62) as Sergeant Steve Nelson opposite star Robert Taylor in 30 episodes.

fiction and horror stuff the titles of which he doesn't remember – or "want to remember."

Lesser men might have despaired and allowed their private demons to overtake them, but West claims he has chased away the mental villains and kept his perspective in balance.

There is a touch of irony that the serious actor crying to be discovered within West has had to settle for a buffonish comedy role in "The Last Precinct," a *Mad Magazine*-style parody of "Hill Street Blues" and other serious-minded TV police series. It's his first series since "Batman" and it was "a helluva long time to wait."

Adam West and Elizabeth Ashley in the 1971 drama "Marriage of a Young Stockbroker."

THE CAREER THAT DRIPPED WITH HORROR

His role is Captain Rob Wright, a precinct chief who is about as adroit and dexterous as Peter Sellers' Inspector Clouseau. "My challenge is to make Wright as much fun as Batman," admits West, seated in a darkened corner of his favorite Sunset Strip restaurant, The Cock 'n Bull. "Which is a tough assignment because while Batman was surrounded by costumes, gimmicks, colorful villains and some pretty strange locations, Captain Wright has less to work with. In fact, it's a humongous challenge, a tricky job because the ambience, people and props don't vary. It's hard when you're working on static, standing sets to find craziness and gags and physical humor that isn't tiresome and snorable."

Making Captain Wright (or any of the dozen bizarre characters within the 56th Precinct) work may be more humongous than even West realizes. "The Last Precinct" is so cracked and mad in its lampoonery, vacillating between tastelessness one moment and cleverness the next, it is having a difficult time finding a lasting audience. While three weeks ago it fared well, it was arrested and jailed to 58th place in the ratings on the night it ran opposite Stacy Keach's return as Mike Hammer on CBS-TV.

Even acknowledging all of this, and arriving at the interview site with an undercurrent of disappointment about the ratings number, which he had just read that morning, West finds joy in being back: "It's been too long and I can't tell you how good it feels to be relocated in the mainstream of action." West takes a sip from his Bullshot, a concoction of beef bouillon cube and a slug of vodka. "Even if it is a show with an ensemble of 12 human beings, I can't be the star all the time." West is kidding, of course, displaying a sharp sense of humor that often slides off into the very comedy camp for which Batman is famous.

Adam West at lunch with me at the Cock'n Bull on the Sunset Strip.

Humor on TV, he feels, "is something with many tastes and ingredients . . . good funny comedy usually has to come from something very real. The characters must believe what they're doing and never think they're being funny, but they must think funny. Thinking funny is the most important ingredient of humor. It's looking at life and people and yourself in a skewered, slanted way."

West sips again from his Bullshot, gazing over the rim of his glass with an elfin smile. "It's important for me to be back in prime time. I mean, it's been years. You know, I've done countless pilots that didn't work for one reason or another. So when something does work, I give it scrupulous attention. Even if this series were to be cancelled, at least I had visibility in a starring role. That's better than not being on prime time at all."

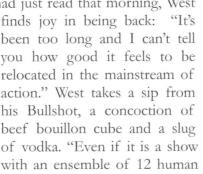

That's Randi Brooks showing off her gams alongside "The Last Precinct" castmates Ernie Hudson, Keenan Wynn and my great friend Adam West.

The pilot episode of "The Last Precinct" carved out an impressive rating when it was aired following the Super Bowl 20 in January 1986. NBC and executive producers Stephen Cannell (the mastermind behind "The A Team") and Frank Lupo decided to wait until early April to begin the series on a weekly basis.

The intention: to counter reruns on the other networks. It didn't quite work out since CBS threw Mike Hammer into the breech and ABC countered with a new comedy, "Mr. Sunshine."

Come to think of it, West tells me, "This isn't a matter of life or death. You can't put your whole life on the chopping block over one show. I feel an actor has to act, he has to keep moving. Stay alive, baby, you gotta move. You can't sit home and say, 'Hey, I'm a star. That phone is gonna ring and I'm gonna be given a stunning role.' You have to get out and shake the trees in the orchard. I mean, that's what I did after 'Batman.' I didn't sit around. That's why I tried to sell your 'Sarge' script to the best producers in Hollywood. Well, each is a unique learning experience. If you can do the kind of crap I've done and survive as I've survived . . . "

West has always maintained a happy-go-lucky image and remains dedicated to his wife and six children. How genuine is this image of good cheer? "I feel that behind the facade is bound to be some injury and profound feelings. Anyone worth his salt in acting has to have a certain sensitivity. But even the finest performer doesn't have to suffer in anguish on the set to do his or her best work.

"In fact, you have to get rid of all that baloney somewhere in your career so you can work without restrictions and handicaps. You have to be open and abandoned and a little crazy and enjoy what you do. Otherwise, nobody else will enjoy it and you won't bring dimension to it. But if you're able to take what's around you, those little breezes, and make them work . . . "

Standing tall is Adam West in the role of Captain Rob Wright in "The Last Precinct," a role that has been compared to Peter Sellers' Inspector Clouseau. Mama mia!

Another sip of his Bullshot, and he continues: "You have to visualize. I see entire films or programs in my head, from start to finish, and I know if I'm malleable enough to the director's vision, we're going to work well together and each of us will have part of the vision come true. But if you're fighting and suffering and being Dostoevsky, all that stands in your way."

Most actors, he continues, "have their own methods, a way of getting at resources, at the tools of the trade. Each human being is capable of so many facets and levels. You don't have to worry about giving too much or giving it all away too often. Get at it. Dig and you'll find plenty of stuff."

Whatever detriment Batman may have brought Adam West, he still loves the character and the values he stood for. "I'm very proud of Batman. It's a TV classic that will last. Yes, it has prevented me from doing more substantial projects, major Hollywood films. If I hang on in the saddle, maybe those bigger things will happen yet . . . and who knows, maybe 'Batman' will happen to me again."

"Batman" is returning? Maybe . . . maybe not. "When Fox bought the rights from DC Comics back in 1965 to produce a series, for some inexplicable, cuckoo reason the studio didn't buy the rights to do additional material. So DC Comics subsequently resold the rights to Warner Bros., and for four years a project has been underway. Little is known about that project, even by me, Batman."

West shakes his head. "I've some very salient ideas about how Batman should be played in the 1980s. For one thing, his tights shouldn't be quite so lavender. I think he should return to his origins, fighting crime only at night. I think a new Batman would be different but the movie would still have to acknowledge the TV series that made the merchandising and comic book such successes.

"The Wall Street Journal recently said that if Leonard Nimoy hadn't played Spock in the 'Star Trek' movies, the films would have instantly lost $15 million apiece. I suggest that Warner Brothers heed this as a warning."

AFTERWORDS

Adam West's series was dumped after only seven episodes. Although West would spend a good share of his time in one-shot roles for television, the Batman imagery never quite went away. He ended up doing voiceover work for "Family Guy" for many seasons as the amusing Mayor. The 2013 documentary "Starring Adam West" covers many elements of his life and career. As for Warner Brothers and Batman . . . they never got the Batmobile out of reverse.

Frank Gorshin (famous for portraying The Riddler" on Adam West's "Batman" series) is seated on my "Creature Features" set in 1979 when I devoted an entire show to his career and he was doing his comedy act at the Fairmont Hotel. He returned a year later for a second interview for the Chronicle. That was when he signed this on-set photo to me. It reads: "John: Good luck with your book! Gorshin '80." At that time, I was still working on my first edition in the "Creature Features Movie Guide" series. Frank died in 2005 at age 72 with seventy feature films to his credit.

UP NEXT: THE MOST STUNNING, BELOVED
E.T. IN CINEMATIC HISTORY!

A SINGULAR PRELUDE WITH A DUEL PURPOSE

For me it all starts in November, 1978, when I am taken for a ride. No, I'm not being conned. I'm in a limousine with British-born producer David Puttnam who made "The Duellists" in England and is now taking me to see the film at the Four-Star Theater. Oddly, this will be the only theater in America where it will be shown, and the Chronicle has assigned me to review it.

Puttnam, who would go on to produce "Chariots of Fire" and "The Killing Fields" and run Columbia Studios in Hollywood from 1986-88, tells me he doesn't understand why

"Duellists" producer David Puttnam, who went on to become chairman and CEO of Columbia Pictures between June 1986 and September 1987.

Paramount isn't giving "The Duellists" a wider release, for it had won an award at the Cannes Film Festival and was well reviewed in Europe.

Starring in the film are Keith Carradine and Harvey Keitel as French officers in the early 19th Century who hate each other and engage in a series of duels. It's a strong mixture of characterization and action and after the screening, as we drive through the Richmond District, Puttnam begins telling me about something that was going to become very important in a few months. "Here's the story," he says, "and listen good. Ridley Scott, whose excellent directorial work you just saw in 'The Duellists,' is a genius behind the camera. Right now, he's back in England working on a science-fiction thriller unlike anything I've seen before.

"I predict it'll become a major hit all over the world in the coming year. The real star of the film is an extraterrestrial. An extraterrestrial that's going to be the most frightening outer-space creature you've ever seen in a motion picture."

"What's the title?" I have to ask, my curiosity at a high point.

Putnam literally shouts. "'ALIEN!' Remember that title. Once you see it, you'll never forget it! It's going to hit viewers directly on the chin and send them rocketing into another universe."

HOW AN ALIEN PARASITE FROM GREAT BRITAIN WAS CREATED AND IS READY TO ATTACK AMERICA

IT IS NOW May 1979, exactly two years since "Star Wars" premiered at theaters throughout America. It was a massively popular science-fiction thriller but of a kind remarkably different from the film that is opening this week across America. It is a bizarre mixture of horror and science-fiction. One magazine writer has already dubbed it "space gothic," marveling at its makers' ability to intermix elements of two genres. The story has been described by its director, Ridley Scott, as "linear," so fast-moving it took only 40 minutes for him to read the original screenplay. When he put the script down, he was stunned. "I just felt it was an amazing piece of entertainment. Also, to me it is more than a horror film. It's a film about terror."

THE CAREER THAT DRIPPED WITH HORROR

"Alien" has every indication of being a most unusual space movie, far removed from the fun-and-games attitude of "Star Wars" or the recent "Buck Rogers in the 25th Century." This one was designed to scare you right out of your spacesuit. The refinery-freighter Nostromo (named after a ship in a Joseph Conrad story) is deep in the Universe when it receives a strange transmission. The crew of five men and two women lands in a nightmarish landscape where they find fossilized extraterrestrials aboard a derelict spacecraft.

When they return to their own ship, they bring with them – attached to the body of one of the crew members – a horrible parasitic entity that threatens the entire crew. "Alien," which reportedly cost $9 million because of its complex special effects and enormously stylized alien world sets, was filmed in England under the direction of Scott.

Scott, whose background is largely in TV commercials, was developing "Tristan and Isolde" for

H.R. Giger with a metal version of the monster he created for "Alien." They say Giger suffered from nightmares and kept a drawing pad next to his bed so he could sketch the horror he had just experienced upon waking. Thus was created the "Alien."

Paramount when he first read Dan O'Bannon's screenplay. He immediately shifted his focus to the making of "Alien." He has been quoted as saying, "I'm not usually impressed by horror or science-fiction. I was never enthusiast as a kid, but O'Bannon had written an excellent script."

O'Bannon had previously written, directed and starred in "Dark Star," a 1975 low-budget feature that had kicked off at the University of Southern California as a student project, then escalated into a $60,000 venture when investors became impressed with the special effects. However, O'Bannon's script was reworked by Walter Hill and David Giler after 20th Century Fox executives expressed disapproval. (Actually, their contribution may not have been all that much since O'Bannon received sole writing credit for "Dark Star.")

From the beginning O'Bannon had wanted to hire Swiss painter/designer H. R. Giger to design the sets and costumes for "Alien." They had worked together on an ill-fated attempt to film Frank Herbert's classic science-fiction novel "Dune." Once Scott was involved with the project, O'Bannon convinced him that Giger was the man for the job, and in turn Scott convinced Fox.

Who is Giger? He's a painter whose work often defies description, combining eroticism, symbolism and death into a freakish mixture. Giger also designed the alien planet, the interior and exterior of the derelict spacecraft . . . and of course the titular monster. "The alien," Giger has said, "is elegant, fast and terrible. It exists only to destroy–and destroys to exist. Once you see it it will never be forgotten. It will remain with people who have seen it, perhaps in their dreams or nightmares, for a long, long time. Perhaps for all time. I even dream about the alien myself–so much that I'm afraid of going to sleep."

The studio initially released no photos of the alien and kept tight security around the production. O'Bannon told writer Bob Martin (*Starlog Magazine*), that he was glad Fox was "playing their card so close to the vest."

"People are going to come in, sit down and say 'Show me.' And are we gonna show 'em. I grew up on all the horror movies and scary books there were and, with 'Alien,' I just wanted to see how frightening I could make something without a lot of violence and gore."

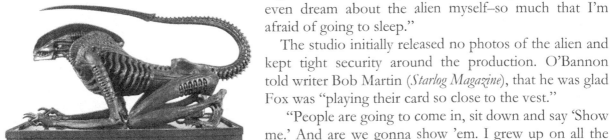

Word to the wise: if you see this creature heading your way, plan on going the other way!

Members of the cast include (L-R) John Hurt, Veronica Cartwright, Tom Skerritt, Yaphet Kotto, Signourney Weaver, Harry Dean Stanton, and Ian Holm. Cartwright, a child TV star of the 1950s, co-starred with Donald Sutherland in the 1978 remake of "Invasion of the Body Snatchers." She says of "Alien": "The special effects are the most amazing thing I've ever seen. They had the same people from 'Star Wars' working. The monster breathes and moves its arms and head. It's the most hideous thing I've ever seen. Grotesque beyond belief."

Attention! On Guard! You're About to Meet A Rising Film Director Who Gave Us the Most Terrifying Outer Space Monster Conceived by Mankind for Motion Pictures. So Freeze . . . And Stand Fast. No Running to Mama!

THE CAREER THAT DRIPPED WITH HORROR

JUNE 10, 1979:
THE DAY "ALIEN" DIRECTOR RIDLEY SCOTT AND I MET AT THE SAN FRANCISCO CINEMA SHOP

RIDLEY SCOTT has burst onto the motion picture market so suddenly that while thousands of Americans are flocking to see his first major feature, "Alien," they are only vaguely aware of his name, or not aware at all.

Before "2001: A Space Odyssey" Stanley Kubrick had "Dr. Strangelove." Before "Star Wars" George Lucas had "American Graffiti." Before "Close Encounters of the Third Kind" Steven Spielberg had "Jaws." Before "Alien" all Ridley Scott had was a British feature film, "The Duellists," which Paramount released for just a few days in a San Francisco theater (see page 76). In no other U.S. theater did anyone get to see it despite good box office in foreign markets.

"Alien" is a classic mixture of horror and science-fiction depicting how a hideous E.T. breaks loose aboard the space freighter Nostromo and makes human mincemeat of the crew members, one by one. It is strictly stuff for nightmares, with director Scott cleverly playing off all our primal fears, always to the screaming point. As that producer Puttnam predicted, that ugly creature really makes your skin crawl.

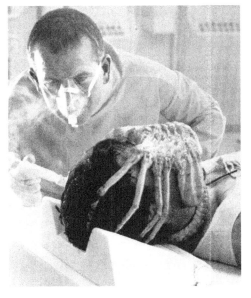

When the initial rave reviews for "Alien" erupted, 20th Century Fox decided it was time to bring Scott out of his cocoon of anonymity and he breezes into San Francisco, bright-eyed and cheerful, dressed in blue jeans. We meet at the Cinema Shop, where my cameraman awaits. In a voice tinged with a Scottish accent, he reflects on a directing career that is only now exploding after years of hard work and dedication to film.

"The important thing about science-fiction," he begins, rubbing his fingers through his reddish beard, "is that it be made well so it will retain its respectability and not become something stodgy or undesirable. Science-fiction . . . what an amazing theater to work in. Actually, 'Alien' is a thriller, isn't it? I mean, '2001: A Space Odyssey' is a religious film, very real. 'Star Wars' is on the other end of the scale. Anything goes in science-fiction as long as you do it right and make it stick. Otherwise, it turns into hokum and we don't need that."

The alien entity in Scott's $9 million film (for which Fox is pumping out an additional $6 million in advertising and promotion money) is so nightmarishly unforgettable that one wonders how it was conceived. Scott explains that while Dan O'Bannon wrote the screenplay, it was the Swiss painter, H. R. Giger, who conceived the external appearance of the alien. "The monster evolved out of several discussions, some of them on an intellectual level regarding alien shapes and societies, some of them on a biological level about the various stages of gestation and evolution. We also asked ourselves key questions about our inner-most fears. What scares man on a primal level?

THE CAREER THAT DRIPPED WITH HORROR   *PAGE 79*

"The answer can be very complex, certainly is something more than a killer with a knife, isn't it? It's something deeply rooted within all of us. And that something is what I've tried to touch when you see 'Alien.'

"We didn't think about traditional movie monsters. We approached the problem from a biological point of view. Once that was established, we could work backward or forward. The monster is seen in various shapes and sizes as it passes through some form of speeded-up evolutionary process. It's reptilian, amphibian, humanoid, metallic . . .'"

Scott also admits that the characters were portrayed as realistically as possible to allow the audience to identify with them. This was achieved by ordinary clothing and a naturalistic flow of dialogue. The sets, all built to scale without the trickery of matte paintings, were also designed to be functional and realistic so that the eventual horror would take place in a believable setting.

And, stresses Scott, no animation, no Ray Harryhausen stop-motion effects, were used in the monster sequences. "It was a combination of gears and the human element. The teeth, for example, are mechanical--a cable system partly manual, partly air pressure. For the scenes where you see the entire body, we used a real human being who was 7-feet-3-inches tall." That man was Nigerian visual artist Bolaji Badejo.

Director Ridley Scott

The sets of the alien planet, where the astronauts first land and find the alien within the remnants of a derelict spaceship, were also accomplished by Giger. "Yes," admits Scott, "they are full of sexual symbols. That's not the way we set out to do it but the idea evolved after lengthy discussions. One gets quite evil-minded. The creature is very phallic at one point. Outrageously effective, which again hits a primal chord. You must plan these things . . . give them a background and a purpose. Otherwise, you get bad, hokey characters."

At one point, an unhappy ending was considered for "Alien," but O'Bannon and Scott concurred it was important that audiences leave the theater feeling fulfilled and not let down. Would Scott consider directing a sequel? "Sequels are dangerous, aren't they?" he responds. "Rarely are they very good. 'Godfather II' was an exception. A sequel to 'Alien' would have to be speculative and deal with the motives of the alien. What will it do away from its home planet? What are the possible relationships with humans beside butcher-victim? It might be worthwhile to direct a sequel and I'll consider it." Ultimately, he did, directing "Prometheus" (2012) and "Alien: Covenant" (2017).

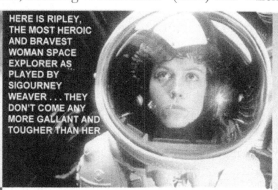

HERE IS RIPLEY, THE MOST HEROIC AND BRAVEST WOMAN SPACE EXPLORER AS PLAYED BY SIGOURNEY WEAVER . . . THEY DON'T COME ANY MORE GALLANT AND TOUGHER THAN HER

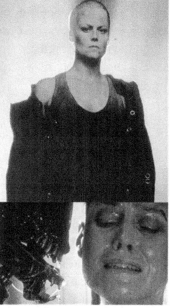

Sigourney Weaver has been described as "the most significant female protagonist in motion picture history." She was nominated for an Oscar in 1986 for the sequel "Aliens," in which her Ellen Ripley once again armed herself to fight against E.T. evil. She also starred in 1992's "Alien3" and scores of other films (including "Ghostbusters"). A British TV service called Channel 4 chose her as No. 20 among "The 100 Greatest Stars of All Time."

RIDLEY SCOTT was born in 1939 in South Shields, England. His father was a British officer in charge of the Mulberry docking units during the D-Day invasion. Eventually he was promoted to brigadier general. Ridley was considering the Royal Marines when his father advised him to seek a non-military career of his choice. So, Ridley ended up studying at the Royal College of Art in London and was being trained as a TV set designer when he made his first short in 16mm, "Boy on a Bicycle." From that his interest in photography became overwhelming and he worked his way into directing TV commercials. He was making so much money he decided to start his own production company.

HARRY DEAN STANTON AS BRETT IN "ALIEN" —TOO BAD HE DIDN'T LIKE SCI-FI FLICKS

"I had 40 people working for me, I had an office in Paris, I had everywhere to go. Suddenly I realized I was blossoming off in the wrong direction, getting farther and farther away from the little movie I so wanted to make." With hundreds of TV commercials under his belt, and with a reputation unsurpassed in some parts of the world, Scott gave it all up to seek the most difficult thing of all: financing for a feature film.

He turned his company over to his brother Tony Scott and began the long, lonely search for dough. And his determination finally paid off when he was offered 150,000 pounds to produce an historical TV drama. Knowing such a production could be expensive, he turned to public domain material, finding possibilities in Joseph Conrad's short story "The Duel," based on a true incident from French history in which two Napoleonic generals feuded over a 40-year period, ending of course with one final face-to-face showdown with rapiers aimed at each other's heart.

Scott reveals that "four or five" major British directors had turned down "Alien" before he was shown the script. After a single reading he immediately accepted the job. "I saw a germ of something big in the screenplay and I immediately wanted to do it. I somehow knew 'Alien' was going to be an important film. The story's linear and it's lean and it unfurls quickly."

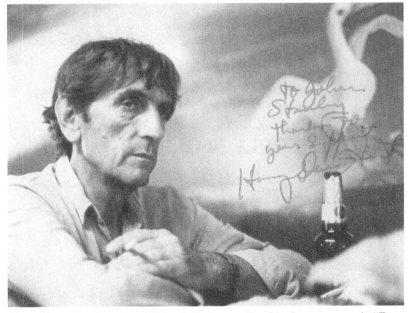

Scott has one regret: not being a bigger science-fiction fan. "I never could get into the literature. It was only after '2001: A Space Odyssey' that I began to get the bug. Some fans have said I should be turned on to movie classics such as 'The Thing' and 'Them.' But they didn't quite have the elements of reality that make a classic, or even a good film. Establish your realism, then the monster. It will come off. And so will the film."

Harry Dean Stanton signed this photo (promoting his then-new movie "Repo Man") on the same day I cut the show in which I announced the coming death of "Creature Features." He remained very busy in movies and TV series right up to the time of his death in 2017 at the age of 91. That same year he appeared in the series "Twin Peaks: The Return" as Carl Rodd.

During my in-studio "Creature Features" interview with Harry Dean Stanton, who had portrayed Brett in "Alien," he candidly told me: "This is a dangerous thing to say on this show but I've never been a fan of sci-fi or space films. Except maybe for '2001: A Space Odyssey.' But Ridley Scott was an ace in the hole. He's extremely talented. It was worth going to England to work with him. In fact, he told me himself he didn't like sci-fi movies. And then he added, 'But I think I'm making something very worthwhile out of this.' He certainly did."

AFTERWORDS

Alien opened the door to incredible success for Scott, who has worked on numerous TV series such as "The Good Life" (2009-2016) and "The Terror" (2018-19). His classic follow-up to "Alien" was "Blade Runner" in 1982, which has grown in popularity and is now considered a sci-fi classic.

That was followed by so many other features including "Thelma and Louise" (1991), "Gladiator" (2000) and "Blackhawk Down" (2001). Often working at his side was his brother Tony Scott, who also had a very successful directing career in TV and films.

The sad element to their shared successes: At the age of 68, in the year 2012, Tony leaped from a bridge in San Pedro, CA. It was assumed to be suicide, but the cause has never been determined. Nevertheless, Ridley Scott has continued working like never before.

Director Tony Scott directed "Top Gun," "True Romance" and "Crimson Tide." He formed Scott Free Productions with brother Ridley in 1970. The company has earned over 100 Emmy nominations.

WHY ARE THESE PEOPLE SMILING?

Because they know what is on the very next page . . .
IN
A
GALAXY
NEAR YOU!

THE CAREER THAT DRIPPED WITH HORROR

GEORGE LUCAS STRIKES AGAIN
AND A HORROR HOST MEETS
LUKE, LEIA, LANDO AND DARTH VADER HIMSELF!

BEING A HORROR HOST, I was invited to two movie premieres that I still consider the most exciting of all the special events I attended. One of them, the critics' screening of Paramount's "Star Trek II: The Wrath of Khan," occurred in May 1982 and I have included my interviews from that event with Leonard Nimoy, William Shatner, Ricardo Montalban and producer Harve Bennett in my book "I Was a TV Horror Host."

The other super-memorable premiere was the critics' screening of 20th Century Fox's "Star Wars: The Empire Strikes Back" (aka "Star Wars: Episode V") which took place in Hollywood in May 1980. I had personal moments on film with Mark Hamill, Carrie Fisher, Billy Dee Williams, producer Gary Kurtz and director Irvin Kerschner which I now want to share with you. We were in a hotel showroom when the film camera beside me began rolling . . .

MEET MARK HAMILL
AKA LUKE SKYWALKER

"I PREFER NOT TO DRINK A LOT OF WHISKEY AND GET DRUNK. YOU SEE, I PREFER TO STAY SABER AT ALL TIMES"

Stanley: What does The Force mean to you on a personal level?

Hamill: I always felt there was a challenge in absorbing the deeper meanings of The Force in the "Star Wars" feature, and I feel the same about "Empire Strikes Back," although The Force has taken on an even deeper philosophy. But each of us is different and each viewer can absorb the Force in his or her own special way. For some it's a religion, for others it's an emotion, a feeling that jettisons each of us into a different part of the Universe. Getting all the specifics is a challenge, and for some of us it can seem a little bit dangerous. It might not jive with the feelings of others.

Stanley: How much of Mark Hamill is Luke Skywalker?

Hamill: When I tried out for the part George Lucas wouldn't tell me what it was all about. He simply handed me six pages of script for my screen test. But he never sat down and explained to me it was going to be a homage to the Saturday matinees we had enjoyed in our younger years. His attitude was: Just do it. Show me what you've got. I think I was very lucky to possess enough qualities of Luke . . . and it still amazes me that I almost immediately was chosen for the role. How lucky for me, because from the moments of that screen test I wanted to work for George Lucas because I regarded him as a part of a whole new breed of filmmaker. His is a unique presence in the world of movies.

Stanley: Why do you think "Star Wars" was so successful at the box office?

Hamill: There was a lack in our lives as movie-goers. There was no new mythology. George Lucas feels that the Western was the last form of entertainment that was mythical. It had heroes, heroes in a galaxy a long time ago and far away. So, I feel that George filled a void. That's just a theory but it is mine. And I will always see George in that light. My light!

CARRIE FISHER AKA PRINCESS LEIA

Stanley: What are your deepest feelings about portraying a princess of the future?

Fisher: Portraying Princess Leia has taken me to the height of my career. And in "Empire Strikes Back" you get to know her better than you did in "Star Wars." She's now less stubborn, and she undergoes a succession of close calls. Also, she has a sharper romantic interest, and she can relate more warmly to those around her.

Stanley: And that makes Princess Leia more satisfying to portray?

Fisher: She's the child that's in all of us. She has an appeal that harkens back to the films of the 1930s and '40s. That's when we had heroes and heroines of a more memorable nature. You have never seen things in films that you are seeing in "Star Trek" in terms of the special effects. And you can identify with each of the characters. The princess, the Wise Old Sage, they take on a fairy tale-like quality. By God, Jesus Christ and the Empire are out there.

Stanley: What's it like working on a futuristic "Star Wars" set?

Fisher: Challenging, because you work with things that aren't really there. You stare at the camera and say "The Empire's out there!" or "It's an asteroid field!" And you're looking at nothing. You're looking at members of the crew and you're working in tight quarters. I especially don't like the cockpit. But when I sit down to watch the finished film, I see it like the audience sees it and I'm experiencing the same reaction they experience. And it's like a brand-new experience, creating emotions I never felt during the filming.

Stanley: When you fire a hand-held weapon but nothing really comes out, how do you build your inner reaction?

Fisher: There is something coming out of the weapon. Not a laser, of course, but they do load charges, or a kind of blank. It's a 'big bang,' not a puff of smoke. I guess you could say your imagination does make you think you're firing a weapon.

BILLY DEE WILLIAMS AKA LANDO CALRISSIAN

Stanley: How did you get chosen to play the new character of Lando Calrissian?

Williams: Irvin Kerschner the director came to my home and we sat and talked for a couple of hours about some of the underlying philosophy of "Star Wars." Eastern philosophy, European-Western philosophy. He told me the name of the character and I really loved that name. He explained the character and instantly I told him I'd love to do it. I wanted to be Lando Calrissian. I realized I was in for something unique. I felt I had to grasp and run with this career opening. And I wanted to work for Kerschner because I have great respect for him. And I wanted to work with George Lucas because I regard him as part of a new breed of film-maker that I think represents the future of film. In short, how do you turn down a "Star Wars"? You cannot turn it down. It's an incredible phenomenon.

Gary Kurtz on the set of "The Empire Strikes Back" with (L-R) Darth Vader (David Prowse), bounty hunter IG-88 (Nick Tate), and Boba Fett (Jeremy Bulloch)

GARY KURTZ, PRODUCER OF "THE EMPIRE STRIKES BACK"

Stanley: How did you feel about doing a sequel to "Star Wars"?

Kurtz: I never had the feeling this was just going to be another sequel, like so many other follow-up films. This was to be a continuation of "Star Wars." There had been too much story material to get into one film, and because "Star Wars" had done so well, we felt a second segment was needed. To do a sequel just to capitalize on the first one was never the motivation.

We wanted the characters to be further developed. It's not a sequel, it's a second act. Attitude can be bad and we tried our best to avoid that. We wanted to do a film that stood on its own.

IRVIN KERSHNER, DIRECTOR OF "THE EMPIRE STRIKES BACK"

Stanley: What was a major issue for you in directing this sequel?

Kershner: Dialogue, especially Yoda's. It's fascinating to me. As he says, "Clear your mind of questions. There is no try. Either do or do not." We worked Yoda's dialogue over more carefully than any other dialogue. Yoda has reached a plain of enlightenment that is rare for us poor mortals on planet Earth, or in this particular galaxy. I've learned so much from Yoda. I wish I could meet him sometime and just have a conversation with him. Create a space in my mind so I can learn something. He's talking about inner space while living in outer space.

Stanley: What's in the "Star Wars" films that attracts the younger generation?

Kershner: We're deeply rooted in fairy tales and mythology, going all the way back into our history. Notice that the younger viewers enjoy the dreamlike quality and the scary elements. Call it horror if you will. Our films have roots in the irrational and unconscious. Because of that, it has an appeal that goes beyond pure entertainment. It's buried away in the room and you can talk or dream about it.

Stanley: Is a third film in the series being worked on already?

Kershner: Yes, but this project is less a sequel and more a continuing story. In the second act we've shown all the problems in their total complexity. The third act will be brighter because it will have a climax that will be romantic and satisfying and bring things to a satisfactory conclusion.

Stanley: What are your personal feelings about your boss, George Lucas?

Kershner: George doesn't stand over my shoulder. He gives me great freedom as a director. He's too intelligent and experienced not to. George is a story man. I would call him if I wanted to discuss plot problems. I am careful because this is an ongoing series and I don't want to make any mistakes.

DAVID PROWSE AKA DARTH VADER
(AT LEAST THE MAN IN THE COSTUME IF NOT THE VOICE)

Stanley: The real you in not seen on screen. Does that bother you?

Prowse: No, not when I'm a villain of epic proportions, seen by millions.

Stanley: Having done two "Star Wars" films, what is your overall view?

Prowse: I'm a married man with three children and I personally feel "Star Wars" brought family entertainment back to the cinema on a level we have never experienced before. We have made motion picture history.

I love to go to the movies but eventually I got tired of always looking but only finding sex and violence and bloodthirsty films I couldn't take my children to see. But "Star Wars" opened the door to a whole new kind of genre. And I'm so proud to be part of it all. And the kids, mine and everybody's, are loving it!

Above Right: My most memorable moment with David Prowse, following our interview in a San Francisco hotel. That was the night in 1982 he told me he was never happy about James Earl Jones being the official voice of Darth Vader. Even among movie stars, jealousy reigns.

THE CAREER THAT DRIPPED WITH HORROR

MEET BILLY DEE WILLIAMS

. . . AND LEARN HOW PLAYING LANDO FULFILLED HIS GREATEST DREAMS

SINCE THE DAYS of "The Empire Strikes Back" and "Return of the Jedi," Billy Dee Williams can't walk one block of a busy street without being spotted and mobbed by a never-ending collection of fans who love the adventurous character he brought to life as Lando Calrissian.

In November 1983, on a San Francisco street, his attraction is no exception. The kids know a hero when they see one, especially a "Star Wars" space-rogue-adventure-hero, so they are closing in fast from two directions. So Williams and the long-limbed, blond-haired publicist escorting him hurriedly duck into the front entrance of KPIX-TV, San Francisco's CBS affiliate station.

Williams' face tells you he is enjoying the adulation and a few minutes later he is relaxing in a cafeteria-like area. He looks sleek and sexy, in keeping with the image that has made him an esteemed TV and film actor, but he's also laid back, taking a relaxed, sometimes bemused attitude toward his duties. One of those duties is to promote an upcoming TV special by appearing this afternoon on "People Are Talking," the station's morning-afternoon variety series.

Williams speaks in a soft, even voice and soon props his feet up on a coffee table and becomes animated. "I'll confess that I pick only choice roles and that's why my appearances are infrequent and sometimes a year goes by without viewers seeing a lot of Billy Dee Williams." He thinks of himself as a "character actor" more than a leading man, sex symbol or iconic star.

Suddenly there's a new kind of sparkle in Williams' eyes when he talks about that upcoming TV special. "You gotta see this. It's called 'Classic Creatures: Return of the Jedi,' a CBS show I co-host with Princess Leia. Or should I say Carrie Fisher. It was produced for Lucasfilm Ltd. by Sid Ganis and Howard Kazanjian, and it represents the fun side—the side that's brought me recognition with a younger audience. And it's a part of the 'Star Wars' fraternity."

On the program, he reveals, "I'm in the company of Salacious Crumb, Jabba the Hutt's court jester in 'Return of the Jedi.' He leads me on a guided tour of special-effects genius Phil Tippett's 'Monster Shop,' where a team of designers and effects artists created the scaly beasts, hulking monsters and other E.T. life-forms for 'Return of the Jedi.'"

That is to be followed by a discussion about how the Ewoks evolved out of the Wookies, how Admiral Ackbar was made to "articulate," how Jabba the Hutt was constructed and how the art of puppeteering gave the "vile gangster" his crowning touches. The special doesn't end there.

In addition to examples of "men-in-suits" characters, such as Anthony Daniels as C-3PO and Peter Mayhew as Chewbacca, the documentary will highlight monster footage from past decades. "That includes," says Williams, "Godzilla, the Creature from the Black Lagoon, lizards and dinosaurs created by Ray Harryhausen in his stop-motion animation fantasy films, real-life lizards magnified to look like rampaging tyrannosaurs, and such full-scale mechanical creatures as the giant ants in 'Them.' What's amazing is all that I've described to you is all in one show."

Williams considers himself lucky to have become part of the "Star Wars" cast and feels he is a part of a special "family" that George Lucas was able to bring together because "he knows how to hire people who will lend themselves to what he wants to achieve. It wasn't easy for George in 'Jedi'

because he had to keep the action moving without too much exposition and still resolve the trilogy. We tend to think of George as having reached ultimate success in movies, yet there are great conflicts within him; there must be or he wouldn't be taking a leave of absence. Success can become a tremendous burden. And it's hard for those around George because their lives have to continue without the protection of his endeavors."

Williams has also portrayed Calrissian in a radio version of "Return of the Jedi" and has been pleased to see his likeness in comic books and on the cover of a Ballantine paperback novel, "Lando Calrissian and the Mindshape of Sharu." He even harbors hope that the character might one day be used in a spin-off for a TV series. He sees Lando as a "sweet rogue," a PG-rated version of the sexually attractive males he's famous for portraying, which once earned him the dubious title as one of the "12 Most-Watched Men in the World."

But, Williams says, he does not want to be a role model for anyone and says he has a hard time dealing with people who "create their own fantasies and want me to be part of them. It's an invasion of my privacy. It's frightening and weird. We live in a difficult time. A lot of us don't know who we are or where we belong in today's world. This is not an age of innocence. When I was a kid growing up in Harlem, we knew very little about what was happening in the world. Today, with TV and satellites, we know too much. We see the world as it really is."

Those growing-up days in Harlem were on a street inhabited by hustlers, whores, junkies and

thieves. He could have ended up the kind of convict he portrayed in the 1972 TV movie "The Glass House" were it not for his hard-working mother, who was an elevator operator. And then there was a reformed prostitute who brought him out of an emotional slump at the age of 27 and introduced him to Eastern philosophy and LSD. He has called their year of living together "a rebirth."

Whatever he may think of today's world, Lando Calrissian is very much alive within him. "I want him to last forever. Still, it's like being a major part of movie history."

AFTERWORDS

The voice of Lando Calrissian would live on in video games and several TV specials including 2010's "Robot Chicken: Star Wars III." And finally, Williams reappeared as Lando in 2019's "Star Wars: The Rise of Skywalker." His dream had finally come true.

A FEW MORE STAR WARS MEMORIES

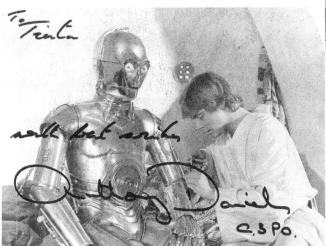

Above: Bob Wilkins' "Creature Features" set sometime in 1977 when Anthony Daniels discussed portraying C-3PO in "Star Wars." Seated with Daniels (left) was my daughter Trista and (right) son Russ. A stand-up C-3PO hovers in the middle.

Left: During his visit to Bob Wilkins, Anthony Daniels signed this "Star Wars" photo of him and Mark Hamill to my daughter Trista.

Right: Peter Mayhew signed this Chewbacca portrait to me and my wife Erica.

Left: Peter Mayhew, famous for his portrayal of Chewbacca, an alien Wookie who was 200 years old, allowed me to sit at his products table at a Wondercon and interview him. Right: Prior to that, I was lucky enough to first meet and interview Peter Mayhew on my "Creature Features" set, while promoting "Return of the Jedi" in 1983.

Below: At a hotel on Market Street in 1982,
I had the pleasure of interviewing David Prowse
(aka Darth Vader) during a science-fiction convention.
Middle: He was also a guest on my
"Creature Features" show that same week,
and he proved to be a fun-filled personality.

To Russ
MAY THE FORCE BE WITH
YOU
DARTH VADER
Dave Prowse

Above: I was lucky enough to
get David Prowse to sign this
photo to my son Russ.
OR WAS IT DARTH VADER
WHO SIGNED???

To Trista
love
Jeremy Bulloch
(Boba Fett)

Jeremy Bullock was attending a Wondercon in San Francisco when he signed
this Boba Fett photo to my daughter Trista. Jeremy loved conventions
and loved talking about his character, a deadly bounty hunter who performed
martial arts. Bullock passed away in England in December, 2020, at the age of 75.

THE CAREER THAT DRIPPED WITH HORROR

Aloha John-
Someday I'll take
you for a swim in my
"Black Lagoon."
[signature]
Hawaii
8-27-99

Stay out of that
lagoon!
Julie Adams

The Tall Man From the Black Lagoon
Who Showed Off His Bare Legs . . .
But They Weren't Insured by Lloyds of London
. . . And Julie Just Sat There, Wearing Her Pants

I T REMAINS one of the most popular monster movies of its kind since the 1950s and it will forever be the one movie that Julia Adams will be remembered for. (After 1955 she changed the spelling to Julie). Mainly because she was wearing a sexy bathing suit and was under attack from one of the most credible-looking creatures in the history of cinema. You wanted to cry out for her survival from this flesh-eater aka the Gill Man.

Yes yes, that thing under the water swimming toward us, eager to rip us to pieces, is the star of "The Creature From the Black Lagoon," released by Universal-International in the spring of 1954. By then the 3-D craze that burst across movie theaters in 1953 had seen its best days and theaters had already begun to revert back to "flat" 2-D projection, allowing only a lucky handful to see this horror-monster programmer in true 3-D. So historically "Creature" was never a success because of its format.

But because of rave reviews by critics who felt the monster was one of the most convincing Hollywood had yet created, the film was a major success in its opening months. While on the surface "Creature" appears to be a typical class-B Universal-International product, it actually plays out well in depicting a group of scientists on an expedition along the Amazon River. Scientists portrayed by Richard Carlson, Richard Denning, Julia Adams and Whit Bissell are in search of a prehistoric Gill Man that could be "the missing link" between fish and animal life.

As for the monster, all the underwater sequences were performed by swimming-lover Ricou Browning, a one-time producer of underwater shows who went on to work as producer for "Sea Hunt," "The Aquanauts" and "Flipper." Ben Chapman, a native of Oakland, CA., who broke into films in "Pagan Love Song," acted out all the monster scenes set on dry land.

Directing was Jack Arnold, who had previously made "It Came From Outer Space," a sci-fier so well received that Universal had no trouble in assigning him to film the Gill Man. In "Science Fiction in the Cinema," author John Baxter writes of director Arnold: "No imprint lingers so indelibly on the face of modern fantasy film as that of this obscure yet brilliant artist."

He credits Arnold, who went on to direct "Tarantula" (1955), "The Incredible Shrinking Man" (1957), "The Space Children" (1958), and "Monster on Campus" (1958), with "raising the Gill Man to the level of Frankenstein and Dracula." Thus is "Creature" added to the cinematic mythology of the 20th Century.

"Creature From The Black Lagoon" director Jack Arnold

On October 14, 2006, the film would enter my life thanks to Bay Area producer Bob Johnson, who had invited me to a weekend event at the Castro Theater. "Creature" was going to be shown in its original 3-D format and Julie Adams and Ben Chapman, who had worn the monster costume in all the sequences filmed on land, would be guests of honor. And I would interview them on the Castro stage.

Before I share that 45-minute exchange with Adams and Chapman I must explain a hilarious irony. When she became a studio icon in the early 1950s Julia Adams' legs were insured for $125,000 by Lloyds of London and were described as "the most perfectly symmetrical legs in the world."

And yet when she walked onto the Castro stage, she was wearing black pants that stretched from her waist all the way down to her flat, non-high heel shoes. (Well, at least her bulging red blouse was something to see.) But her male co-star, six-foot-five Chapman, he was wearing a pair of shorts without pants that exposed his 78-year-old legs up to here and down to there. I burst out laughing inside, but didn't bother to mention it to the large fan-audience that had gathered to see this unique interview.

That's me (left) at the Castro interviewing "Creature" stars Julie Adams and (land monster) Ben Chapman.

"I loved playing that beast," began Chapman, "because it was designed exclusively to fit me. A mold was made to fit my stomach and each arm and leg was a separate piece. The head was also separate and I could slip it on and off at will. What's amazing, it was all done by hand by Bud Westmore and his gang, without all that high-technology we have today. Made of foam rubber, the costume turned very hot if I wore it for too long. But was it cool looking." He added, "Because Ricou Browning and I were of different heights, each suit had to be especially designed."

Julie Adams burst out laughing. "I'll always remember the white bathing suit my character Kay Lawrence wore in the attack scenes, and so will audiences given that the one-piece – like Ben's monster costume – was made exclusively for me," she said.

"And I loved working at Universal-International, doing 'Bend of the River' with James Stewart. Plus other Westerns with Rock Hudson, Tyrone Power, Glenn Ford. Prior to that I had made six low-budget Westerns for Robert L. Lippert under my real name of Betty Adams. We did it in five weeks and I was the leading lady in all of them. It's where I learned to ride. But the film that opened the door to Universal was 'Bright Victory' opposite Arthur Kennedy."

According to Adams, the initial idea for the Black Lagoon monster came from a meeting between the film's producer William Alland and Orson Welles. They had overheard a legendary story about a half-fish/half-man creature on the Amazon River. Welles proposed that mankind was always searching for a link to its creation so why shouldn't a group of scientists investigate the Amazon origins. From that Alland hired Harry Essex and Arthur A. Ross to develop the initial screenplay.

Adams emerges in "Creature" as a statuesque, busty brunette. In the film's best sequence, she dons that historic virginal white one-piece bathing suit to perform an erotic aquatic ballet, unaware that the monster is beneath her, moving in rhythm to her movements. (Actually, the woman in those scenes was stunt double Ginger Stanley, no relation.) The sequence has the appearance of a mating ritual.

The "danse macabre" is climaxed by a linking of sexual past and present when the Gill Man reaches up to touch Kay's foot. This is a "touch" of sensual horror that the rest of the film's underwater duels, savage brawls and gashing brutality can never approach.

Julie went on to explain that she never wanted to be in the two sequels, "Return of the Creature" (1955) and "The Creature Walks Among Us" (1956). "They needed someone new and different so the character could be shocked and terrorized by the sight of the creature. Look, sometimes when movies work, we don't always know exactly why. It becomes a little mystery because it's a combination of script, acting, directing, and music."

I reminded everyone at this point that five pieces of music had been written by Henry Mancini when he was just starting out as a film composer at Universal-International Studios.

Like Julie, Chapman only worked in the first film and "eventually I gave up working in films and moved to Tahiti in 1970. And then in 1975, I moved to Hawaii to work out my days in the travel business."

When Universal-International produced "Revenge of the Creature" (1955), they selected Arnold once again to direct, but "The Creature Walks Among Us" (1956) was helmed by second-unit director John Sherwood, who only handled five films during his career at Universal.

As the old joke goes, it was a case of the Gill Man swimming all the way to the bank.

AFTERWORDS

Julie Adams was kind enough to have dinner with me and Erica the night before the 3-D screening of "The Creature From the Black Lagoon." She would go on to write an autobiography (with help from her son Mitchell Dante) entitled "The Lucky Southern Star: Reflections From the Black Lagoon" which was published in 2011. She died at the age of 92 on February 3, 2019. Ben Chapman, who returned to the Hawaiian Islands, died shortly after the Castro screening at the age of 79. Fans of the film should seek out "Lady from the Black Lagoon: Hollywood Monsters and the Lost Legacy of Milicent Patrick," a history by film producer Mallory O'Meara that chronicles the career of a one-time Walt Disney animation designer who helped in developing the Gill Man, and who went on an extended promotional trip across America prior to the film's release to promote the hell out of it. Both books are great reads.

Back in 1982 at a fantasy convention in San Francisco I had the pleasure of introducing director Jack Arnold to the audience. At that time, he had been stricken by arteriosclerosis and was confined to a wheel chair, yet was still directing episodes of TV's "Love Boat." Arnold loved to talk about his love for science-fiction. He grew up reading sci-fi pulp magazines and seeing horror films. "I'm so glad Universal allowed me to direct those films. It was exactly what I had wanted to do as a director. And in the case of 'Black Lagoon,' I have always considered it among my best work." Arnold died in 1992 at the age of 76.

A Fantastic Dialogue With a Master of the Fantastic:
Ray Bradbury in His Deepest Study of the Universe

M Y FIRST MEETING with Ray Bradbury is at his sixth-floor office overlooking Wilshire Boulevard in downtown Beverly Hills in the summer of 1968, and some of that interview appears in my autobiographic "I Was a TV Horror Host" (Creatures at Large Press, 2007). But there is so much more to be told about one of the most famous science-fiction/fantasy authors in American history. I had first begun to read his short stories in the pulp magazines *Planet Stories* and *Fantastic Adventures* and then, as a fan of the E.C. Comics of the early 1950s, discovered illustrated adaptations of his short stories in the comic books *Weird Fantasy* and *Weird Science*.

Now, enjoying his 48th year on Planet Earth, he has invited me to join him. I want to get into the depth of Bradbury's imagination. Probe those areas of thought that have enabled him to create such books as "The Illustrated Man" and "The Martian Chronicles." While the pulp magazines died away in the early 1950s, Bradbury has gone on to countless writing achievements. And questions about that are what drives me this fabulous morning as I sit down with him. Seated at his typewriter, working on page 162 of a screenplay entitled "And the Rock Cried Out," he seems more than eager to answer my questions.

Stanley: Mr. Bradbury–

Bradbury: Please, call me Ray.

Stanley: Ray . . . this is an exciting time for science-fiction films. There's been a noticeable upsurge due to such releases as "Fantastic Voyage," "Planet of the Apes," and, most recently, Stanley Kubrick's "2001: A Space Odyssey." However, many fans were surprised when you panned the latter film in a magazine review.

Bradbury: I panned part of it. Only part of it. I think overall it's a gorgeous film. One of the most beautifully photographed pictures in the history of motion pictures. Unfortunately, there's no well-directed scenes and dialogue is banal to the point of extinction.

Stanley: I read somewhere that was part of director Stanley Kubrick's intention.

Bradbury (sighing): I hope not. I'd like to believe Kubrick is more intelligent than that. I just think he's a bad writer who got in the way of Arthur C. Clarke, who is a wonderful writer. There's the irony. I know Arthur and I sent him a copy of my review and I said, "Look, we've had a long friendship, we've known each other 17 years or so, and I've written this review. But, I'm sending it to you myself so it won't come through someone else. And I hope you won't be hurt."

Stanley: I don't think he was because Clarke recently told a San Francisco newsman, and I quote: "I don't worry about Ray. He'll come around. They all do." . . . Were you thrown any by the wildly abstract ending of "Space Odyssey"?

Bradbury: I wasn't thrown off. I just didn't understand it. I described it as that wonderful moment on the ceiling of the Sistine Chapel where God reaches out to touch the finger of Adam and doesn't quite make it. Doesn't touch. The spark doesn't leap the gap. You see, if it were just me coming out of the theater a dumbkoff, that would be one thing. But when dozens and hundreds of viewers come out and I find they can't explain it to me either, then Kubrick has failed. You know what I wanted? I wanted to come out of that theater and jump up and down and yell and say this was the best Goddamn film ever made – period. That's the way I felt when I saw "Fantasia" when I was 21. I felt that way about "Citizen Kane." I gathered up my friends and drove them to the theater. I even paid their way. And I wanted so badly to come out of "Space Odyssey" crying with joy. When the film started and there was all that beautiful material with the apes, I said to myself "Boy oh boy, if he continues like this . . . "

And then they bring on the banal scenes. With a false intellectual concept which I'm surprised Kubrick allowed himself to repeat. Intellectuals have been saying to themselves that the future will dehumanize . . . crap. Not necessarily. Not proven. In fact, the astronauts whom I've met and who are around machines all the time are more human than people who're not around machines. So where's the argument? Come on now, cut it out. These easy cliches about machines. Not true. The most humanizing thing that's happened to the world is the invention of the motion picture machine. A robot that instructs us about ourselves, that's what it is. It has done more good in the world than any other machine I can name.

Stanley: And other new science-fiction films . . . how do you feel about them?

Bradbury: I can't really say. I've only seen half of "Planet of the Apes" and what I saw was so primitive . . . sort of like the old Tarzan movies. Nelson Bond was doing this sort of thing long before Gerald Kersh. Stephen Vincent Benet exploited this same theme in "By the Waters of Babylon." So where's there anything new?

Stanley: Aren't some of your own stories being produced by Hollywood?

Bradbury: I just got a call from a producer over at MGM this morning, inviting me to see a rough cut of "The Illustrated Man." Rod Steiger and Claire Bloom head the cast.

Stanley: You wrote the script?

Bradbury: No. And I never got to read the adaptation. Nobody asked me to. *(Laughing)* I'll certainly tell them what I think of it.

Stanley: What stories from "The Illustrated Man" have been adapted?

Bradbury: "The Long Rain," "The Veldt," and "The Last Night of the World."

Stanley: About the screenplay for "The Martian Chronicles." I know it's been a long, involved history. I know that Edward Dymtryk was once involved with its development. What's the latest?

Bradbury: Well, I wrote it for Richard Mulligan about two years ago. I was on it for almost two years, off and on. But none of the studios are interested and I now own the screen rights. It's a perfect time to make the film because here we'll be taking off for the moon next year and "Space Odyssey" is going to be the most profitable film in the history of MGM.

Stanley: I see you have a copy of Nostalgia Press' "Flash Gordon" on your desk.

Bradbury: A beautiful book. I have many of the actual Sunday newspaper pages at home. I have a complete collection of *Prince Valiant* Sunday panels. I have *Buck Rogers* daily strips from 1929 up through 1935. I have the Sunday *Rogers* panels from roughly 1930 on.

Stanley: Some of your short stories came to be illustrated in the E. C. Comics in the early 1950s. I was once told it started over a case of plagiarism. Is that right?

Bradbury: Yes, true. E. C. adapted "Kaleidoscope" under the title "Home to Stay" in *Weird Fantasy #12.* Someone sent me a copy so I wrote a letter to the E. C. editors and congratulated them on the brilliance of the adaptation. I didn't mention any plagiarism, or that my name wasn't on it. I thought, every once in a while, one who pretends to be a Christian should adapt to Christian principles. Turn the other cheek and see how people respond. At the end of the letter I added, "Gee, you forgot to send me the adaptation check. I know how busy you people are but as soon as you could get around to it, I would appreciate a check." The next week a check came through. So you see, there are happy endings to unpleasant occurrences. I wrote back and thanked them for the check. Now, I said, I have an idea. Why don't you adapt more of my stories, giving me credit and thereby protecting my copyright?

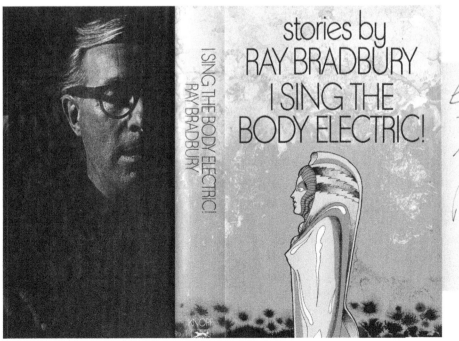

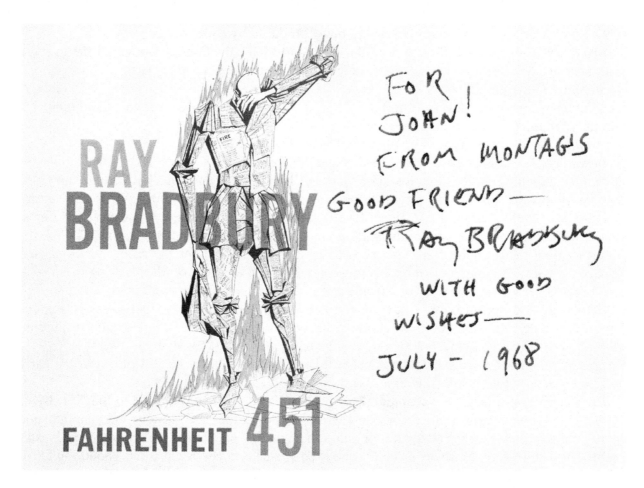

For John! From Montag's good friend — Ray Bradbury with good wishes — July – 1968

RAY BRADBURY
FAHRENHEIT 451

Thus, editor William Gaines and I formed a partnership and E. C. adapted about 30 of my stories and put my name on the covers. It was a helluva lot of fun. Much of it was fine work. Al Williamson, an E.C. artist, did some wonderful things. So did Wally Wood. I'll always admire his "There Will Come Soft Rains."

Stanley: Do you still live by the axiom of doing one story per week?

Bradbury: Yes. This last week I've done the equivalent of a short story. I've been working on a screenplay, "And the Rock Cried Out." I first did it 17 years ago for Sir Carol Reed but it was too far ahead of its time. Civil rights were nowhere in those days. People didn't want to look into a future where possibly the white man's supremacy might be challenged; a future where we might be waiting on tables or shining shoes; a future wherein the shoe would be on the other foot. But then, that's why you write science fiction. To insure that the future you write about will not come to pass. You don't write it because it's going to happen. A lot of people misinterpret that. I've also been working on a new play, "Leviathan 90," based on the legend and mythology of "Moby Dick," but laid in the future.

Stanley: What do you express in plays that you feel you can't in the short-story form?

Bradbury: There's nothing you can say on the stage that can't be said in stories. It just depends on where your love lies at a certain moment. And for the past few years I've focused on the theater with my Pandemonium Playhouse. You see, I'm a child of many forms. I'm a child of motion pictures. I grew up in a time when movies were really coming to birth. (They're still pretty primitive today.) The first film that I remember is "The Hunchback of Notre Dame" of 1923. I fell in love with all the Lon Chaney films and all the Douglas Fairbanks films. So I grew up wanting to have something to do with movies one day.

Stanley: Didn't you write the original version of "It Came From Outer Space" for Universal-International in 1953?

Bradbury: Yes, and I did a very foolish thing. I was supposed to write an idea for them and then do a treatment. But the treatment got away with me and turned into a script. You see, I can't do anything half way. First of all, a treatment is a lie. Anyone who writes a treatment for a studio is lying to himself and to the studio. You don't have to prove anything in a treatment. You just write: "And then the monster is there and everyone is frightened." That's a lie. In order to prove a thing you have to get in there and write it. So, I wrote a 110-page screenplay. I turned it in and they paid me $3,000 for it. Then they brought in a screenwriter who worked over my treatment.

"It Came From Outer Space," the first draft of which was written by Ray Bradbury, was released in 1953. The 3-D sci-fi movie starred an alien that scared the hell out of Barbara Rush and Richard Carlson (clinging to each other)

Stanley: How did you feel about the finished product?

Bradbury: It was only fair. They don't really know how to build an atmosphere. They don't know how to work with a scene. That's one of the great things wrong with film-making in this country. So often they won't take the time to establish the world so you, the audience, can feel surrounded by the feeling of the scene. Someone like Robert Wise knows how to do this. His "The Haunting" is a beautiful picture.

Stanley: And then, of course, you wrote "Moby Dick" for director John Huston, with Gregory Peck portraying Captain Ahab.

Bradbury: It was a case of the blind leading the blind. John didn't know any more about "Moby Dick" than I did. So, we learned together. I'd write ten pages a day and we'd go over them together, then discuss Melville's novel some more. I read the novel at least ten times. Finally, after I'd been in Ireland on the project for four months, I woke up one morning in Dublin and said: "I'm Herman Melville." That same morning, I wrote the last 40 pages and it came terrifically. This is the secret of all good writing. It has to come fast. If you go slow on anything it's automatically bad. In an art form, if you slow down you begin to intellectualize and destroy and pontificate and become self-conscious and make up reasons for what you're doing. You must never make up any reasons for anything. It's there coming out of your fingers because it must come out. That's

Gregory Peck as Captain Ahab in "Moby Dick"

one of the dangers in the country today – we're getting so intellectual and super-intellectual and quasi-intellectual and fake-intellectual that we're in great danger of destroying all our creative talent. All the intuitive process, which is the great truth. That's what you must work with. That's what you must let happen.

Stanley: Do you have any criticism of the final cut of "Moby Dick"?

Bradbury: Only on the casting. John Huston didn't work with Gregory Peck correctly as a director. On the first day of shooting, Huston walked up to Peck and said, "Great, Greg. Now give me just a little more." And I think it was that "little more" that killed it. See, Ahab is a paranoic, a driven man, a very wild kind of insane person. It had to be played, on one level, with great dedication and fierceness. You could get a great performance out of Sir Ralph Richardson or Sir Laurence Olivier. Whom I wanted. Walter Huston when he was alive [Huston, John's father, had died in 1950.] Even Burt Lancaster could do Ahab. But with a man like Peck, he's basically a quiet individual. Therefore, you must think in terms of catatonia. In terms of the kind of madness that turns away and in. Therefore, you must allow Peck to be a colder, quieter kind of madman, and work on that level. Huston never exploited Ahab quite in that way.

"Moby Dick" director John Huston

Stanley: In your short story "Almost the End of the World," you make a personal, abstract statement about the quality of television. That it's turning us into zombies. Come on now. Don't you really enjoy many of the things TV has to offer?

Bradbury: Oh, of course. The thing I enjoy most of all is Bugs Bunny. In fact, that's my favorite show, watching old Warner Brothers' cartoons. People think I'm pulling their legs when I say that, but I'm serious. TV is turning out to be the best purveyor of old films that I have wanted to see over and over. For example, the other night I saw "The Lady Vanishes" [1938, with Michael Redgrave and Margaret Lockwood], and it holds up extremely well. I'm a big [Alfred] Hitchcock fan. I would say, in fact, that 95 per cent of the time the reason I like TV is simply for old films. Every Sunday morning you can be sure I'll be up at 10:30 watching Bugs Bunny.

Stanley: Do you read much science-fiction nowadays?

Bradbury: Not as much as I used to, because I feel it's dangerous to read in your own field. I think it's better to read in poetry, psychology, philosophy, etc., and bring back into your own field things from other fields. First of all, if you read something that's already been done you don't want to do it. Right? Reading what others have written can often discourage you. So it's not wise to read in your own field. That way you stay fresh and original. Of course, there are times I will read certain favorites. Leigh Brackett is an old, old friend. Ed Hamilton, I like. Catherine Moore. Henry Kuttner, when he was alive.

Stanley: You always seem to have an incredible number of projects in the works. How do you do it?

Bradbury: I don't, really. If there were three of me, there still wouldn't be enough to do all the things there are to do.

Stanley: Didn't you once have ambitions to be an actor?

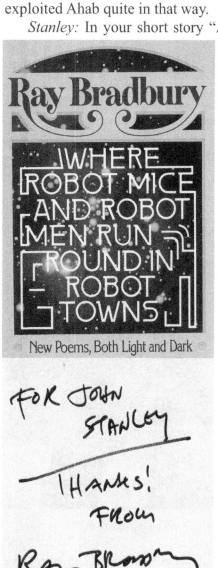

Ray Bradbury

WHERE ROBOT MICE AND ROBOT MEN RUN ROUND IN ROBOT TOWNS

New Poems, Both Light and Dark

FOR JOHN STANLEY

THANKS! FROM

Ray Bradbury

Bradbury: In high school I was very active in the drama society and after I left high school I worked with Laraine Day's little theater group here in Los Angels until I was 21. But all through the latter part of my teens I knew I could have only one career – and that was writing.

Stanley: And don't you do quite a bit of lecturing?

Bradbury: It's one of my biggest kicks. It gives me a chance to act, you see. To sense an audience, to know how it's thinking and how it's reacting.

Stanley: What criteria do you follow in selecting a subject?

Bradbury: I never prepare a topic in advance. No matter where I speak. I just go in and, if I'm on a campus say, I get a sense of what the campus is like or how the tastes run. I find generally if I speak on the things we're discussing now, everything goes well. What is creativity? How do you work with it? How do you stay enthused with life in the face of so much that is brutal and dehumanizing and unhappy? How do you not growl in a world of sorrow and destruction? How do you control your own violence and hostility? . . . All these things are of vast interest. These are the subjects common to us all.

Stanley: Regarding your many short stories. Do you have a favorite?

Bradbury: "Something Wicked This Way Comes" [published in 1962] is my favorite book. I think it says more about my own life, about my father. "Dandelion Wine" is based on my experiences with my brother and much of it is so basic to me. ["Dandelion Wine" began as a 1953 short story set in the fictional town of Green Town, Illinois, patterned after Waukegan, where Bradbury grew up. "Something Wicked This Way Comes" expanded on that beginning.]

(Note: "Something Wicked This Way Comes" was made by Disney into a full-length feature in 1983 starring Jason Robards and Jonathan Pryce - above as Mr. Dark. I met with Ray and his wife Maggie at the Fairmont Hotel in San Francisco just prior to the opening and interviewed Ray for a two-part interview that ran in the San Francisco Chronicle, and which can be found in "I Was a TV Horror Host.")

Stanley: In his "Seekers of Tomorrow," Sam Moskowitz accused you of writing less and less science-fiction in more recent times.

Bradbury: It's not really true. Remember, it's only been a year since I had a long short story in Playboy called "The Lost City of Mars." Playboy wants another story but recently rejected two. And there are other fantasies in the marketplace . . .

Stanley: What do you feel is your main weakness as a writer, given the rejections?

Bradbury: If I knew I would correct it. I don't think I really know. I don't think you can analyze and correct weaknesses. All you can do is have hindsight and keep writing and reading and hope to learn more about people, atmosphere, things. The greatest thing, though, is to develop a style that is totally suitable. That is totally yourself. In other words, style is not worthwhile unless it's absolute truth. And truth, after all, develops its own style. They're one and the same, actually. When I read something, I ask myself, "What kind of truth does this man tell me of himself? Is he lying to me?" If he is lying, then he has a false style. If he's telling the truth, then he has his own style automatically. What you're trying to do is bring out all the truths at various levels. Your fear of the dark, your fear of violence, your hostility toward this, your love of that.

Stanley: You've written many stories about machines. How do you feel toward today's gadgetry and inventions?

Bradbury: I think machines can be fabulous teachers. We're so primitive, still, in our ability to teach one another. I write about machines to show how we can use them to humanize ourselves. Jesus, a hundred years from this very day we'll have robots the likes of which you can't even begin to imagine.

Think what lies ahead. You'll be able to program a robot to carry on a dialogue. I see the proliferation of millions of robots who'll be teaching us history, philosophy and sociology in colleges all over the world. It sounds impossible right now. It sounds silly. It sounds stupid. But it will happen.

Stanley: You have a file bulging with stories that have never been submitted to publications. Is there any one characteristic about them that makes them unsalable?

Bradbury: No, no, I'm not keeping them there because they won't sell. I'm keeping them there because I can only work on them one at a time. There are just so many hours in the day and so many stories you can finish in a year. These are all fragments I've put away. There's a beginning, middle or end. In the last month I've taken two stories out of that file that I began 16 years ago. One story just went off and the other I finished two weeks ago. I go through my file and if a fragment cries out to me in any way . . . if the idea speaks and says, "Father, it's time, clap me on the back and bring me to life," then I take it out.

Stanley: Do you find you have to be in a certain mood for a certain story?

Bradbury: Yes, I use my file as a Rorschach Test for myself. I just keep going through it, and as these stories flash past I remember a title and I say, "Yeah, yeah, yeah, this is good but I never did like that ending." And if the ending comes to me in that instant, success. A lot of times I go with instinct, with intuition. I believe all great creative things have happened on a subliminal level. I do not believe in the intellectual writer. I do, however, believe in the ideas he writes about. A lot of my ideas, I find when I'm finished, are intellectually accepted.

They are of my time. "There Will Come Soft Rains" is a poetic exposition on an idea that has to do with hydrogen bombs, people and machinery. But I didn't set out to write that kind of story. It wrote itself. My subconscious thought it up on its own terms. But this is where there'll always be continuing conflict. The fight will be between creative persons and intellectuals. And the intellectual, per se, is not a creative person. Can't be. I do not know of any solutions to problems that have ever been thought out. I think these things happen intuitively. That part of the process I'm afraid of is the one setting on top of the mind, guiding and steering. This is the destroyer of the creative process.

Stanley: Do you do much rewriting?

Bradbury: Very rarely. I retype a story three or four times. And as I retype, I might throw in a word or take one out. These are just the minor truths. You see, you nail down the big truth first. But if you start fussing with those little truths while you're still writing the story, you'll never finish it. You'll be messing with grammar and single words and adjectives. Who cares? Not important. The whole story finished, that's what is important. Get it down, get a skin around it, then make your changes. The art of cutting, of course, is the Great Art. The second Great Art is Knowing. Knowing when to stop cutting before you deball it. You have to write every day to learn both arts. And the more you write the more enthusiasm and fun you have and the better your work gets. There's a direct relationship between quantity and quality. It's a flat rule: There's just no way to contradict it.

AFTERWORDS

It was the month of June in the year 2012, in the town of Palo Alto, and I was on my way with my wife and son Russ to see John Wayne in "The Quiet Man" at a theater specializing in reviving old films, the Stanford. As we passed a drugstore on University Avenue I saw a newspaper headline, declaring the death of famed science-fiction author Ray Bradbury. Miraculously, he had lived to be 91 years old. To the very end he had devoted his career to writing superb science-fiction and fantasy. I took a deep breath and thanked Ray for all the hours he had granted me during the four times we met.

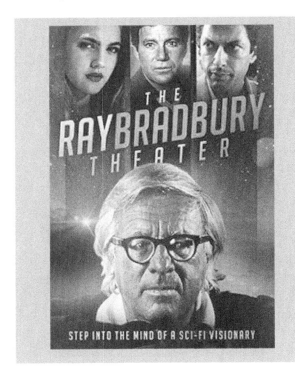

One of Ray Bradbury's great successes was a Canadian-produced TV series "The Ray Bradbury Theater," which ran 65 episodes from 1985 through 1992. Sixty of these shows were written by Bradbury himself. Each fantasy tale opened with Bradbury stepping off an elevator and entering a horribly-cluttered office overflowing with posters, books and other scattered memorabilia – a symbol of all the literary work he had accomplished. His voiceover told us: "
People ask: "Where do you get your ideas?" Right here! All this is mine. Martian landscape . . . somewhere in this room is an African veldt. Just beyond perhaps is a small Illinois town where I grew up. I'm surrounded on every side by a magician's toyshop. I'll never starve here. I just look around and find what I need and begin. "I'm Ray Bradbury and this is . . . "

HERE COMES THE
COOLEST FANTASY
AUTHOR OF ALL
. . . WHO DROVE
EVERYBODY
ABSOLUTELY

PSYCHO!

A lonely hillside road, of the kind that usually harbors unutterable horrors for the characters in suspense and terror tales, is the only route to the home of Robert Bloch. As one warily drives the tortuous lane that winds through the Hollywood Hills, searching for unlit street signs and nocturnal pedestrians who tend to loom suddenly out of the darkness, there comes to mind a Bloch anecdote about the killer who threw his murder weapon into a culvert on a lonely hillside road. Later, after he confessed his crime, police searched the culvert and found not only the gun in question but several murder weapons which, apparently, had been discarded by other criminals with equal dispatch. This very winding road could well be where Bloch got the inspiration for his little tale. And who knows how many other stories of horror for which he has become known world-wide. It's the year 1969 when I finally arrive.

Bloch's residence is modest in design but large in size. There are well-tended shrubs and flowers. All very suburbanite, except for the quietude and the isolation. Bloch, for whom I have been searching, comes to the front door dressed in a black turtleneck sweater, immediately conveying an air of tranquility. Perhaps a hint of modesty? Not really. There is nothing modest about this man. The beginning of an ironic smile seems to be perpetually pulling at the corners of his mouth, but it only fully emerges when irony finally smashes home.

Robert Bloch seems to be a man filled with curiosity about me, a man capable of deep introspection. The look of an interrogator who has yet to ask any questions.

THE CAREER THAT DRIPPED WITH HORROR

He looks strangely different from most of his photographs, and he is quick to explain he recently gave up his horn-rimmed glasses for contact lenses. It has resulted, he believes, in an entirely new image. How ironic, I think, he gave up glasses, which tend to make one look literary. Possibly even intellectual?

He leads the way into his library, a neat, orderly room where he does all of his writing. He lights up a St. Moritz cigarette in a lengthy holder and sits behind his typewriter which has been covered for the night. The desk is remarkably clean. The only other objects in view: a blotter in the shape of a human skull and a letter opener made to resemble a decomposing corpse. He sips from a glass of lemonade, giving me time to scan the library. On one wall are a Count Dracula Society Award and a Hugo – the latter presented to him in 1959 at the 17th World Science Fiction Convention for his short story, "That Hell-Bound Train." In a bookcase are all the publications which contain his writings. The top shelf consists of hardcover anthologies;

below those are yellowing pulp magazines from the 1940s and '50s. *Fantastic Adventures, Planet Stories*, those kind of publications from a bygone era. Bloch, not looking bygone at all, leans back in his swivel chair, indicating he is ready for the interview. So I start asking …

Stanley: One of the things that rocked the world of horror and imagination was the death of Boris Karloff earlier this year. [Karloff had died in England on February 2, 1969, at the age of 81, of both emphysema and pneumonia.] Karloff, he made history as the actor who first conceived Universal's Frankenstein Monster. What was your initial thought when you heard of his death?

Bloch: My immediate thought was that I had lost a close friend. The kind difficult to replace.

Stanley: Did Karloff have any personal interests in the supernatural?

Bloch: Despite all those characters he portrayed – no. He was a total skeptic. I remember once that my wife Eleanor and I were visiting his summer place and he took us for a drive through the English countryside. Along the way he pointed to a so-called "haunted house" and told some amusing stories about it, concluding with the comment: "If it's haunted by anything, it must be by insects." Still, Karloff had a great love for the literature of the macabre. He had a wide reading background and was acquainted with most of the classic writers of his time. He compiled his own anthologies, and a close examination of them will reveal those writers he thought the most of.

Stanley: Did Karloff have a sense of humor?

Bloch: A tremendous sense of humor. On that same drive I was telling you about, Mrs. Karloff was pointing out tea shoppes and other businesses along the way. Suddenly, Boris leaned out the window and shouted: "Oh look, there's Ye Olde Woolworth's."

He didn't take himself pompously; he was always self-deprecating. One of the last funny stories told of Karloff concerns a science-fiction film he was making last year in Mexico [this would have been "Alien Terror," which would not be released until 1971]. Boris was portraying a scientist of some kind and had a lengthy speech in the final scene that went something like this: "The aliens have left now, but where have they gone? Will they be back? I hope we've seen the last of them!" Then he turned to the camera and the crew and added: "Because if they do come back, we'll have to do the whole damn picture all over again!"

Stanley: Did he take his films seriously, or did he look upon them as just a way of making a living?

Bloch: That depended on the film. Certainly, he took the Frankenstein Monster seriously, for

This photograph, taken in the 60s, of Boris Karloff with his daughter Sara was given to me by Sara when she appeared with me at the 2007 WonderCon in San Francisco. She was his only child.

he often said, "Frankenstein was the best friend I ever had. It's given me everything." And certainly, Karloff appreciated such films as "The Body Snatchers" and "Bedlam." And "The Isle of the Dead." However, in his later years Karloff realized he was a limited actor and became a working professional who would accept almost anything just to keep working. Even though he had to spend most of his time in a wheelchair during his last years, he worked right up to the time of his death.

Stanley: And what was his general attitude toward the horror film genre?

Bloch: Close to my own personal feelings. He felt horror and science-fiction had been degraded by substitutes of shock and sensationalism. He often commented, "There just isn't enough genuine feeling for the supernatural."

Stanley: Was there any goal Karloff failed to reach during his lifetime that you are aware of?

Bloch: Yes, there was one unrealized ambition, though it had nothing to do with films. Karloff, as you know, started as a stock company actor in Canada. From time to time he would

Boris Karloff, playing Jonathan Brewster in the stage version of "Arsenic and Old Lace," one of his finest performances.

take small parts in Hollywood. He did "The Criminal Code" in 1930. Later he did "Arsenic and Old Lace" for two years on Broadway. [He was unable to play his role of Jonathan Brewster in the movie version because he was still doing the play when Frank Capra was shooting the footage.] He also co-starred with Jean Arthur in "Peter Pan" on Broadway and with Julie Harris in "Skylark." But he always had wanted to appear in a West End production in London, which would be the equivalent to our Broadway. By the

time it was possible, however, he was too well along in years and couldn't sustain the night-after-night pressures. But despite not achieving this goal, Karloff, in both thought and action, expressed the attitude that life had always been extra good to him.

Stanley: Since you're the man who's given the word "psycho" entirely new dimensions, I wanted to tell you that Calvin T. Beck, editor of the *Castle of Frankenstein* magazine, heard I was coming to see you and wanted me to ask you some questions. So, if you don't mind . . .

Bloch: I want to hear what he said. I'm ready to give you an answer. Fire away, young man. Fire away!

Stanley: Calvin Beck has said this, and I quote: "Robert Bloch, you may have been pretty damned good 17 or 20 years ago, but the quality of your technique has declined and gone heavily commercial. Your zest has dwindled away." Beck also believes that [screenwriter] Joseph Stefano and [producer-director] Alfred Hitchcock turned an otherwise routine potboiler novel into a very fine film by embellishing it. "Psycho," of course. And he further believes that you, Robert Bloch, have lost your love of art for art's sake. How do you respond to Beck's beliefs?

Bloch: Let's take that point by point. I don't think my zest has dwindled in the slightest; I don't think whatever craft I've possessed has diminished at all. Markets have changed. I will say quite candidly that in the past year I've written five short stories – three of them haven't been placed because the markets have changed for that sort of material. I would like to write a great deal more fiction, but there is the problem of market availability. So, I write to specification.

This is the issue of *Castle of Frankenstein* (#16, published in 1971) that contained my Robert Bloch interview featuring questions editor Calvin T. Beck had requested that I ask. And Bloch gave it back to him good.

Now this is no different, really, from how I wrote 20 or 30 years ago when there were pulp magazines like *Weird Tales*, *Strange Stories*, *Unknown Worlds* and *Fantastic Adventures*. They wanted a certain kind of story and I wrote those stories.

I don't feel I've changed; I feel the times have changed. And they change for every writer. There is no writer living today who will end up ten years later with the same market conditions and the same reading audience and the same media. Now, regarding the film version of "Psycho." Ninety per cent of that movie *was* my book.

There was an extended prologue, showing the relationship between the hero and the woman which was not presented dramatically in my book. But after those scenes, the characters and story development remained the same.

Stanley: Could you briefly trace the film's creation for us?

Bloch: Certainly. When Hitchcock bought the book, he bought it blind from my agent in New York. I was not told who bought it. All I received was a flat offer.

Once I learned it was Hitchcock, he asked if I would be available to write the screenplay. The person he talked to was an agent for the Music Corporation of America. It took that agent three seconds to say, "No, Bloch is not available."

Because at that time MCA wanted one of its own clients to do the writing. Well, someone else got the assignment and handed Hitchcock a treatment that he turned down. Hitch then hired Joseph Stefano, who worked three weeks on a new version Stefano's only previous script was "Black Orchid" (1958). Hitchcock did the rest.

Calvin T. Beck, editor of *Castle of Frankenstein* magazines published from 1962 through 1975.

Top: Alfred Hitchcock and Janet Leigh in the most memorable Robert Bloch environment of them all – the stall of falling water at the Bates Motel.
Below: Leigh in her Golden Globe-wining role as Marion Crane, the woman murdered in a motel shower by Norman Bates (Anthony Perkins). As for Mr. Bates, he would be remembered as one of the most fascinating cinema killers of all time.

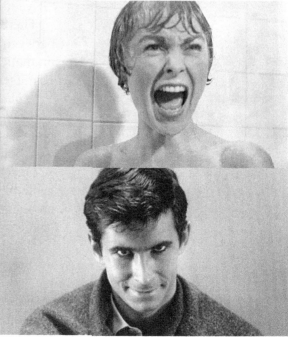

For the nudity scenes in the shower sequence of "Psycho," showgirl Marli Renfro substituted for Janet Leigh. Marli signed a photo for me when I met her at the 2011 WonderCon in San Francisco. Robert Graysmith's "The Girl in Alfred Hitchcock's Shower" had just been published highlighting how she came to be the stand-in.

"When that knife went into me in that shower scene, I could almost feel it."

Bloch: From the start I wanted "Psycho" to be made. It was an aggravation to Paramount Studios. It was considered too far out, too shocking, too daring for its time. The studio wanted to change the title, the story, everything. But fortunately, Hitchcock had the kind of contract by which he could exercise complete control. I call it power. Strength of character. I like to feel that "Psycho" the novel contributed to a breakthrough in cinema fare.

Stanley: What was your own personal reaction to the film on first viewing?

Bloch: I can remember the studio screening vividly. Sitting behind me was Hitch and Janet Leigh, who played the girl [in the shower]. When the lights went up, Hitch asked Janet what she thought of the picture. She told him: "When that knife went into me in that shower scene, I could almost feel it." As for myself, I was very, very pleased. There were many reasons why I was pleased. The first reason: I can remember a silent motion picture, "Seven Footprints to Satan," which was made from a popular A. Merritt novel in 1927. When Merritt saw the film he sat there and cried. And after reading the book and seeing the film, I can understand why. There was nothing of the story, characters or concept left in that movie. It was an atrocious disaster, even though it had been directed by Benjamin Christensen, who had also directed "Witchcraft," a fine Danish film of 1920. But . . . there was my book, up there on the screen. That is something that seldom happens today. I was also pleased for various tangential reasons. I'd always admired the work of Bernard Herrmann, who did the music for "Psycho." And I thought he was at his best in an atmosphere of horror. The fact it was done in black and white pleased me. Certain things have to be done that way for effect. Many so-called horror and psychological suspense films have been ruined by color because color has emotional overtones that sometimes overshadow the essential starkness of black and white. When

Alfred Hitchcock with "Pyscho" composer Bernard Hermann, a master of music filled with utter horror. Hitch received an Oscar nomination but Hermann didn't. He should have!

you get the warm flesh tones you just lose something. Then there is the temptation by some producers to substitute shock color for actual horror. They turn a man green, or show tomato catsup flowing by the bottles. It becomes lurid, unreal, comic-strippish, disgusting in many cases.

Stanley: Bill Castle did that in "The Tingler." He inserted a single color sequence in a black-and-white film that showed a bathtub filled with blood.

Bloch: Now, about Calvin Beck's feeling that I've lost my love of art for art's sake. Unfortunately for the idealistic *Castle of Frankenstein* editorship, I've never had any idea of art for art's sake. I always approached writing as I approached doing plays in high school. I want to entertain my audience. I want only to entertain. I've never had any notion doing anything more than that. If I interject a personal message this is still a form of entertainment rather than an artistic endeavor. I think my primary duty is to satisfy the demands of an audience.

Stanley: Well, whatever Calvin thinks, I wanted you to know this about your work: Nothing I've ever read from your pen has been dull. And I've been reading you since the days of the pulp magazines. You're also why I bought a set of bound issues of *Fantastic Adventures*.

Bloch: Well, thank you. To me that's the highest compliment you could pay me. I might be bad, maybe. But dull? Never.

Stanley: Though you did not write the film version of "Psycho," you have written a number of motion pictures. "The Couch" [1952], "The Night Walker" [1964], "The Cabinet of Dr. Caligari" [1962], to name a few. Do you have a favorite?

Bloch: Most certainly not "Cabinet." In fact, I've never seen it. I was displeased with the way the screenplay was revised. [Final credits listed Bloch as screenwriter, which had further angered him.] You see, I used basically the same plot as in the silent film classic, but I updated it into a realistic setting. The dialogue and direction in the first three-quarters of my screenplay version emphasized a real atmosphere. You actually thought this woman was in the hands of some kind of madman. You never realized her aberration until the last of the film. Then the rug is pulled out and we see she is a psychiatric patient and this man is the doctor treating her, and the man she is in love with is really her son. With an added touch, the psychiatrist is perhaps a little crazy. But that's not quite the way it ended up. You begin to see the constant war between writers and film-makers.

But you asked me for my favorite. I would say the only film segment I have really had any complete enjoyment from is a twelve-minute section of William Castle's "Strait-Jacket" [1964]. It was filmed exactly as I conceived it, and it conveyed precisely the effect I wanted. This is the part in which we establish there is a murderess running around with an axe upstairs in a mansion. The father leaves the wife downstairs and goes up to get ready for bed. Step by step the tension builds because we think something is going to happen. There are half a dozen little places where the audience is quite certain that the axe killer is going to strike. But I keep playing with the audience. Teasing it. Then, when everyone is completely lulled, it happens.

Everyone jumps. This is what they want, and this is what I delivered. It's primarily a matter of timing. And bad timing is what makes so many films misfire nowadays. The director, in many cases, decides to superimpose his own angles and his own tempo on the film, but he rarely knows the medium that well. He confuses suspense with brutal shock. He confuses excitement with gore and he doesn't know how to build to it. There are too many producers and directors and cameramen who do horror films who invalidate what they are trying to achieve. That's why for every good film of this sort, there are innumerable bad ones. They just keep coming.

Joan Crawford preparing to bury the axe in William Castle's "Strait-Jacket," which was written by Robert Bloch.

Stanley: What about your most recent film, "Torture Garden," which starred Burgess Meredith and Jack Palance?

Bloch: They only did about 60 or 70 per cent of what I had written. There is a general tendency – I hate to sound repetitive, but it's true – to confuse visual shock with psychological build-up and this has become so characteristic you grow to expect it. It's par for the course in this business.

Peter Cushing and Jack Palance in "Torture Garden."

Stanley: "Torture Garden" seemed terribly muddled. Many things were left unclear, despite some excellent acting.

Bloch: Definitely so. There is a longer version for TV in which there are twelve minutes more of clarification. But even with that, there are still changes I don't feel are effective. But what's the use of complaining about it? It's too late to go back and do it again.

Stanley: Now, about your writing for TV. You did ten "Thriller" episodes in the early 1960s which came off rather well, with Boris Karloff as host.

Bloch: In general, TV never quite comes off. There are too many fingers in that particular pie. But "Thriller" was a different proposition altogether. Almost invariably my first-draft teleplay was shot exactly as I wrote it. The director didn't try to change the shots or angles or anything regarding the story.

Stanley: You've also done three "Star Trek" scripts ["Catspaw," "Wolf in the Fold," and "What Are Little Girls Made Of?"]. What are your feelings about that series' prominent characters?

Bloch: In a series you're married to certain concepts. You have a continuation hero and secondary hero or heroes. You have a set location. You can seldom stray from that. When you have a star that star must be a prime mover in each story. If you follow a guest star's viewpoint too closely your star, the star's agent and the network will object because they're not paying to build up a one-shot character. And, finally, you are married to the drudgery of a formula. So, your stories go out the window. The rest is watered-down concept.

Stanley: What, in your opinion, was wrong with TV's "Journey to the Unknown"?

Bloch: The series [which ran in the fall of 1968 for only seventeen episodes] failed because the producer, Joan Harrison, was boxed in by ABC. The network decided early in the game it wanted none of the traditional supernatural elements. It was like doing a Western series without six-guns or horses. Therefore, there was no atmosphere, suspense or any of the other qualities fans of the genre have come to expect.

Stanley: What films or TV are you currently involved with?

Bloch: Nothing in TV at the moment. Amicus Films of England will soon be releasing a film that is much like "Torture Garden" in that it consists of four separate short stories of mine: "Method for Murder," "Living End," "Sweets to the Sweet" and "The Cloak." I hate to tell you that the film is currently entitled "The House That Dripped Blood." But I do pray it will be changed before the release date. (The title was not changed.)

Stanley: Are there any forthcoming series of supernatural, horror or science-fiction to take the place of "Star Trek" and "Journey to the Unknown"?

Bloch: There are always rumors of myriad projects, but I've heard of nothing definite.

Stanley: Do you think there's any hope for any more series like "Thriller"?

Bloch: It may be attempted eventually, but only as a last resort. It's so much easier for all concerned to go the way of the series – it's much simpler to write, produce and direct.

Stanley: You've written some semi-satirical short stories about Hollywood: "Terror Over Hollywood," "Is Betsy Blake Still Alive?", "Sock Finish," "The Dream Makers." Do these reflect a certain cynicism toward what makes the film industry tick?

The terrors, grotesques, nightmares and **BOGEY MEN** that haunt the unique world of **ROBERT BLOCH** Ten tales by the author of PSYCHO With a note on the author by Sam Moskowitz

Bloch: More of a love, I think. I started out as a movie man of the silent era. When I was in England recently, I joined the National Film Society so I could catch up on a whole lot of old films which I hadn't seen for forty years. I spent my youth in the Midwest in theaters. The first film that shocked me out of my wits was 1925's "Phantom of the Opera." Lon Chaney had a traumatic effect on me. All during the 1930s I carried on a private romance with Hollywood. Movies were an outlet during the Depression. An escape for millions of Americans. For a dime you saw a double feature. Dream stuff. Escapism par excellence. When I came to Hollywood in 1959, it was like coming into a world I had always dreamed of seeing. It was a great thrill to meet these people, to work with them. To get to know them. I still feel that way. Part of me is still extremely naive – eight years old, wandering around and gawking at the stars. Those short stories you cited. They were written before I came to Hollywood, so they are not tinged with cynicism.

Stanley: And now that you are embedded deeply in the Hollywood community, how do you feel about motion pictures in your genres of choice?

Bloch: I was impressed with "2000: A Space Odyssey," naturally. But I thought it was 90 per cent Kubrick and only ten per cent Arthur C. Clarke. I would like to see the original shooting script someday just to verify whether I am right. Anyway, I felt there were four styles of science-fiction. The ape sequence and the initial spaceship material were in the old Hugo Gernsback technological style.

"Everything scientifically accurate and beautifully done. This was written to satisfy the hardcore sci-fi enthusiasts. The second section, to me, was an American-International parody of the computer, with the Vincent Price overtones. The third dressing up, of course, was for the hippies, and this is the trip through the Stargate – the psychedelic experience. The fourth was metaphysical. The ambiguous finale. So, it was a film done in four divergent styles. Designed to hook just about every potential level of an audience. Commercially this is sound, but I don't know how aesthetic it is."

Stanley: Is it true that you wife Eleanor never reads any of your stories?

Bloch: (chuckling) It's true. She doesn't care to know that side of me. She hasn't even seen "Psycho" the movie. In fact, I never discuss with her what I've written. While she enjoys Christopher Lee and others as friends, she doesn't follow their work either.

Stanley: You sold your first story to *Weird Tales* when you were just 17 years old. Many of those early stories, "Feast in the Abbey" and others, were pretty well considered imitative of the H. P. Lovecraft tradition.

Bloch: I was very definitely a Lovecraft follower and a Lovecraft pupil. He read and criticized those first few stories I did. Naturally I admired his work and so, for the first four or five years, my work was reminiscent of Lovecraft.

Stanley: In his "Searchers of Tomorrow," Sam Moskowitz states: "In science fiction, Robert Bloch felt uninhibited, under no obligation to be anything but himself. In weird fiction the ghost of Lovecraft bound him in a literary straitjacket that would take him years to completely extricate himself from." Do you agree?

Bloch: I agree partially. I would say that regarding science fiction, Moskowitz is referring primarily to my Lefty Feep stories, which were broad farces utilizing the Damon Runyon idiom of the early 1940s with fantastic locales. This was the first time I totally cut loose from time-honored horror stories in search of a different style. But I had also done humor in *Weird Tales* that was just as uninhibited and I had already begun to develop what eventually became my natural style (for better or worse) in *Weird Tales*. Then there are the mystery and suspense novels. "The Scarf" was the big breakthrough for me because I hadn't done anything like it before. I began to inject more and more pseudo-psychology and psychiatry into my works. And nobody has yet discovered that although I've dealt with psychotherapy in 50 or more of my stories, I'm totally unsympathetic to the Freudian concept. Almost in every instance the psychiatrist's attitudes are exposed or downgraded. And from that, of course, comes the final phase of my career: writing films and TV shows. To specification, of course.

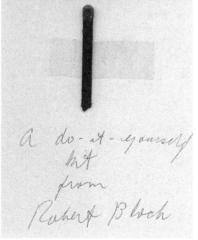

a do-it-yourself kit from Robert Bloch

Stanley: What percentage of your material in the last few years would you say is pure science fiction?

Bloch: Very very little . . . unfortunately.

Stanley: Has, then, the bulk of your stories been in the horror genre?

Bloch: Always has been. I think I'm only a science-fiction writer by sufferance. After the decline of *Weird Tales*, the sci-fi magazines would print fantasy and label it sci-fi. But I know nothing about science at all. I never have.

Stanley: The same is true of Ray Bradbury.

Bloch: Yes, but Ray is a stylist. That's his strength. And so he must write a Bradbury story. There is no such thing as a Bloch story. I've written in too many fields. Bradbury always consciously plays the role of a child in an adult world. The sense of wonder in a child. The innocence of a child. The insight of a child. This may seem a downgrading of his talent, but it is more an explanation of it. He gives to young people a voice. He is their spokesman. He looks at the Emperor and sees that he is naked. Behind the computer is some poor fellow who has to feed it data. Ray sees only the man, he doesn't see all the technological front.

Stanley: A moment ago you said there's no such thing as a Bloch story. Why?

Bloch: I've always suffered from a shortage of talent. I've very limited. Secondly, I have a very inadequate educational background. I must therefore improvise, invent and augment. Thirdly, I'm faced with the problem that faces every writer: the necessity to keep up with trends. It's not a matter of growing stale. It's a matter of growing out of touch. Actually, empathy is the only strength I have. The ability to put myself inside the characters and understand their motivations. This is a matter of acting in print. I impersonate the people as I write them.

Stanley: What kind of writing schedule do you follow? Do you have a set pattern or do you work only when you feel like it?

Bloch: If I only worked when I felt like it, nothing would ever get done. If I have something going, I sit down at the typewriter at 9 in the morning. I get up for lunch. I keep working until I get tired. When I get tired, I quit. I've learned I can force myself to go on, but the next day I'll have to re-do those pages.

Stanley: How long does it usually take you to write a novel, say, like "Firebug" or "Terror"?

Bloch: Usually five or six weeks. I revise as I go. I used to have eyestrain before contact

lenses, so I tried to save myself by having as few drafts as possible. I've trained myself to write first draft. I'm lazy, you see. And the sooner I get it over with, the more time I have to loaf and complain. If it's a screenplay I don't get a good night's sleep. I write in my sleep. A kind of half-dream, half-awake state. When I get up to my typewriter, suddenly it's all there again, working at me. I want to get that succulence off my back. That 40-pound monkey of manuscript! I want to get it done with. Not that there's any craftsmanship involved.

Stanley: How much reading do you have time for nowadays?

Bloch: In recent years I haven't been reading one-tenth of what I once read. Or should be reading. I don't have any time.

Stanley: Describe your feelings about the so-called "new wave" of sci-fi writers. Those who seem to be more concerned with style and ambiguity than anything else . . .

Bloch: I'm not sold on it, though right now it's the vogue. There's such a deficiency in content and concept. Because I'm so ancient I can reflect on all the great moments in science fiction. I know when sci-fi really began to work. I can cite you half a dozen breakthroughs in concepts that were quite staggering, within a contemporary frame of reference. Isaac Asimov developed the robot stories; A. E. Van Vogt developed things that were based on general semantics theories. Theodore Sturgeon did "More Than Human." Alfie Bester came along with "The Demolished Man." Phil Farmer with "The Lovers."

These were always matters of not only technique but ideas that were departures from what had previously been done. What I'm attempting to say is that in recent years I have seen no such breakthroughs in stories. I have seen stylists come along and adapt style tricks and nuances from so-called mainstream fiction or avante garde fiction. We've had nothing to shake up readers or broaden the field. Only stylists.

Robert Bloch, author of
PSYCHO II
(Mass Market Original, September 1982, $3.50)
Warner Books/75 Rockefeller Plaza/NYC 10019/212-484-8630

Bloch: And what are they writing about, really? The atomic holocaust; the end of the world; the reconstructed man; attitudes of aliens; totalitarian societies on other planets. They are still preaching such miraculous new concepts as bigotry, intolerance, brotherhood. This is all fine and dandy but it is not an explication of the best that could be done. There's going to have to be some very new directions taken. Not toward outer space, but toward inner space. The strange gray world inside our cranium. That is the microcosm and macrocosm we've just begun to touch upon. We must become obsessed with the miracle of man's thoughts, his consciousness. This to me is where it's all at. This is what should be happening, baby. When writers turn on themselves to examine the subliminal and think of ESP in terms of cerebral connotation, rather than its external effect, then we'll have something to wax lyrical about.

Stanley: In many of your stories you paint an ugly portrait of mankind. Why?

Bloch: I started writing 35 years ago and, until the late 1950s, was always very much a part of the mass and had ample opportunity to live with it first-hand. Some were very fine people, but others gave nothing to the world and had no desire to do so. They lived for sensations, for kicks, for today only. And in them I've never been able to completely excuse these weaknesses. Perhaps this is an unjust viewpoint. I've never been victimized, I've never been paranoid. My parents were good to me. I suppose I'm just idealistic. I must say this about my writing: You'll find almost always, in the final analysis, I'm writing a morality piece. My villains don't triumph. They don't really enjoy their frustrations or perversions.

The grotesqueries that I write about are merely illustrative. I never had believed that anyone who's read "Psycho" would want to go out and become another Norman Bates. There's no percentage in it. [Bloch points toward the bookcase behind him.] You can see my problem as a writer on those shelves there. I've written in too many fields and people interested in one don't know anything about the other. People who read mysteries don't read science fiction, and vice versa.

Stanley: To wrap this up . . . what advice would you offer to young writers today?

Bloch: That which most of us writers try to avoid: Sit down at the typewriter and write! I've found that 90 per cent of the would-be writers don't want to write. What they want is to be known as writers. They want the label. But the actual act is something they dread deep inside. To me, all writing is communication, self-expression. Or should be. My objection to atonality in music, to glorified Rorschach Tests which pass as pieces of Modern Art, and to so much written today is that it does not communicate. I still believe it is the prime duty of the writer or the artist to hold the attention of an audience. To entertain or to enlighten. I've always had this desire to communicate with people. Share a viewpoint, evoke a reaction. The switch, the punch, the gimmick, the mystification, the joke, sight or verbal – even the pun. The slant or twist on the obvious. Beyond that, there isn't much else to say.

On the "Creature Features" set in 1981 with Robert Bloch

AFTERWORDS

There was plenty more to say in years to come. I established a friendship with Bloch and years later, in the fall of 1982, he would be one of my guests on "Creature Features," discussing the publication of his novel "Psycho II." He revealed to me then that when Hitchcock had purchased the rights to the first "Psycho" book, his agent had not handled the contract properly and he had not been entitled to any monies from movie sequels. So, as a form of revenge, he had written "Psycho II."

At the end of our interview, I asked him a question: "In the past, you've said that in reality, you have the heart of a small child. Is that true?"

Bloch's answer: "Well, I just want to show you, my heart is in the right place."

He removed a covering placed over a bottle next to him. Inside was the heart of an animal my wife had purchased earlier that morning. Bloch added, "I was taking a chance bringing it here tonight, because if a cop had seen me, I would have been the victim of cardiac arrest."

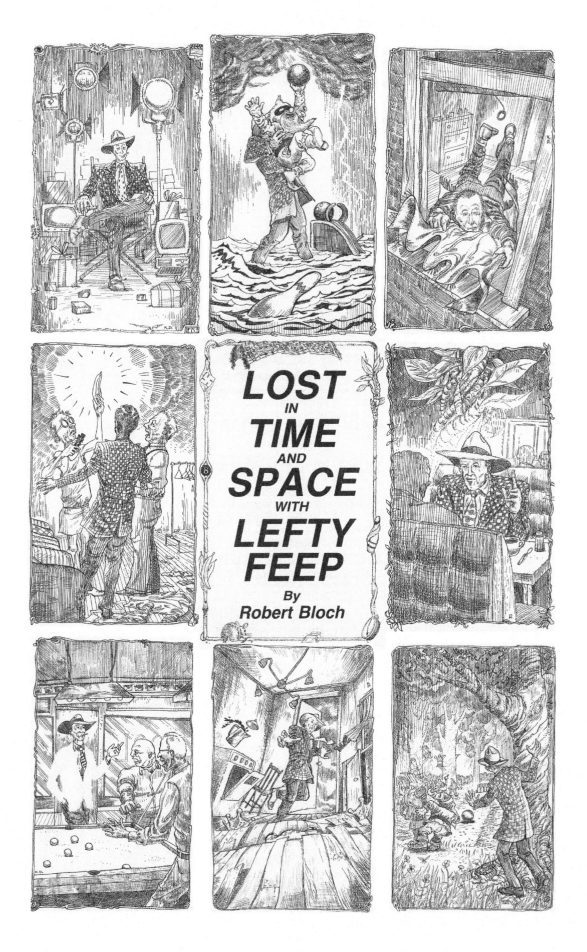

LOST
IN
TIME
AND
SPACE
WITH
LEFTY
FEEP

By
Robert Bloch

THE CAREER THAT DRIPPED WITH HORROR

A VISIT TO A PSYCHO KING TO PLACE BETS ON A RACETRACK TOUT

In January 1986 I paid Robert Bloch a surprise visit at his home on Sunset Crest Drive in the Hollywood Hills and proposed that we publish a collection of his short stories that had originally appeared in the pulp magazine *Fantastic Adventures* back in the 1940s.

They focused on a racetrack tout, Lefty Feep (see right), who was always entangling himself in bizarre situations. Always engaged in close encounters with crazy inventors and mad scientists ... and always displaced in time and space.

Thus, the title "Lost in Time and Space With Lefty Feep."

Although well-remembered by readers, these comedic tales had never been reprinted. Bloch worked closely with me for the next year. There would be eight short stories and one brand new misadventure.

(A saving grace: Back in the year 1979 I had discovered several collections of old pulp magazines were for sale at a bookstore in downtown San Francisco. By pure luck, one of the sets was made up of

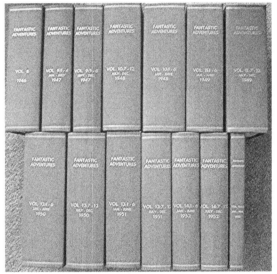

My collection of bound volumes of *Fantastic Adventures* magazines of the 1940s.

bound volumes of almost all the *Fantastic Adventure* magazines. And that included all the issues that contained Lefty Feep stories.)

For original illustrations to be included in "Lost in Time and Space With Lefty Feep" I turned to Kenn Davis, whom I had met in the mid-1960s in the San Francisco Chronicle's art department where he worked as a photo retoucher and artist. Our love of films had brought us together to produce the 1978 motion picture "Nightmare in Blood," which depicts a San Francisco horror convention whose guest star is a Hollywood actor who portrays a vampire named Malakai in his films.

It had been based on our love for horror and fantasy movies. (More about "Nightmare" on pages 219-223). Kenn and I had also co-written a novel, "The Dark Side," starring Carver Bascombe, a black private eye in San Francisco, published by Avon Books in 1976 as a paperback (the book was nominated for an Edgar Award but did not win). We also co-wrote "Bogart '48," a mystery thriller published by Dell in 1980 in which Humphrey Bogart and Peter Lorre join ranks to track down a killer in Hollywood 1948.

Kenn was in the process of writing several more Carver Bascombe novels but he still agreed to illustrate the Bloch book. Each piece of art visualized elements from one of the stories in the book. (Kenn had also done illustrations for my "Creature Features Movie Guide" series, creating images to start off each letter of the alphabet. (Many of them are included on pages 139-146.)

Artist Kenn Davis

I contacted several sci-fi and fantasy writers and sent them copies of the stories. Returning short comments I could use in the front of the book were Ray Bradbury, Fritz Leiber, Richard Matheson, Richard Lupoff, William F. Nolan, Richard Christian Matheson and Harlan Ellison. (Good thing I had interviewed Bradbury, Leiber, Lupoff and Ellison on my "Creature Features" TV show and knew which planets they lived on, not to mention their phone numbers.)

Kenn Davis was a good friend of Chelsea Quinn Yarbro, at that time famous for her series of historical horror novels spotlighting Count Saint-Germain, and she agreed to write an introduction about Bloch for my book.

In both hardcover and trade paperback the book arrived in mid-1987. It had been a challenging but pleasing experience. I especially enjoyed driving to Bob's home in the Hollywood hills with all the hardcovers in my trunk and spending a few hours at his side as he signed each one. "You're never going to make any money from all of this," he remarked that afternoon, slapping his signature onto another book. That didn't matter. What mattered was my ego. And the anticipation of doing two more editions in what I now called "The Lefty Feep Collection."

Chelsea Quinn Yarbro

I got really busy putting out the third edition in my movie guide series and working with John Mitchum (the brother of Robert Mitchum, remember?) for almost three years to finish off "Them Ornery Mitchum Boys." It was around the time I had left the Chronicle and begun a new career teaching entertainment classes to the seniors of America that news came of Bob's death. He had passed away in September 1994 at the age of 77. (Just one year earlier he had written what he called his "unauthorized autobiography," "Once Around the Bloch.")

And Lefty Feep? All those other stories we'd planned to reprint remain unreprinted.

Anybody out there want to be a publisher?

The following piece on a major hit in "Star Trek" movie history first appeared in the Sunday Datebook of the San Francisco Chronicle on Dec. 1, 1991. For some inexplicable reason I failed to include it with the rest of my "Star Trek" interviews in my 2007 autobiography, "I Was a TV Horror Host" (which unfortunately is now out of print). My apologies – but at least I'm finally catching up to myself. Thanks for waiting all these years.

HE WENT WHERE NO MAN HAD GONE BEFORE IN THE WORLD OF TV

...AND MADE HISTORY THAT LIVES ON TODAY

Gene Roddenberry
Executive Producer
STAR TREK

"It speaks to basic human needs that there is a tomorrow. It isn't all going to be over with a big flash and bomb. The human race is improving. We have things to be proud of. No, ancient astronauts didn't build the pyramids. Human beings built them because they're clever and they work hard. 'Star Trek' is about those things." – **Gene Roddenberry**

Where "Star Trek" Has Never Gone Before Means the Series Regulars Must Retire ... Maybe!

THE CREATOR of "Star Trek" was dying of heart failure when he uttered those optimistic words above, in the fall of 1991, in what was to be his final interview for a commemorative TV special. Only weeks later, at the age of 70, the world-popular TV and film producer succumbed to a final attack, a blood clot to his heart. So it happened that on October 24, 1991, the entertainment world lost one of its finest creators as he beamed up to ... only God knows which solar system within the Universe.

No combination of modern medicine and science could have saved Roddenberry, but in his own fanciful, advanced world of "Star Trek," there would have been a different outcome. Dr. McCoy's scanning device would have made an immediate diagnosis and injected him seconds later with a life-saving serum. And his soul would have become eternal.

That was the kind of idealization of life Roddenberry had always maintained and was the inspiration behind his sci-fi classic. He had created "Star Trek" in the mid-1960s, during the escalation of the Vietnam War, as a "positive view of our future."

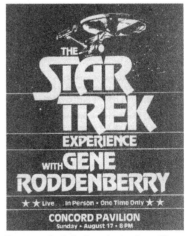

I was scheduled to interview Gene Roddenberry at a show in the early 1980s but Roddenberry had to cancel at the last minute. I thank God that I had met and interviewed Gene in 1966 three months before "Star Trek" premiered on NBC-TV.

It was a depiction of "mankind's ability to overcome its earthly problems to conquer diseases as well as space and the territories beyond."

Although Roddenberry the dreamer has taken that ultimate voyage to the most unexplored country of all, he leaves a legacy for Trekkers worldwide. It is a legacy that seems never to die. Syndicated TV's "Star Trek – The Next Generation" has begun its fifth season, drawing top ratings as always. And now comes this newest star burst of cinematic excitement, "Star Trek VI: The Undiscovered Country," the sixth entry in the motion picture series.

As always with a new "Star Trek" movie, there's been much anticipation among Trekkers for another high-tech, action-strewn science-fiction epic with the familiar crew of the Starship Enterprise . . . and that anticipation has been extra-keen because early publicity about the

picture described it as "the final adventure of the Starship Enterprise." Indeed, it does appear in 1991 A.D. that the old crew is retiring to make room for replacements. (Would that by any chance be "The Next Generation" gang, such as Patrick Stewart as Captain Jean-Luc Picard, Jonathan Frakes as Commander William Riker and other prominent members of the cast?)

Chatting with "Undiscovered Country" director Nicholas Meyer in Hollywood shortly before the film's release.

The new "Star Trek" is darker than the earlier films. The basic premise: Just when Captain Kirk (William Shatner) and Dr. McCoy (DeForest Kelley) are scheduled to retire, they are among those assigned to escort the Klingon High Chancellor into peace talks only to see the elder statesman assassinated instead. They are captured and face execution. It's going to be up to the rest of the USS Enterprise crew to help them escape and to prevent a conspiracy to destroy all hopes for peace.

Its very heavily textured plot was first conceived by Leonard Nimoy himself and director-to-be Nicholas Meyer. Then it became a screenplay by Meyer and Denny Martin Flinn. Ultimately it would feature less of the playful bantering between cast regulars and some of the buffoonery that earmarked the previous entry, "Star Trek V: The Final Frontier" (1989). There are Shakespearean touches in its dialogue and a sense of tragic doom about its characters that even reaches out and touches Captain Kirk, who is forced to look within himself and face his own deep hatred for Klingons.

This time out the major catalysts – ramrod co-writer/director Meyer and executive producer Leonard Nimoy – have done much to preserve "the franchise" (a phrase that director Meyer uses to describe the continuing existence of the series).

Nicholas Meyer

THE CAREER THAT DRIPPED WITH HORROR

Meyer was responsible for writing-directing "Star Trek II: The Wrath of Khan" – an act that in 1982 got the series back on a popular footing with those who had hated the first film so much. And Meyer, although he had refused to work on the third film in the series ("Star Trek III: The Search for Spock") because he thought bringing Spock back to life was a "cop-out," had been instrumental in shaping up the excellent script for "Star Trek IV: The Voyage Home."

As popular as the films have been since 1979, when "Star Trek – The Motion Picture" got the series moving again after a decade of inactivity (the original TV series left NBC in 1969), "Star Trek VI: The Undiscovered Country" faces a basic problem that was expressed recently by Meyer in his modest office at Paramount Studios. Dressed casually in blue jeans, blue shirt and Nike running shoes, bearded Meyer was in his customary no-nonsense mood.

Meyer all but shouted at me, as our lengthy exchange began, that "The Final Frontier" was about "searching for God in the depths of the Universe and it was an unresolved theme." His face

Christopher Plummer portrays the duplicitous Klingon General Chang in "The Undiscovered Country"

suddenly became grim. "Why? Because what do you do if you find God? So you don't find him and that lets the audience down, which suspected it was being tricked all along.

"Let's face it," the director continued. "Not all of the 'Star Trek' movies have been great. And when you follow a lesser entry, you have a problem of building the faith of the fandom audience again." The new adventure (stardate 8679.14) is, according to Meyer, "about the future and how we face that future, but it also relates to things that have been happening recently in our world." In Meyer's own words, "Futuristic perestroika." (The term "perestroika" was a political movement within Russia during the 1980s brought on by Soviet master Mikhail Gorbachev.)

The Klingon Empire, after an energy explosion reminiscent of the Chernobyl disaster, is on the verge of collapse, its economy drained by military over-indulgence. (Hey Russia, does that sound familiar?) A Klingon figurehead (a parallel to Soviet President Gorbachev?) wants to forge a new alliance with the Federation, a long-avowed enemy, and a wary Starfleet sends the USS Enterprise to spearhead peace negotiations.

David Warner plays Gorkon, the benevolent alien ruler. Other guest stars include Christopher Plummer as Chang, a fierce Klingon warrior, Kurtwood Smith as the Federation commander in chief, and John Schuck as the Klingon he first portrayed in "Star Trek IV." Michael Dorn, who portrays Worf in the current "Next Generation" series, appears as Lieutenant Worf's great-grandfather, a trial defense attorney.

These historic photos of me with Leonard Nimoy on my "Creature Features" set were taken in 1980 when Nimoy was in San Francisco doing the one-man play "Theo," about the brother of painter Vincent Van Gogh. It was one of the most memorable moments during my six years as a TV horror host.

All the regular crew members are back. Top row: George Takei, Nichelle Nichols James Doohan. Bottom Row: Walter Koenig, DeForest Kelley, William Shatner, Leonard Nimoy.

In setting the film up as a "finale," the Enterprise is three months from being decommissioned and its crew on the verge of retirement. Meanwhile, former helmsman Sulu (Takei) has taken his own command aboard the Starship Excelsior.

"After the last film," said Meyer, "[producer] Harve Bennett decided the cast was costing too much. He thought the answer to keeping the budget down was to make a prequel – that is, a film about Captain Kirk, Mr. Spock and Dr. McCoy in their younger cadet days. A gimmick that would have required the casting of inexpensive unknowns. But the idea never got off the ground, and Bennett resigned from the film series."

Enter Nimoy, who contacted Meyer from Cape Cod, where he was vacationing in June 1990. "We walked along the beach together," Meyer recalled, "while Leonard told me his idea about linking a 'Star Trek' adventure to current events. We kept walking up and down that stretch of beach, exchanging ideas. It was all very solid in our minds."

Meyer returned to London (where he has lived since 1988) and developed the mixture of ideas into a story line. Then Meyer turned to his assistant, Denny Martin Flinn, for a first draft. "Then I took that and worked it over to finish it off. Leonard and I kept probing to make it better. He's relentless, close to a perfectionist. And his dissatisfaction with the early versions is responsible for this adventure getting to a better place."

The captain during a casual moment.

THE CAREER THAT DRIPPED WITH HORROR

Meyer, a onetime movie publicist for Paramount who went on to write the best-selling "The Seven Percent Solution" (a spinoff on the Sherlock Holmes character), broke into a more creative part of Hollywood by directing 1979's "Time After Time," featuring H.G. Wells in a time machine.

He directed "Star Trek VI" at Paramount on sets that had been recycled from the current TV series. (Estimated cost is said to be around $27 million, including the special effects carried out by George Lucas' Industrial Light and Magic shop in San Rafael.) "I'd like to think that I've gotten better as a director since 'Star Trek II.' I do know I'm more precise than I used to be. I've learned that the more time you spend setting up the shots, the more you achieve in terms of what you envision yourself achieving."

Meyer believes it's the actors who have kept the series so popular, despite its ups and downs at the box office, and despite a mixture of critical opinions. "They've created characters that have become American icons. Icons that have seduced us. We feel we know them so well. We feel comfortable with them. And it's a challenge as writer and director to discover nuances about Kirk and Spock and Scotty and the rest of them. Creating new bits of business is like adding pieces onto the legend."

AFTERWORDS

Wow! "Star Trek VI: The Undiscovered Country" made around $75 million in American box office and received excellent reviews. It came to be considered one of the best entries in the series and made up for the weaknesses of the previous entry. Patrick Stewart would continue in "The Next Generation" series through 1994, and make four feature films as Captain Picard. Fifty years on, "Star Trek" continues to thrive on TV with "Star Trek: Discovery," "Star Trek: Picard," "Star Trek: Lower Decks" and "Strange New Worlds."

Gene Roddenberry, wherever he is, has to be smiling.

Left: Leonard Nimoy signed this photo for me in 1980 when guesting on "Creature Features."
Right: This is the opening for the special I did in June 1982 with interviews I had recorded at the 3-day world premiere of "Star Trek II: The Wrath of Khan" with William Shatner, Leonard Nimoy, Ricardo Montalban, DeForest Kelley, James Doohan, and producer Harve Bennett.

Top row: William Shatner as Captain James T. Kirk, Jimmy Doohan as Lieutenant Commander Montgomery Scott, aka "Scotty," and DeForest Kelley as Dr. Leonard "Bones" McCoy; Middle Row: Ricardo Montalban as the villianous Khan Noonien Singh, Laura Banks as one of Khan's space groupies, and Harve Bennett, executive producer of "The Wrath of Khan." Bottom Row: Nichelle Nichols as communications officer Lieutenant Nyota Uhura, "Khan" co-producer Robert Sallin, and Walter Koenig as Ensign Pavel Chekov.

THE CAREER THAT DRIPPED WITH HORROR

Broadcast Legends is a Bay Area group devoted to personalities who have been on local radio and TV stations. I was able to become a member because of my "Creature Features" years. It continues to hold several special luncheon programs a year featuring retirees or those still active in media, with each show offering a theme, such as old-time radio, news broadcasting, disc jockeys or the histories of certain local celebs. In 2003 Bob Wilkins and I were invited to be guest stars, with an afternoon devoted to our careers. I decided to write an original poem devoted to Bob, tongue-in-cheek perhaps, but sincere. And after a grand lunch, I got up before the group and let fly. I've been soaring ever since.

TO BOB WILKINS, AN ODE, WHICH I HOPE ISN'T TOO BIG A LOAD BUT WHAT THE HELL, LET'S HIT THE ROAD

To my loyal fans hail and hearty,
welcome to a most unusual party.
To my loyal fans hearty and hail,
listen now to a most unusual TV tale.

It's about one of our very own
who created an exclusive Bay Area
"Twilight Zone."

I think it would even please Dr. Demento
for it begins in a place known as Sacramento.
And so to begin my horrific foray,
I now take you to a station known as KCRA.

Yes, that's Channel 3,
an NBC affiliate about to go on a spree
with tingling, scary imagery.
Setting a horror trend to be
watched by you and me,
ghastly images on Saturday night TV.

Let's get a fix on this narrative mix—
time is September '66.
Inside Channel 3 works a devoted advertising man
about to step out with a life-changing plan.
Taking care of sponsors is his job . . .
you know him as Mr. Wilkins . . . Bob.

He'd tell you, "I'm just a working slob,
serving up a lot of corn on the TV cob."
But soon he had a job very macabre,
this fella who called himself Wilkins, Bob.

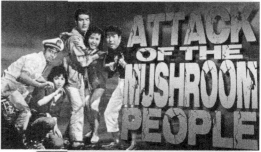

One Saturday night he climbs onto a
media-high steeple.
When he introduces Japan's
"Attack of the Mushroom People."

He makes wisecracks and puts the movie down,
even though his advertisers will surely frown.
But what the hell, the flick's a clinker.
No, he decides, it's an utter stinker.
It was made, he thinks, by cinematic fools
who turn Asian tourists into decaying toadstools.

"Turn to another channel," he says with pride,
reading other station choices from a TV Guide.
The sponsors call the next day, it's time to sob,
a sponsor wants to kill Bob Wilkins' job.
He swears, "I'm going to make you squeal, son."
And then he hears about the ratings
—you know, the Nielsen.

Suddenly the irate sponsor thinks Bob is sweet.
"Mr. Wilkins, you can't be beat.
Can you do it again and draw viewers back?"
"Sure," says Bob, "because I'm no hack.
I'll make you and the station a lotta jack."

The sponsor: "Hey kid, you've got the knack.
I'll ask the station not to give you the sack."
"I enjoy this," says Bob, "so I'll give it another
whack."

And so did Bob Wilkins, TV host extraordinary,
continue that day without having a coronary.

And thus was the "Creature Features" formula born
putting down bad horror movies
Wilkins had to an oath sworn.
No monster's garb, no hideous make-up,
no ghastly cries.
He wore business suits, plain-toed shoes
and colorful striped ties.

The show's opening, it was never to be dull
for Bob shed light on things with a candle
stuck atop a human skull.

His movies had many a killing.
And some were spine-chilling.
And others generally thrilling.
Some even blood-spilling.
And Bob was the star, he got top billing.

This kid from Hammond, Indiana, he did it with grace,
always with a wry grin upon that
deceptively young face.
He had a sense of humor decidedly low-key
while in his fingers he clutched a
House of Windsor stog-ie.

To his psychiatrist he once said,
and this is something I've only read,
"I never puffed on a single cigar,
I never scattered ashes,
I held that thing to keep from having
terrible nervous flashes."

Yeah, nervous he was and not ashamed to declare:
"I hid my shaking from fans by rocking in a
yellow wooden chair."

He needed a motto and decided that he
couldn't go wrong
with "Watch Horror Films—Keep America Strong."
He put this saying up on his wall on a sign.
And smiled his smile of the utter benign.

Some of the titles to come
sounded like terrible fodder,
Yet even a hit was that awful
"Jesse James Meets Frankenstein's Daughter."

THE CAREER THAT DRIPPED WITH HORROR

For the insatiable fans
there were entities of evil galore,
Godzilla, Rodan,
Monster From the Ocean Floor.

Some of it evoked many a shriek,
manic and panic and diabolique.
Killers all, mean and psychotic.
Enough to make your psychic go neurotic.

Nielsen kept smiling in the ratings race
even when Bob showed
"Killers From Space."

Now at Channel 3 was a man
who was tall and lean.
There wasn't a bone in his body
you would ever call mean.
This sharp-thinking exec,
he dressed like a college dean.
And everyone saluted this man,
this man called Tom Breen (see right).

An ex-Marine from the Pacific war,
he had easy-going style.
And he encouraged Mr. Wilkins,
often with a warm smile.
Then one day Breen was forced to tell
his good friend Bob "hail and farewell."
Said Breen: "Keep up your horrific style
and do take care.
I'm off to a place in Oakland
called Jack London Square."

"Holy Toledo," cried Bob, "this can't be true!
You're forsaking this job here
for that station, KTVU?"
Replied Tom: "A new brew, a new crew.
I'm off to that place called Channel 2."

KTVU, Channel 2
was in store for a grue.
And more than one or two
helpings of vulture's stew.
Horror movie derring-do,
murder, mayhem, even voodoo.
Sci-fi and fantasy, the magical glue.
Yes, a new destiny for KTVU.

THE CAREER THAT DRIPPED WITH HORROR

Tom Breen landed high up in management's Ivory Tower,
and as an exec began to blossom and flower.
And he had this idea: "I'll hire Bob and bring him to the Bay
and we'll do 'Creature Features' in a more intellectual way."

"No more late-night crap for insomniacs.
We'll do horror movie stuff
for prime-time maniacs.
If we put the show in a 9 p.m. setting,
a larger audience I think we'll be getting.
Counter-programming, that's my show-biz reach.
And I'll start out with that turkey,
'Horror of Party Beach.'"

And so Tom stole Wilkins
from Sacramento kooks
and settled him down with movies
about zombies and spooks.

Every Saturday night at nine,
oh, the results were just fine.
Followed soon by "Frankenstein."

This Wilkins, he was no dummy
as he offered up Karloff's historic Mummy.
A hideous thing in bandages enwrapped
that caused your brain to be utterly snapped.

There was Wolfman and Black Cat,
and a creature called Willard—what a rat.
It was all so wonderful spectula
when Bob played "Billy the Kid vs. Dracula."

And he really hit a rating one June
when he played "Creature From the Black Lagoon."

This new-mangled show, part of our culture.
But I ask you: the Black Scorpion, Tarantula
and the Vulture?
Many a devoted fan was sent to bed,
head filled with images from
"Night of the Living Dead."

Among the fans, spearheading the nucleus
was a guy from Marin, name of George Lucas.
He came running to Bob, like a sly fox
to tell him: "'Creature Features'" has knocked off my socks.

You inspired me, Bob, and helped to open new doors
so I could go on to make my first 'Star Wars.'"

In 1974 I underwent a surprise blow
when Mr. Wilkins invited me to be on his show.
I had a new book, "Movie Monster Game,"
and Bob formed a panel
that brought him great fame.

It was a book I'd co-written with Malcolm Whyte,
a publisher I considered to be extremely bright.
Troubadour Press had given him literary might.

Helping out in the studio
to avoid knowledge flaw
was a devoted movie-lover
named Bob Shaw (see right).
Tipping off Wilkins with
behind-the-scene facts,
allowing through his lips
occasional wisecracks.

He was a giant help to Bob,
who knew little about cinema stuff.
"I'm no expert," Bob admitted,
"just a sparkling diamond-in-the-rough."

Overlooking all this business,
an executive who often saved the day,
was an Iwo Jima Marine
by the name of Jacobs, Ray (see right).

He did on-air editorials in those days,
and oversaw Bob's show.
He wanted to be certain it had a spectral glow.

And the guests and the interviews,
they were a hellish-like chorus,
Especially the night Bob questioned
Karloff, Boris.
And fans turned out to watch with Britannica glee,
Bob's interview with England's vampire star,
Christopher Lee.

There was always a big name
he would somehow muster.
One night he had Flash Gordon—
remember Crabbe, Buster?
The Force was with him one night
with David Prowse,
Who came to re-enact Darth Vader,
villainous louse.

THE CAREER THAT DRIPPED WITH HORROR

Sometimes there was a beautiful bod.
How about that sexy gal Adams, Maud (top).
The stars were so darn many . . .
Anthony Daniels, Leonard Nimoy,
even Jack Benny (second from top)

It was a special effect as he was seen browsin'
with stop-motion animator Ray Harryhausen.

And if you did a careful check,
you'd know that on the set of "MacArthur"
he saluted one-and-only Gregory Peck.

In 1977 Bob made a brand-new pick
when he decided to play Captain Cosmic.
Standing beside him was a robot, 2T2.
And to the late afternoon show the fans really flew.

Wife Sally, she didn't care for his costume design,
and one time at a show to us she did whine,
"I'll never be seen at his side on any day,
should he decide to go public dressed that way."

"And now comes the day,"
to me the TV horror host did say,
"When I want to do the thing I love most:
Return to the advertising world!" That was his boast.

After the Channel 2 reign was finished and over,
Bob went back to his advertising agency,
his four-leaf clover.

The bills had to be paid, and this he appeases
by landing a giant national account,
Chuck E Cheese's.

He promoted these pizza parlors all over the land.
The income from pepperoni and anchovies
was oh so grand.

And then in the '90s Bob went to Reno,
to a place called Sparks.
There he obeyed John Ascuaga's
commands and barks.

And do you know the reason he really dug it?
He was advertising boss
at the swingin' casino, Nugget.

Now he's retired and living in the Big Little City.
But Bob, I gotta tell ya, it's time to end this ghastly ditty.

Congratulations, Bob, for a job well done,
during which time you had a lotta fun.
Those glorious days when you were Channel 2's greatest gun.

So everyone put their hands together and clap
for this man who really put Channel 2 on the map.
It's time to acknowledge Wilkins' spectacular show.
Just put your lips together and blow . . .

But no matter your poise
or your choice of noise,
you cannot deny it,
you cannot defy it . . .

Creature Features lives on,
a monster most infernal,
and Bob Wilkins is the guy
who made it eternal.
About one thing,
he was never wrong.

That was how he had made
America so strong.
On that note, folks,
I'll just say "So long."

Bob is interviewing special effects artist Ray Harryhausen and producer Charles H. Schneer in the lobby of a San Francisco screening room after a critics' showing of "Sinbad and the Eye of the Tiger" in 1977. That's me seated in the background with my son Russ, who snored so loud he woke Bob up.

THE CAREER THAT DRIPPED WITH HORROR

THE
DARK
SIDE
OF
BLACK
. . .

. . . AND HOW
SHE AND HER
SON HUNTER
FACED AN
ATTACK BY
MARTIANS

A Homely Moment with a Beautiful Actress Who
Faces a Martian Invasion with Her Son

KAREN BLACK is singing Diana Ross' "Touch Me in the Morning" in the kitchen, toasting wholewheat bread and slicing grapefruits in half. Out of the room scampers her ten-year-old son Hunter, carrying a white cat whose long tail lashes the air. Hunter, who played the young boy named Hunter in "Paris, Texas," a film written by his father I. M. Kit Carson (now divorced from Black), scratches the cat's head and disappears into a hallway.

The setting is Black's home only a couple of blocks south of Griffin Park in Hollywood. It's a large house but not opulent by movieland standards. A couple of beat-up cars are parked in the driveway. This is a home that looks lived in, no pretensions in sight.

Black returns to the living room, still singing lightly under her breath as she sets a tray of food down and plunks herself onto a sofa. Before she has a chance to pour orange spice tea, Hunter's wailing voice cuts through the house, holding on a high note. The ululation is a single word: "Mmmmmo-o-o-mmmmmm." Black refers to it as a "war cry" and springs up, hurrying into the next room to see what Hunter wants.

I snapped these photos of Karen Black when I dropped into her Hollywood home in the summer of 1986
to interview her regarding "Invaders From Mars," in which she stars with her son Hunter Carson.

She returns in a minute and stands limned against the hallway opening, a figure in gray pedal-pushers and a pale-yellow sweatshirt with a drawing of the Chateau Marmont of Hollywood emblazoned on the front. She plunks back on the couch, pours the tea, and then scrunches her feet beneath her. Her left wrist, adorned with three red-and-white bracelets, kerplunks on her thigh. She's wearing no make-up yet her famous eyes stand out, locking on her visitor with penetrating curiosity. Black's blond hair is coarse and frizzy, her attitude ultra-casual. Just an average day for Hollywood actress Karen Black.

Hers has been a career of award-winning roles scattered among some 30 movies. It started with the box-office smash "Easy Rider" in 1969, which featured Jack Nicholson. She appeared with Nicholson again the next year in "Five Easy Pieces," which gave her an Academy Award nomination and a Golden Globe. She was to receive another Golden Globe for "The Great Gatsby" (1974).

Karen did go into her kitchen to get tea and grapefruit while I was visiting her but she didn't look like this at all when she came back.

Many of these parts have been kooky and eccentric, qualities carried over from her personal life, earning her a reputation as being colorful, iconoclastic and unpredictable. Her visits to the altar are good examples: she married her first husband, actor Skip Burton, in a white bedsheet, and wed Hunter's father in a 6 a.m. outdoor ceremony.

I have dropped into Black's home so she can tell me about her latest film, "Invaders From Mars," a $10 million production from Cannon in which she plays the school nurse who helps a young boy convince the military and people in his rural town that the Martians are coming, turning everyone into mind-controlled zombies. "Invaders" is a potentially major event in science-fiction because it's a remake of a 1953 cult classic directed and designed by William Cameron Menzies, the Hollywood cameraman famous for "Gone With the Wind."

This new version was directed by Tobe Hooper, that mild-mannered sentimentalist who gave us "The Texas Chainsaw Massacre" and "Poltergeist." The film retains the basic plot: David MacLean, son of a rocket scientist, is awakened from sleep by a flying saucer as it burrows into a sand pit behind a hill near his home. Nobody believes the boy's wild story. Later the youth sees people being sucked into the sand pit by unseen forces and realizes that the citizens in his town (including his father) have implants in their necks, making them subservient to the alien invaders. His only help is a child psychologist.

While the 1953 film had only mediocre special effects, in keeping with most low-budget films of its time, this new version has state-of-the-art effects by John Dykstra, with Martian creatures designed by Stan Winston.

The 1953 poster for the original "Invaders From Mars."

THE CAREER THAT DRIPPED WITH HORROR

Since Black's son Hunter plays the film's young hero–the character originally played by Jimmy Hunt, with whom millions of young viewers have identified for the past 33 years–would Hunter care to discuss his role with me? Black shakes her head. "He's devoting himself to cartoons this afternoon," she tells me, thereby closing the subject.

I show Karen a current issue of *Cinefantastique* magazine, which contains color photos of Hunter on the set with director Hooper. She hasn't seen the article or pictures before and she flips through the pages curiously. "Funny," she

Tobe Hooper, director of "Invaders From Mars," will no doubt be remembered for directing "The Texas Chainsaw Massacre" (1974) and its 1986 sequel. Hooper passed in 2017 at the age of 74.

says, somewhat cryptically, "how when you see things in a magazine it makes everything seem real . . . I see my son here with Tobe. It's actual, it's real."

One of the reasons "Invaders from Mars" has remained a favorite of so many generations is its air of paranoia as experienced by a youth. Powers of authority (police and military) are part of the conspiracy, symbolizing the eternal gap between youth and adults. David is a voice crying out into the night and, as experienced by so many young time throughout time, it is a voice that goes unheard.

"I would agree with that interpretation," says Black in her soft, wispy voice, which sometimes falls away to inaudibility, "but there's more. Sometimes people remember things that they identified with but which they resisted as children. To have parents become something that will harm you in the worst possible way, worse than death even, in a sense you're killing that child."

The Norwegian-born actress stirs on the sofa, lowering her legs back to the floor. "I want a grapefruit. I need a grapefruit," she says. "I'm going to get a grapefruit." She wanders away to the kitchen, where she resumes singing "Touch Me in the Morning." Pretty quickly she is back. Between bites of the grapefruit: "Tobe [Hooper] called one day and said he wanted my son to play the lead role in 'Invaders.' Tobe has been a friend of the family for a long time. Meanwhile, I was having trouble making a deal for another picture with Cannon's producer. My lawyer told me 'Forget the other film. Focus on this. You play the nurse opposite Hunter.' That sounded like a great idea. Mother and son together. And so I accepted the offer."

Karen Black's son Hunter Carson facing the Martians in Tobe Hooper's "Invaders From Mars."

Knowing Hooper also convinced her to let Hunter do the film. "I didn't want my son to have unhappy experiences making movies . . . When you get a clunker it's a terrible ordeal because the ethics are so bad. Terrible. Uggghhh . . . Clunkers have destructive people at work, destroying the artistic efforts of others."

Black did not go back to look at the original "Invaders From Mars." "I'd be afraid of imitation," she says. "I'd rather have it all fresh. Sometimes I think it's the wrong idea to read the book a movie is based on. I'm not always sure about that; it's something I wrestle with."

Karen thinks the movie is going to be "real scary. I've done some spooky things. 'Burnt Offerings' and 'Trilogy of Terror.' I like science-fiction but I don't like horror." And why not? "I don't like witches or vampires. As a matter of fact, I don't like war pictures or Westerns. I like character movies with real people and places." She doesn't know why sci-fi appeals to her. "I don't think people can tell why they like something. Like, I like the color red . . . ask me to explain and I'd have to make something up."

Interestingly, Karen is not clear where "Invaders" was filmed. "I don't know the name of the place. It's a huge, huge, huge thing by the ocean. It's the biggest soundstage ever in movies. Once upon a time it was a hangar for airplanes [Howard Hughes' Spruce Goose], and it's just endless. The spaceship is like the inside of someone's body: there are veins along the wall which Tobe wanted to get to beat and glow and really, they could have done it for another $50,000, but they didn't. Parts look like eyeballs, vessel-like, organic, rib-shaped.

"Then there's these expensive working things I call droids . . . just brilliant, wonderful. One man inside each with a TV camera so he can see where he's going. Red skin, wrinkly in a blobby shape, tiny little eyes. And these droids have a horrible needle, which Hunter says zombied everyone out."

Karen Black in "Five Easy Pieces" as Rayette Dipesto, a diner waitress who becomes involved with a troubled oil well worker played by Jack Nicholson.

Karen unstretches her lean body and stands up to pour more tea. But she suddenly discovers the tea is all gone and the grapefruit halves have been squeezed wrinkly, and the afternoon will soon be twilight. You get the feeling she wants to go make dinner for Hunter.

On my way to the front door she tells me, "I think I'm one of the luckiest persons in the world. I have a nice life. Nice house, wonderful son. I'm going to be doing another movie, playing a Sheena-type aboard an airliner that is going to be held up. I have my own script, 'Deep Purple,' a Robert Redford project. Then I'm doing 'Indian Summer' with Hoyt Axton and I have another movie in September I can't talk about now, except to say . . ." – Karen Black pauses for effect as she opens the door – "I can tell you it's a wowzer, a bowzer-wowzer."

AFTERWORDS

Karen Black continued to work steadily in feature films and TV roles. Karen married one more time and had a daughter with producer-film editor Stephen Eckelberry. Regrettably she was diagnosed with ampullary cancer in November 2010 and underwent surgery that left her cancer-free. But the cancer resurged and she died in 2012. "Invaders from Mars" did okay at the box office, grossing nearly $5 million. It encouraged son Hunter to pursue a Hollywood career and he enjoyed limited success as actor, producer and writer.

YOU WERE introduced to my co-author/co-producer Kenn Davis in the Robert Bloch piece on how I published Bloch's short story collection, "Lost in Time and Space With Lefty Feep."

In 1981 when I was preparing to self-publish the first edition of "The Creature Features Movie Guide" I asked Kenn if he would create an image to introduce each letter of the alphabet. A, for example, could depict "Alien" or an alligator, since there have been films about gators. E, for example, could refer to the movie "E.T." or to a creature like an elf. Kenn agreed and drew me a sample for the letter "C" (see below) and went on to draw the A-to-Z sketches and covers for the first, third and fourth editions.

Kenn continued to write novels in the Carver Bascombe private eye paperback series and continued to create surrealistic paintings, a specialty that had attracted him for most of his life. Sad to report that in January 2010 Kenn passed away at the age of 77 in an apartment on the outskirts of Sacramento, CA.

KENN DAVIS: THE KING OF SKETCH ARTISTRY

I want to thank Kenn one more time for contributing so many wonderful sci-fi and horror images based on motion picture history.

Above left: That's me and Kenn editing "Nightmare in Blood" in the early stages of post-production.

Above right: Scouting locations in downtown San Francisco prior to the production of "Nightmare in Blood."

IT'S A TO Z TIME!
TURN THE PAGE AND ROLL YOUR EYEBALLS!

THE A-TO-Z FANTASYTHON

THE CAREER THAT DRIPPED WITH HORROR

THE CAREER THAT DRIPPED WITH HORROR

KENN'S VISION OF HORROR STARS

VINCENT PRICE   CHRISTOPHER LEE   LIONEL ATWILL   BORIS KARLOFF   BELA LUGOSI

THE CAREER THAT DRIPPED WITH HORROR

THE CAREER THAT DRIPPED WITH HORROR

ALTHOUGH this chapter on some of the TV products made by one of Hollywood's most successful producers of fantasy and science-fiction will end with a negative, I positively want to describe Irwin Allen (above) with the historic truth: He stood tall for 30-odd years as a devoted maker of popular and well-remembered TV series. In my case that included "Voyage to the Bottom of the Sea," "Lost in Space" and "Time Tunnel." Each was colorful fantasy with emphasis on alien life forms and spectacular special effects. There was never anything boring about Allen's choices. He also made fortunes with such box-office hits as "The Poseidon Adventure" ($84 million worldwide) and "The Towering Inferno" ($116 million worldwide). Hold that attitude in your mind as you now enter the production kingdom of the one and only, Irwin Allen. Be patient: Allen himself will sit in front of me behind his massive desk during a 1967 interview which will conclude this segment.

STAND BY ON DECK! ALL HANDS!
THE CAPTAIN IS APPROACHING!
TEN-SHUT!

THE FLY has joined a private naval force, at least that's the buzz in Hollywood. To the TV viewer this means David Hedison, who terrorized movie-goers a few years back (1958 to be precise) as a mad scientist emerging from a disintegrating machine as half-man, half-insect, has graduated ("dived" would be better) to deeper pursuits as Commander Lee B. Crane, skipper of the submarine Seaview. This futuristic craft is the focal point of "Voyage to the Bottom of the Sea," a series being produced during my visit to Los Angeles in the summer of 1964. And it begins my exposure to the work of the show's producer Irwin Allen, whom I have already introduced to you above, sitting behind his giant office desk.

The Seaview is a trouble-shooting nuclear sub, similar to Captain Nemo's Nautilus, travelling the depths of the Seven Seas in the year 1973 to help mankind solve its underwater problems. Simultaneously, it is conducting an unrelenting search for a force of evil that is bent on destroying world peace and led by an evil being known as Dr. Gamma.

For those who didn't see the 1961 Walter Pidgeon movie of the same title, co-written and directed by Irwin Allen, "Voyage" now features Richard Basehart in the role of Admiral Harriman Nelson, the designer of the sub and head of the Nelson Institute of Marine Research in Santa Barbara, where the craft is harbored during quieter moments.

Hedison, in a studio at 20th Century Fox, thrusts his hands into the pockets of his khaki uniform and steps away from a mock-up interior of the Seaview's control room, where producer-director Allen has just finished bawling out an extra for crookedly wearing his sailor's

David Hedison as Capt. Crane

cap, and where an "officer" was rehearsing at the top of his voice the line: "Commander Crane! There's an unidentified object coming in on our starboard side."

"Today we're filming an adventure taking place at the North Pole," Hedison tells me. "Scientists up there have been injecting octopuses with a special serum, turning them into creatures that're half-fish, half-animal. One of them gets big enough to destroy a Norwegian shipping vessel. Talk about having too many legs. The Seaview's been called on the scene to find out what the hell's going on. As you can gather, this is going to be an exciting series, with emphasis on visual creatures of a frightening nature. And we're pulling out all the stops as far as credulity is concerned."

Viewing the set of "Voyage" is like trying to put together the pieces of a gigantic jigsaw puzzle. Sections of the ship's interior and exterior are scattered all over the sound stage so there is ample space for camera and lighting equipment to maneuver in and out.

A diving bell, an escape hatch, racks of spear guns and diving gear, torpedoes, Polaris missile tubes and a two-man miniature scouting sub are just a few of the fascinating props. Hedison points to an eye-catching, modernistic panel of gadgets and flashing red, green and yellow lights which serve as the Seaview's control board. "Looks complicated, huh? But don't let it fool you. We used that same contraption when we made 'The Fly.' All we had to do was have the technical boys readapt it from a disintegrating machine into a submarine control board. Isn't technology exciting!

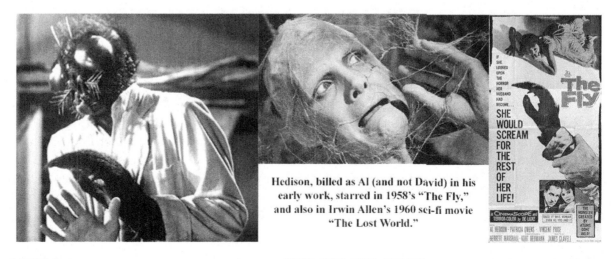

Hedison, billed as Al (and not David) in his early work, starred in 1958's "The Fly," and also in Irwin Allen's 1960 sci-fi movie "The Lost World."

THE CAREER THAT DRIPPED WITH HORROR

Hedison, under contract with Fox since appearing in an off-Broadway production which won him a Theater World Award as "promising newcomer," starred in a previous TV series, "Five Fingers." But the spy thriller, in which Hedison portrayed undercover agent Victor Sebastian and costarred with Paul Burke and Luciana Paluzzi, only lasted 16 episodes.

"People were just getting used to my character when they yanked the series," he says with more than just a touch of bitterness. Since then, he religiously played the Apostle Philip (see left) in George Stevens' 1965 feature film "The Greatest Story Ever Told."

"When I was signed to play Commander Crane, I spent some time aboard a real nuclear sub, the Scamp, while it was docked in San Diego. I wanted to see how a real Commander operated, and to pick up pointers on military matters," he explains. "Realism always adds to the nature of total fantasy."

Back on the set, producer Irwin Allen has apparently straightened out the extra's crooked cap and is ready to roll the camera again. "If you'll excuse me," says Hedison dutifully, taking his hands out of his pockets and ambling slowly toward the control room. "I've got to find out what that unidentified object coming in on our starboard side is all about. Watch our series when it debuts in a few weeks and you'll find out for yourself."

AFTERWORDS

Playing Commander Crane, David Hedison would complete 110 episodes over a four-season period, moving on to a never-ending line-up of appearances on TV series and in movies.

Because Roger Moore liked his work he was cast as CIA agent Felix Leiter in two James Bond features: "Live and Let Die" (1973, see right) and "License to Kill" (1989). He would also score big as Arthur Hendricks in the soap opera "The Young and the Restless," appearing in 50 episodes. It was a full life that ended in the summer of 2019, at the age of 92.

Meeting him was just the beginning of my exposure to the making of "Voyage to the Bottom of the Sea." Next up would be the major star of the series, Richard Basehart.

Stand by! You're also going to take a trip into space, and you are going to find yourself trapped in a time tunnel. And then will come the most unforgettable . . . my brief but unforgettable meeting with producer Irwin Allen. Brief? Unforgettable? You'll find out why. And now . . .

ATTENTION! ALL HANDS ON DECK! THE ADMIRAL'S TRAPPED IN THE TUMMY OF A SEA CREATURE WITH A GIANT TAIL!

IT IS an historic moment when I arrive at 20th Century Fox in the summer of 1965 to interview Richard Basehart, star of "Voyage to the Bottom of the Sea." Historic because the episode being produced that week, "Jonah and the Whale," will turn into one of the most memorable plots of the series. It starts when I see one of the most unusual sets ever created for a TV series.

"This," says Basehart, as he leads me onto the Studio B sound stage, "is the internal stomach of a whale." I stand there stunned as I gaze upward at a huge oval-shaped object. "A whale's stomach?" I ask. "You could put a ton of food in that. Amazing anatomy re-construction."

Basehart frowns. "I might be part of the diet. Let me explain. Me and a Soviet scientist [she's played by Gia Scala] are inside a diving bell when suddenly this whale swims up. Unexpectedly of course. And swallows the bell and both of us whole. Good thing the whale has a level bottom to his stomach, otherwise we'd be potential dinner rolling all over the place."

IT'S THE ADMIRAL! STAND BY FOR A WHALE OF A TALE!

I want to ask Basehart "Where's Captain Ahab when you need him?" but keep quiet.

"At least you have a beautiful actress with you. Gia, she's something. But how the hell are you going to get out of a whale's stomach?" I ask, swallowing some bile and somewhat stunned.

"I can't give away all of the plot, that would anger Irwin our producer. But I can tell you, me and the doctor have about 90 minutes of oxygen and it's going to be up to Commander Lee Crane–that would be David Hedison, my co-star–to get us out before we suffocate. And the only

way is for him to swim into the whale's mouth . . . well, I can't really give away any more details. That would totally piss off Irwin. He does have his moments."

We stroll back to Basehart's dressing room where he settles down and braces himself for all my questions. I begin by telling him that I have seen his most recent screen portrayal in John Sturges' suspense thriller "The Satan Bug," and I'm of the opinion he has distinguished himself with a career that spans stage and screen. And almost all of his films have been first-rate endeavors. And now he has entered a new phase of acting: as Admiral Harriman Nelson, designer-commander of the trouble-shooting submarine Seaview. Hence "Voyage to the Bottom of the Sea" will always stand out among his credits.

He is currently filming episodes for the second season and I tell him, having seen the first season, that I felt "Voyage" had turned into an amusing offering, often capturing the spirit of an old-time movie serial with its unique underwater characters and on-land weirdos. And I hoped Basehart wasn't suffering from claustrophobia by being confined aboard an atomic sub week after week.

Basehart, soft-spoken but still rugged-looking, nods his head. "We were all playing around with a different kind of adventure and we were trying to find credulity without a tongue-in-cheek flavor. It takes some probing to find out what is successful and what is not."

Basehart admits that during the first season the series was a "a somewhat slow experience. Partly because of our very cardboard characterizations. The human element was seldom stressed. Instead, the focus was on outlandish plots involving 'certain undivulged powers' bent on world disorder and eventual conquest of mankind. Okay, so maybe being trapped in a whale's stomach is outlandish, but it's a unique idea and I think it will strengthen the series, being it will play first for our second season."

Richard Basehart will be remembered for starring in the 1948 film noir "He Walked By Night" (check out the noirish lighting above). He also portrayed Der Fuhrer in the 1962 biographic thriller "Hitler" without one hint of goodness.

Basehart does not feel that running opposite Walt Disney's show on another network hurts "Voyage." "We appeal to a different kind of viewer, one who I like to call a Jules Verne adventure nut who loves imaginative science-fiction and cliff-hanging situations."

Suddenly Basehart breaks out laughing. "I'm going to have fun with this character Nelson. I think I'm finally adjusting to the tedious grind this film industry always seems to demand. You may wonder why I switched to television after more than a decade of making movies and theater work. I did it for the money, period. I don't suppose that's the answer I should give, or the answer you expected, but it does happen to be a question of economics. Call it survival."

Basehart was raised in Zanesville, Ohio, and after a failed attempt at journalism served his acting apprenticeship with the Hedgerow Theater in Philadelphia. Plenty of "door knocking" in New York eventually led to an important role in "Counterattack" on Broadway and he soon after secured the role of the doomed Scot in John Patrick's "The Hasty Heart," for which he was awarded the 1945 New York Critics' Award as the most promising newcomer to the stage.

His first film role was in the low-budget quickie "Repeat Performance" (1947). Things got better in "Cry Wolf" (1947). And then he really struck pay dirt as David Morgan, a cop-killer and hold-up man in "He Walked by Night," a highly popular and dark film noir of 1948. The film was based on an actual Los Angeles police case in which Morgan used the city's sewer system to emerge on a street, perform a crime, and then duck back in the sewer before police arrived.

Basehart also vividly remembers his first film for 20th Century Fox, "14 Hours," recalling how most of his performance in that 1951 feature consisted of close-ups without dialogue—an ability that impressed many movie critics. His character was a man on a high ledge of a tall building, threatening to commit suicide.

At the height of his success as one of Fox's leading stars, tragedy struck. Basehart's 34-year-old wife Stephanie died of a brain injury, and soon after, broken-heartedly, he left to live in Europe. "I had to escape to live in a new place and try to put the loss behind me." In Europe he met Italian actress Valentina Cortese

Richard Basehart playing a clown with Guilietta Masina in Federico Fellini's "La Strada," the first movie awarded the Best Foreign Film Oscar in 1954.

and married her before appearing as a circus clown in Federico Fellini's "La Strada" (1954).

Two years later he returned to America and was chosen to portray Ishmael in John Huston's "Moby Dick" (1956), followed by the role of Ivan in "The Brothers Karamazov" (1958). "I was away for so long. I was very happy to get back and resettle here in L.A. I've become very enchanted with this part of the country again. I'm more at home here because, after all, this is where I got my start in motion pictures. I like the climate; I like the people. I also prefer Hollywood's business procedures to those overseas."

Basehart is always the deliberate gentleman, in no way attempting to insult or be snide, and

he proves his lighter side when he jokes of his experiences with director Samuel Fuller making "Fixed Bayonets" at Fox in 1951.

"Sam actually treated us like dogface soldiers. All of the cast had to carry heavy equipment and go on long marches when we weren't shooting scenes. Always wearing what he called 'steel hats' and always 'jackassing' to get somewhere. He wanted us to feel some of the pain soldiers undergo when stuck in a snow-covered landscape. It was the toughest role of my life."

Jokingly he tells me: "About that whale we saw earlier. We give it a massive dosage of bicarbonate so it'll burp up the bell. Don't put that in your story."

AFTERWORDS

Irwin Allen's "Voyage to the Bottom of the Sea" would last for a total of four seasons and keep Basehart busy through 1968. After that his powerful voice was used for many voice-over jobs and documentaries, but he seemed stuck doing one-time appearances in TV movies or series without ever again scoring big at the movies.

After several heart attacks and strokes, he died in 1984 at the age of 70. By no means was my exposure to the work of producer Irwin Allen yet ended. Yes, I was about to be projected into a world of science-fiction, fantasy and . . .

"DANGER! DANGER! ATTENTION! ATTENTION!"

THE CAREER THAT DRIPPED WITH HORROR

ATTENTION! DANGER LIES AHEAD! THE SPACE FAMILY ROBINSON AND VIEWERS GET "LOST IN SPACE!"

(L-R) Angela Cartwright, Mark Goddard, Marta Kristen, Robot (performed by Bob May and voiced by Dick Tufeld) Jonathan Harris, June Lockhart, Guy Williams and Bill Mumy.

THERE WAS A TIME, back in the 1930s, when science-fiction consisted largely of Space Opera: pulpy yarns about ray gun-packing spacemen who heroically rescued scantily-clad beauties from the many-tentacled clutches of bug-eyed monsters of the Universe.

The history of motion-picture science-fiction has also offered its share of Space Opera. Young and old alike are familiar with the extraterrestrial adventures of Flash Gordon and we have all winced at one time or another at TV's "Space Patrol" (starring Ed Kemmer as Commander Buzz Corry and Lynn Osborne as Cadet Happy), Buck Rogers and other samples of human beings who meet other-worldly monster creatures far beyond our solar system.

Sci-fi writers in more recent years have abandoned the pulp magazine (*Fantastic Adventures, Planet Stories,* etc.) approach and taken a much more mature look at what-it-will-really-be-like-in-deep-space. So have Hollywood studios with such feature films as "Destination Moon" (1950), "Forbidden Planet" (1956) and "This Island Earth" (1955). Even the medium of television has demonstrated a sophisticated attitude toward the fantastic in "The Twilight Zone" (1959-64) and "The Outer Limits" (1963-65).

However, 20th Century Fox has taken what appears to be a step forward to prove that the more juvenile approach to sci-fi is still popular to a bug-eyed young audience and worth one hour of prime time with "Lost in Space."

The series focuses on the exploits of the John Robinson clan in the year 1997. Professor Robinson is an every-day astrophysicist faced with the depressing reality that Earth is overpopulated, so bravely he volunteers his wife Maureen (played by June Lockhart) and children (Judy, played by Marta Kristen, and Will, played by Billy Mumy) to explore with him other worlds. It is his way of not only visiting unknown planets but also helping the Human Race to make its way across the vastness of the Universe.

Blasting off from Earth, the Robinson rocket Jupiter II suddenly goes berserk, its mechanical malfunction compounded into terms of Light Years. And that puts the Robinson clan in the vicinity of Alpha Centauri. Also aboard the spaceship is a goofy scientist named Dr. Zachary Smith (Jonathan Harris, upper right) and a robot who is reminiscent of Robby the Robot in "Forbidden Planet." (In fact, both robots were designed by the same human, Robert Kinoshita.) In some ways the robot steals some episodes of "Lost in Space" and has become famous for the recurring line: "It does not compute." (Dick Tufeld did the voiceovers.)

 Finally, the Jupiter II lands on a world that is far from underpopulated. Among its extraterrestrial life-form oddities: a 40-foot one-eyed giant with an apparent dislike for intruders and a pet known as The Bloop–a cross between a teddy bear, a puppy dog and a monkey.

It isn't surprising to learn that the creator of "Lost in Space" is Irwin Allen, who delights in bringing flashy adventure spectacles to the screen with little thought content or credulity. Thus far this first season emphasis has been on imaginative ingredients of the future: bizarre costumes, silvery rockets gleaming in the black void of space; the engrossing procedure of Suspended Animation. In short, escapism slanted for the youngest of minds, and those who like their science-fiction unrefined and filled with occasional humor and frequent killer beasts.

Guy Williams is Professor John Robinson, who takes his family to the Alpha Centauri star system and gets lost... yeah, in space.

Another reason that might make the younger set rejoice over this CBS-TV entry is the presence of Guy Williams, the bold caballero who previously portrayed sword-swinging Zorro for Walt Disney (1960-1961) on "The Magical World of Disney." Disney kept Williams under contract beyond the demise of Zorro's success, giving him only a small part in "The Prince and the Pauper" (1962). When Williams finally won his freedom, he found himself type-cast as a villainous swashbuckler in "David and Pythias" (1962) and "Captain Sinbad" (1963), both films made in Europe. He also appeared in a few episodes on "Bonanza" (1964).

Now, although he is still cast as a fearless adventurer, Williams is nonetheless thankful he does not have to carry a sword. He's also happy about not having to play a character of the past, even if it means playing a character of the future. "I originally took up fencing," he explains to me during lunch at the Fox studio commissary, "to get rid of my hostilities. But I've since given up dueling and all the swords are in the closet."

Williams is an actor with a wry, biting sense of humor. He seems patient, well-adjusted and tolerant toward those who kept his range of acting limited. While Williams admits that "Lost in Space" is pure flight-of-fantasy, he does believe that it is "more sophisticated than all those Buck Rogers and Flash Gordon serials. We have much more knowledge now about outer space and how we are going to have to deal with it to reach the moon and beyond."

He takes a deep sigh and looks me squarely in the eyes. "But I suppose 30 years from now another actor in a science-fiction series will look back, as I just did, and say that 'Lost in Space' lacked many values in terms of advance technology regarding rocketships, satellites and other beginnings of our conquest of space. I just hope that whoever that actor is, he doesn't compare me to Buster Crabbe."

June Lockhart on Lassie and her Dog Days in Space

AFTER "Lost in Space" is cancelled in 1968 at the end of the third season, I will have an opportunity to meet June Lockhart, who had portrayed Maureen Robinson for 84 episodes. During our discussion of her busy career, I take time to ask her if she had been disappointed by the cancellation of "Lost in Space."

She burst out laughing. "Personally," she finally said, "all of the cast members were very glad because it had been such nonsense. On the other hand, we all got three years of busy roles that had filled us with fun, screaming and running from E.T.s of wide varieties. We'd get the new dialogue and laugh until tears came out of our eyes, it was all so hilarious. Jonathan Harris, as Dr. Zachary Smith, had the most marvelous wit and during moments away from the cameras could tell dirty stories that were utterly delightful. I've never been in a cast where there were so many stimulating conversations between us. But believe me, the dialogue you had to listen to was pure garbage."

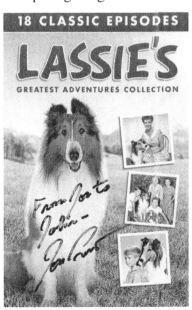

More memorable for June Lockhart were her 207 episodes of "Lassie" (1958-1964), in which she was the mother of Lassie's best pal, Timmy Martin. Timmy was portrayed by Jon Provost (bottom left), who became a best friend back in the days when I was hanging out in Marin County with Tom Wyrsch and Bob Wilkins. Jon signed this DVD set in February 2020, just before the Coronavirus pandemic struck America, when he made a personal appearance at a movie theater in Sonoma, CA.

With him was his wife Laurie Jacobsen, hostess on Wyrsch's "Haunted" DVD sets, shown on page 18.

AFTERWORDS

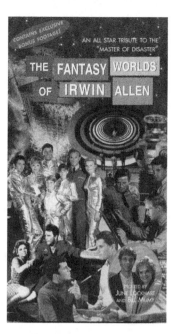

For Guy Williams "Lost in Space" was his final work as an actor. In the 1970s he decided to move to Buenos Aires where he died in 1989 at the age of 65 of a brain aneurysm.

June Lockhart went on to star in 47 episodes of "Petticoat Junction" (1968-1970) as Dr. Janet Craig and in 34 episodes of "General Hospital" (1984-1998) as Mariah Ramirez.

A highlight of her career came in 1995 when she co-hosted with Bill Mumy the VHS documentary "The Fantasy Worlds of Irwin Allen," a fun-packed collection of never-before-seen outtakes from "Lost in Space," bloopers, and footage from Allen's TV shows and movies. Also seen is "special guest star" Jonathan Harris. (Originally this had played as a special on the Sci-Fi Channel.) Lockhart is anything but lost: She still does appearances on TV shows and had her 95th birthday in 2020.

One More Irwin Allen Fantasy Involving Time Travel . . . But Time Will Soon Run Out!

James Darren and Robert Colbert in "The Time Tunnel"

I'M PAYING a visit to 20th Century Fox once again in the summer of 1966. Call it the home of Irwin Allen as the man who gave us "Voyage to the Bottom of the Sea" and "Lost in Space" is busy as hell once again. When I walk into one of the studios I'm amazed at the ingeniously-designed props for Allen's new series "The Time Tunnel," scheduled to begin in the fall. Especially impressive is the tunnel itself, which is a gigantic cylinder that gives the optical illusion of a swirling vortex that seems to recede ad infinitum.

It's a top-secret research project, located eight miles beneath the Arizona desert. Hmm, sounds like a deep plot. Scientists played by Robert Colbert, Whit Bissell and Lee Meriwether are there to transport human beings forward and backward through time. Not always with total success, leading to suspense and uncertainty of safety.

I'm there to meet James Darren, who will always be best remembered for his character of Jeffrey Matthews (aka Moondoggie) in "Gidget" (1959), "Gidget Goes Hawaiian" (1961) and "Gidget Goes to Rome" (1963). He is portraying Dr. Tony Newman, one of the time travelers, when we meet. He's dressed in a green spacesuit for an episode concerning space travel of the future, and after shaking hands he removes a cumbersome helmet encasing his head. "This thing is murder," he mumbles, tapping the face mask. "I wish I could get my hands on the guy who designed this. Every time I speak, the glass fogs up, and so we have to cut after every line of dialogue to get it clean again."

Given that "Gidget" involved romance between young surfers and helped to create the genre of beach party movies, I ask Darren, why is he now in a sci-fi series?

Darren shrugs. "Because it's work. And because I get to travel back and forth through time, living in different eras and places. Me and Doug [Robert Colbert] end up aboard the Titanic. We're at Pearl Harbor on December 7, 1941. We're caught up in the War of 1812. And we get trapped in the war between Trojans and Greeks in 1200 BC. And that's just the beginning!"

This still was taken in 1959 during production of "Gidget." Left to right: Cliff Robertson as Burt aka The Big Kahuna, Sandra Dee as the titular beach babe, and James Darren aka Burt aka Moondoggie.

I ask Darren if he has a favorite sci-fi or fantasy movie. Or perhaps he has a favorite writer of the genres. He shakes his head. "No, not really. I'm not a fan. However, I do like Irwin Allen's movies and TV shows, and I heard he was inspired to do this series after he saw 'The Time Travelers,' which was made two years ago with Preston Foster.

"I think I'm playing a very unusual part. As this young physicist Newman, I'm full of fire and I'll stop at nothing to find my way in and out of the situations I'm thrown into." Darren runs his hands along his spacesuit and grins. "As you can see, I'm getting a chance to do unusual things and wear unusual costumes. I'm in the hands of Irwin Allen, and anything is possible."

AFTERWORDS

"The Time Tunnel" airs 30 episodes on ABC-TV but is cancelled at the end of the first season. Darren co-stars with William Shatner in "T. J. Hooker" (1982-1986) as Officer Jim Corrigan for 66 episodes. He also plays Vic Fontaine (a hologram) in several episodes of "Star Trek: Deep Space Nine" (1998-1999). Oddly, he is the only "Time Tunnel" actor who did not become a cast member of "Land of the Giants," the one Irwin Allen creation that I did not get an opportunity to cover. Darren remains a well-remembered teen idol because of his Gidget movies.

AND NOW HERE IT COMES AT LAST!
SIMILAR TO AN ATOMIC BLAST!

I experience one final interview regarding the Irwin Allen era of television, And it turns out to be one of the worst meetings I have during my 33 years as a newspaper reporter specializing in interviewing movie and TV stars. It takes place in the summer of 1968 at 20ᵗʰ Century Fox in Irwin Allen's vast office. As Burt Lancaster said in "Vera Cruz": "Hang on to your hat, Max, and don't worry about the women and the children." So here it is, in all its gory glory.

The Day the Stuff Hits the Fan In the Office of a Classic Sci-Fi Television Man

WHILE SOME REVIEWERS have not exactly been ecstatic over the content of Irwin Allen productions for television, he continues to be a very successful writer-producer-director of science-fiction genre programs. Financially successful, anyway. Critically? Not when you compare his shows to "Star Trek," which came on the air in the fall of 1966 at the height of Allen's productions.

For Allen it all started with a love for film even though he originally headed toward being a journalist after graduating from the Columbia School of Journalism. For a while he was a magazine editor but that love for movies persisted and he enjoyed the first highlight of a film career when he won an Academy Award for the documentary "The Sea Around Us" in 1953. That's when he decided being producer was everything and he began writing and making feature films. First up: "The Big Circus" (1959), a thriller starring Victor Mature and Red Buttons. After that he allowed his love for science-fiction to prevail with the making of 1960's "The Lost World" (a trek into an Amazon jungle where dinosaurs dwell, a shock for Michael Rennie and Jill St. John.). That was followed by "Five Weeks in a Balloon," based on the Jules Verne novel and starring Fabian, Red Buttons and Barbara Eden. Next up: the 1961 undersea adventure "Voyage to the Bottom of the Sea" starring Walter Pidgeon as Captain Admiral Harriman Nelson. The very character Richard Basehart would play when it became a weekly sci-fi series in 1964.

It's now the late summer of 1968 and in a few weeks Allen's new CBS-TV series "Land of the Giants" is set to premiere. It begins when a spaceship from Earth crash-lands on a far-flung planet inhabited by humans just like us – except everybody is an estimated 12-times bigger.

If you think Allen spent millions for props on "Land of the Giants," getting a giant boot on "Creature Features" cost me plenty of wear and tear.

Animal life is also king-sized and the Earthlings are constantly facing crushing annihilation.

Allen's production office is located at 20th Century Fox. As I enter that office, I notice right away that he loves to surround himself with symbols of his success. Along one wall of his immaculate suite are bound copies of telescripts for "Voyage to the Bottom of the Sea." The title of each is boldly lettered on the binding: "Deadly Dolls" . . . "Werewolf" . . . "Terror" . . . "Shadowman" . . . "The Deadly Amphibians." And outside in the corridor, positioned like some sentinel to ward off bug-eyed creatures of doom, stands the robot from "Lost in Space."

If only the mechanical being had cried aloud: "Danger! Danger!"

Allen, 52, makes a grand entrance into his gleaming sanctuary and takes a position behind his elongated, clean desk, nodding at a ubiquitous production assistant. Nice to have somebody around when you need something. Allen is of medium height, with a receding hairline. He wears glasses and is casually attired. He remarks that he has been ready for 25 years for reporters like me and leans back in his swivel chair.

AND THE TERROR BEGINS . . .

Stanley: The official Fox biography, which I'm told was approved by you, describes you as "The Jules Verne of the Entertainment World." How do you feel about that?

Allen: I'm not responsible for press-agent writing. I'm gracious and humble, but I do insist these bios be accurate.

Stanley: In 1953 you made an Oscar-winning documentary "The Sea Around Us," based on Rachel L. Carson's study of ocean life, which had been a best seller. What led you soon after to pursue science-fiction movies and TV series?

Allen: I made a number of films after "Sea Around Us." All were of an escapist nature. High adventure, fantasy and science fiction. But in all instances brilliantly produced. *(Allen bursts out laughing, aiming his hee-haws in the direction of the stand-by assistant.)* Hey, I don't think he knows we're putting him on. He'll quote me verbatim. *(More Allen laughter as the assistant stands by, stone-faced, not saying a word.)* My films got you away from the normal, humdrum existence of living on Earth. *(He laughs again.)*

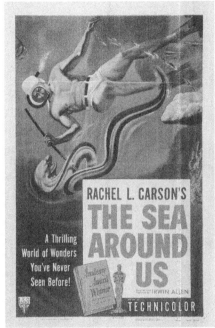

Stanley: How do you feel about the current wave of sci-fi movies playing in theaters?

Allen: I saw "Planet of the Apes" and thoroughly enjoyed it. The story was well told, the make-up was good, the surprise ending was typical of good science-fiction. How's that for building up a Fox production?

Stanley: Do you feel we'll see more like "Planet of the Apes" and "2001: A Space Odyssey"?

Allen: We should, we deserve to see more. Science-fiction has been accepted now as a cut above B pictures. Now they're dealing with adult problems. Expensive movies will attract more sophisticated audiences. Myself, I like to do adult stories against a sci-fi background but with lots of stuff thrown in for the kid audience. The end result is an all-family audience.

Stanley: How do you look upon "Star Trek," your only real TV competitor these evenings?

Allen: *(Frowning)* It would be improper for me to say. I've only seen it in passing, I've been so busy with "Lost in Space" and prior to that with "Voyage to the Bottom of the Sea." I'm not an expert on "Star Trek." It could be important, but I couldn't say.

Stanley: How much sci-fi reading have you done?

Allen: I'm forced to read a great many books these days. That's because I'm always looking for science-fiction properties that I think I can turn into good business. It's a requirement of being a producer these days.

Stanley: What do you think of Ray Bradbury, a personal favorite of mine?

Allen: I like Ray Bradbury a great deal. He's a superb author. *(lengthy pause)* And wait a minute. Who's the other author I'm trying to think of?

Stanley: Isaac Asimov?

Allen: Yes, Asimov. And . . . *(long pause)*

Stanley: Robert Heinlein?

Allen: Yes, Heinlein.

Stanley: Why have you not used professional sci-fi writers for your series? "Star Trek," for example, has used Robert Bloch and–

Allen: Wait a minute. Now you're talking about a more elite kind of writer. Like Bradbury. They have nothing for sale in the teleplay format.

Stanley: Well, Bradbury has done a few teleplays–

Allen: I don't believe that's true.

Stanley: Let's see, he did a "Twilight Zone" entitled "I Sing the Body Electric." And "The Jail" for an "Alcoa Premiere" in 1962. He's also written at least two Alfred Hitchcock shows.

Allen: I refuse to believe that.

Stanley: Well, "Star Trek" has used Norman Spinrad, Theodore Sturgeon, Jerome–

Allen: I never said I used those writers.

Stanley: I didn't mean to say that you did. I–

Allen: *(turning to his nearby assistant)* Say, I thought this interview was supposed to be about my new show, "Land of the Giants," which is coming on the air very soon.

Stanley: Very well. Please tell me about "Land of the Giants." I'm assuming it's going to have a lot of special effects. Giant humanoids vs tiny tiny Earthlings.

Allen: It's set on this strange planet with people 72 feet high. *(Allen stands up from his chair, raising both arms above his head, as if to touch the ceiling.)* Buildings are 100-feet tall. Chairs are 40 feet in height. Seven humans crash on the planet and now have to adjust to a new lifestyle, facing the possibility of being crushed every week. This has been the most expensive series I've ever done: $250,000 per episode. Nothing but special effects. We all knew it was going to be expensive, but not *that expensive*. The optical work is taking far longer than we imagined it would. *(Still standing, Allen proudly spreads a number of photographs depicting some of the optical work across his desk so I can see them close-up.)*

Stanley: These photos are impressive. How were some of these special effects accomplished?

Allen: You don't think I'm going to tell you, do you?

Stanley: Just thought I'd ask.

Allen: See the hand in this photo? *(He taps the photo to single it out.)* That cost $36,000. It was operated by six crew members on piano wire cables. There are no easy ways to get these kinds of scenes.

Stanley: I love this still of your star Gary Conway holding a giant safety pin. It looks like a handy weapon and not just a safety pin.

Allen: That's the heart of the show, how normal things look in a giant format.

Stanley: On my way into your office, I noticed there were many books that contained ratings for your series over several seasons. You must follow the Nielsen Ratings very closely.

Irwin Allen on location in San Francisco producing "The Towering Inferno," a disaster movie that was nominated for eight Academy Awards. It was also the biggest box office hit of 1974, scoring $203 million worldwide.

Allen: Right now, I'm studying Demographics. It's a new system that gives you your own rating plus what else is being televised at the same time. There's included a profile on each viewer. How much money he or she makes? Complete histories.

Stanley: What are some of the statistics about your viewers?

Allen: "Lost in Space" appealed only to the 3-to-12 set. No adult audience to speak of. "Voyage to the Bottom of the Sea" had an audience that averaged 26 to 60. Including many adult women. But why . . . that I don't know.

Stanley: About "Voyage," which I saw a lot of . . . and enjoyed an afternoon on the set with both Richard Basehart and David Hedison. That was a very funny show in its own way. I loved the whale episode. I know many others who watched it faithfully–

Allen: *(Standing up suddenly, frowning)* Funny? You mean so funny it was bad?

Stanley: Well . . . sometimes, not always, yes.

Allen: I didn't know it was bad. I'm used to people liking my shows who come into my office to talk to me.

Stanley: What about "Time Tunnel?" You had a very fine pilot, produced and directed by yourself. Then . . .

Allen: The other 29 episodes went downhill?

Stanley: In the ratings, yes.

Allen: You've got a lot of nerve. Coming into my office and insulting my shows.

Stanley: I thought you'd want to honestly discuss your shows–

Allen: All I can say is, you've got a lot of nerve.

Stanley: Would you rather this interview come to a close?

Allen: I most currently would! Clear out of here! Good-bye.

AFTERWORDS

So went my interview with Irwin Allen. "Land of the Giants" would last two seasons (51 episodes) and prove to be fun to watch, with giant creatures and objects constantly imposing danger to the stranded human beings from Earth. But it brought Allen's TV career to a stop.

He transferred his passion to the big screen and became known as "The Master of Disaster," producing the successful "The Towering Inferno" in San Francisco in 1974. Others: "The Poseidon Adventure" (1972) and "The Swarm" (1978). His final effort was "Aliens From

Gene Hackman in the Oscar-winning 1972 epic "The Poseidon Adventure." An ocean liner is overturned by a tsunami on New Year's Eve, forcing the survivors to battle their way to the top (bottom) of the ship. The movie set the template for all the '70s disaster flicks.

Another Planet," a 1982 TV movie consisting of three re-edited episodes of "The Time Tunnel."

He remained retired from film production for the remainder of his life, which ended in 1991 when he was 75. Rumors have persisted that Allen was on the phone a lot during his final days, trying to convince Jonathan Harris to return to play Dr. Zachary Smith in a remake of "Lost in Space." For Allen that had been the funniest, and most memorable, moment of his career.

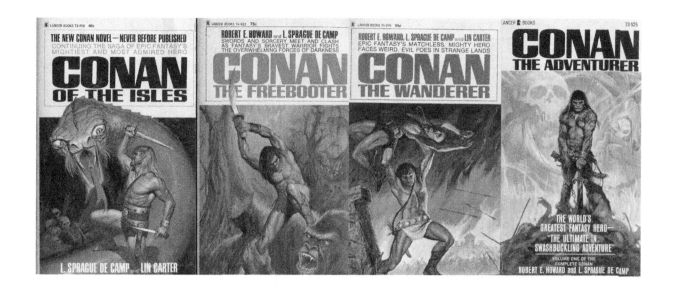

HOW ARNOLD THE WARRIOR BEGAN TO CONQUER HOLLYWOOD AS A BARBARIAN

It is May 1982 when I fly to Los Angeles to cover the world premiere of the sword-and-sorcery adventure "Conan the Barbarian," the first screen adaptation of a famous literary character created by Robert E. Howard in pulp magazines of the 1930s. Conan was a superb warrior from an Indo-European cult dating back to the 8th Century and he constantly faced monsters of every variety and women of unique beauty.

After Howard's death by suicide in 1936, other writers came forward to create new paperback novels and short stories showcasing Conan, the character had grown to be so popular. A small but well-remembered publishing company, Arkham House, had specialized in reprinting much of the Conan-related material. In the 1960s many new Conan paperbacks were issued, so memorable had Howard's character grown.

It is not a happy time for me. My father, Myron Stanley, had just passed away in Napa's Queen of the Valley Hospital from a heart attack. I had been with him the day before he died, sitting next to his bed in the recovery ward. He had already been unconscious for a few days and I had decided to sit quietly with him. Suddenly he rose up, looked at me blankly, looked over toward a window behind us, then settled back down as if nothing unusual was happening.

I called out for a nurse and she rushed in to examine him. "He rose up like he was no longer in a coma," I told her. "He looked at me, he looked over toward the window. Is he really awake?"

The one and only photograph Arnold signed for me during our time together.

She examined my dad's head for a moment, then said, "No, he's still in the coma. It's not unusual for someone to rise up like that. Sometimes they hear something, a noise outside maybe, and that will cause them to react, but it's not caused by coming awake."

And so two days later I'm on a jetliner headed for Hollywood. I keep thinking about Dad and my final hours with him. He had been a terrific father who had taught me the hardwood floor-laying business starting at the age of ten. When I was 18, he wanted to create a father-son business but I told him I was tired of sawdust blowing into my face. I possessed a love for writing and wanted to attend San Francisco State College when I finished high school. There were five daily newspapers in the city and it was my dream to land a job at one of them, being I had already worked at two weekly papers in the Napa Valley.

The San Francisco Chronicle had become that place, and as an entertainment writer I was now headed to meet an up-and-coming star of action and fantasy films, Arnold Schwarzenegger. I had first met him in 1976 when he was filming an episode of "The Streets of San Francisco." (That account can be found in my autobiographical "I Was a TV Horror Host.")

THE SETTING IS UNIVERSAL STUDIOS AS I PEER INTO THE GLEAMING EYES OF CONAN THE BARBARIAN . . .

Stanley: What was the greatest challenge you faced bringing Conan to the screen?

Schwarzenegger: Making the character vulnerable. He has the look of a rugged, dangerous warrior but I wanted to capture some sympathy for him . . . and of course I wanted to make him believable, but then that's always the case with a movie character. Conan is powerful, physically a fighting machine. And of course a barbarian. You have to live up to the title. But, let me say it's not easy to do. I had to work hard on that physical side to him and fortunately I was always in good shape. I was used to doing physical activities. Swinging a ten-pound sword all day long or climbing up ropes or being run over by a galloping horse. All those things made Conan a major challenge in my career.

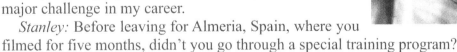

Stanley: Before leaving for Almeria, Spain, where you filmed for five months, didn't you go through a special training program?

Schwarzenegger: The only way to do it well is to put a ton of physical energy and time into it. I spent a year-and-a-half taking kendo lessons and samurai sword fighting and training. Axes, knives, ropes, horseback riding. I had to wear 50 pounds of body armor when I was astride a horse. That's hard to do, especially when you are galloping like crazy. Also just climbing on and off a horse was a challenge, no matter how easy it might have looked.

Stanley: Director John Milius had promised you and the rest of the cast there would be plenty of dirt and pain before production, and it sounds like he lived up to his promises.

Schwarzenegger: Yes, he lived up to his promises. More than lived up to them.

Stanley: Did you get hurt? What were your injuries?

Arnold Schwarzenegger with Leslie Foldvary, credited as "Sacrificial Snake Girl" in "Conan the Barbarian."

Schwarzenegger: Unforgettable. All over my body. On the first day of shooting . . . no, on the first hour, I was attacked by four wolves and pulled over a 12-foot-high rock and then bitten.

This was tremendous action, wonderful. That's what I told Milius afterward. In response, John told me "This is the way I want it all the way through this film." Then I had to fight with a giant snake which threw me all over the set. I told John of my pain. He said "Pain is only temporary. This movie is permanent."

Stanley: So you never had a disagreement with Milius no matter what he demanded of you?

Schwarzenegger: Never, because he knew all the time what he wanted. He had a very clear vision what the film should look like. He brings leadership to the set. We always say he's the dog trainer and we're the dogs. Simple as that, throughout the filming. He's very inspirational.

Stanley: Speaking of inspirational, you have a memorable love scene with Sandahl Bergman and I was wondering . . . what are you thinking about during an emotional moment like that?

Schwarzenegger: A love scene is always very technical. You worry about the lights, your distance away from the camera. From the director: "Okay, now you can kiss . . . stop kissing . . . Arnold, look this way. Sandahl, look that way." You cannot dare to think about love, you merely act as if you are making love. Truly, it is the most difficult of scenes to shoot. Imagine 50 people surrounding you and some of these Spanish guys are peeking at you through the slots. It was supposed to be a closed set but suddenly everyone wanted to help out in some way. "Do you need water? What else can I do for you, hombre?"

Sandahl Bergman holds her own against Arnold's Conan as Valeria, the Queen of the Bandits. They would join forces again in "Red Sonja" (1985).

However, I knew Sandahl well enough, and it became a comfortable thing after a while.

Stanley: In the scene where you're crucified on the Tree of Woe, and a buzzard flies down and actually bites you on the neck, and you in turn bite off the neck of the buzzard. Did I get all that right?

Schwarzenegger: Yeah, only it wasn't a buzzard, it was a vulture. It was already dead when I bit its neck off. Something you don't want to do on a normal basis. It was filled with worms and lice and all kinds of little insects and they all stink like hell. Afterward I had to gargle with alcohol and water. That night, alcohol again. Vodka!

Sandahl Bergman signed this photo and thanked me for my wonderful questions.

Stanley: How do you feel about your film career at this point?

Schwarzenegger: I feel excellent, I love acting. But I feel a hunger to get even better. To keep growing. I always felt that way in bodybuilding, and that became a success for me. In fact, it became the stepping stone that led to acting. And acting I shall do. And an actor I shall be.

AFTERWORDS

The Conan character was a hit, making $79 million gross, and established Schwarzenegger as a leading player in the game of Hollywood. After the sequel ("Conan the Destroyer," 1984), he became internationally famous in five "Terminator" hits, as well as "Predator" (1987), "Total Recall" (1990), and "True Lies" (1994), plus he played Mr. Freeze in 1997's "Batman and Robin."

He dropped actor to become Governor of California from 2003 through 2011. (He preferred you called him "Governator.") He returned to acting and is still starring in many projects, though not as successfully as when he started out.

AS TOUGH AS HE GETS: Schwarzenegger as a Bond-like spy in James Cameron's action comedy "True Lies" (1994), as the iconic "Terminator" (1984), who kept living up to his repeated promise "I'll be back," and the leader of an elite rescue squad that encounters the deadly titular "Predator" (1987).

GILLIAN ANDERSON AS SCULLY: ... BUT SHE DOUBTED THE WHOLE BUSINESS OF E.T. LIFE-FORMS

DAVID DUCHOVNY AS MULDER: HE WANTED TO BELIEVE IN UFOS AND ALIENS ...

(This was written in September 1993 just days before the television premiere of "The X-Files.")

How Chris Carter Gave the World A New Way of Seeing UFOs and Other Modern Phenomena Through The Eyes of Muller and Scully

STRANGE LIGHTS flashing in the night sky, mysterious, alien-like shapes hulking in an eerie forest, an inexplicable force disrupting mechanical devices, motorists disappearing for a few hours and waking up to find their bodies covered with odd punctures . . .

These recurring themes from reported UFO abduction cases have become the stark, sometimes sinister images for the new series dramatizing paranormal phenomena, "The X-Files," premiering on the Fox network. If there is any one word that creator-producer Chris Carter wants to emphasize it's "scary." However, "I don't mean scary in the horror-genre sense, but scary in the way that speculation pushes beyond scientific credibility to enter a realm of 'extreme possibility.' Films like 'Coma' [1978] and 'The Andromeda Strain' [1971] have that quality. It's the idea that shakes up you and your beliefs, not some hideous Frankenstein monster or a hand clasping the heroine's shoulder."

Even so, it was the hideous vampire monster in "The Night Stalker," a highly rated TV-movie of 1973 produced by Dan Curtis, that gave Carter his inspiration to create "The X-Files." "When I saw 'Stalker' with Darren McGavin playing that obsessed newspaperman Carl Kolchak, it really shook me up to think there might be a twilight world of bloodsucking creatures. Of course, that's the spectrum of the supernatural. Today we're all more fascinated by modern phenomena, which has a way of really shaking up that segment of our society that has come to believe in extraterrestrial beings and UFOs."

Carter was having dinner one night with a Yale psychology professor and researcher. "When I found out he had been a consultant on Dan Curtis' 'Intruders,' a 1992 drama about UFO abductions, he told me that three per cent of the public believed in this syndrome. I was astounded. I realized there was a topicality to this theme of the unknown. And so, 'The X-Files' began to grow out of that fascination."

The series depicts two FBI agents–poles apart in their thinking–on the trail of various unsolved mysteries. In upcoming episodes, promises Carter, "they will track biological anomalies, chemical anomalies, twists on genetic engineering and other fanciful spin-offs from modern technological advances." And, of course, UFOs moving at incredible speed across the night sky.

Maverick agent Fox Mulder (David Duchovny, who had briefly portrayed a transvestite DEA agent on "Twin Peaks") is a firm believer in the paranormal, often

"X-Files" Creator/Producer Chris Carter

turning paranoid in his obsessive search to find the answers to baffling phenomena. His partner

Dana Scully (Gillian Anderson), with a degree in medicine and a bent for seeking answers through scientific logic, is a total skeptic. Each week they will be incompatibly thrown together on a new assignment, unaware that their chiefs are part of a top-secret government project using them to further its own clandestine causes.

In real life, the actors are just the opposite in their attitudes toward the paranormal. Duchovny, currently enjoying the theatrical release of his film "Kalifornia," has serious doubts about all those UFO reports. "I accept the possibility of extraterrestrial life-form units in this vast universe of ours. But I don't understand why, if there are aliens, they don't land in Manhattan instead of always choosing unpopulated areas where maybe three people happen to see them."

Duchovny doesn't believe much in conspiracies, either. "It's unlikely any high-level conspiracy could last for very long. The sheer amount of people keeping the secret would eventually crack open; somebody's death-bed confession would expose the whole thing."

Anderson, an award-winning off-Broadway actress whose film/TV career is just beginning, admits that "I have this tendency to believe the most outrageous things. After all, this is a large universe we live in, and UFO stories tend to follow a pattern that, in my eyes, gives them validity."

She finds the role of Scully a challenge to play. "She does everything she can to find a scientific answer to the mysteries, which becomes difficult after a while, because her constant exposure to the weirdest things imaginable eventually have an accumulative effect."

What alien creature did Dana Scully (Gillian Anderson) just see?

Even so, she adds, "That's when she turns to her science and physics the most. In a way, she's shielding herself from the unacceptable."

Carter, whose writing career since 1985 has included episodes for the comedy series "Rags to Riches" and the creation of the comedy show "A Brand New Life," tries to see both sides of each "X Files" enigma.

"One half of me wants to have something set before me so I can see it with my own eyes. But another side, and we all have it, wants to take a leap of faith, wants to believe in wild things. I'd like to be driving one night through the desert or a lonely forest and suddenly see something that couldn't possibly be happening, but it is happening.

"Then I would know these strange things are really going on, and I'd finally be a part of it."

AFTERWORDS

"The X-Files" became a classic TV series and ran without interruption from 1993 through 2002. It returned in 2016 and ran through March 2018 with Chris Carter still at the helm.

In between Carter also created "Millennium" (1996-1999), in which Lance Henriksen (right) portrayed Frank Black, a former FBI agent who had the ability to read the minds of murderers and who investigated the supernatural and possible alien beings.

That was followed by "The Lone Gunmen" (13 episodes in 2001) in which X-File investigators were portrayed in a more comedic, tongue-in-cheek fashion.

Carter has had incredible success in the world of TV and one can only wish him well in a thriving culture of human beings. And possibly alien life forms?

THE CAREER THAT DRIPPED WITH HORROR

STAN LEE
THE MARVEL OF COMIC BOOK HISTORY

With the possible exception of William Gaines, who created the Entertaining Comics (EC) line-up out of which *Mad Magazine* became the most successful publication in American history, Stan Lee stands as an historic personality of the comic-book industry, having also made a more modern reputation for himself in TV and motion pictures.

As for many recent Marvel Movies featuring superheroes, somewhere within you will discover Lee appearing in a cameo role, usually with a comedic overtone. In "Captain America: Civil War" he's a driver for FedEx; in "Deadpool" he's the head disc jockey of a strip club; and in "Ant-Man" he's none other than the bartender. Would you believe at least 100 parts in all? Call him The King of Cameos, or the champion of small parts of an Ant-sized dimension.

Before I tell you about my meeting with Stan Lee back in 1974, allow me to provide a brief outline about my introduction into the world of comic books. It started in the summer of 1949 when I discovered the E.C. comics of Bill Gaines. It began with his horror trio: *The Vault of Horror*, hosted by the Vault-Keeper; *The Haunt of Fear*, hosted by the Old Witch, and *Tales from the Crypt*, hosted by the Crypt Keeper. These horror comics were establishing a new trend in story-telling and artwork. One of the artists, Graham Ingels, became better known as "Ghastly Graham" for his horror artwork.

I also picked up my first copies of *Frontline Combat* and *Two-Fisted Tales*, war comic books written by cartoonist Harvey Kurtzman (who would go on to create *Mad Comics* in 1952). Unlike previous war comics, these depicted various phases of historic warfare (past and present) from a point-of-view that was quite often disturbing in its realism. There was also *Crime Suspenstories* and *Shock Suspenstories* which sometimes even dealt with racial issues.

Stan Lee's cameo of a Hugh Hefner-type playboy in "Iron Man" (2008), the first movie in the Marvel Cinematic Universe feature film series.

I suddenly came across similar comic books bearing the Atlas News Company emblem and all done under the editorship of . . . yep, Stan Lee. It was obvious to me that the war, science fiction and horror/suspense Atlases were spin-offs of the EC comics. But I didn't care. They were close seconds and to me were a compelling read.

Then in 1954 came a political investigation of comic books through Senator Estes Kefauver's sub-committee. Rather than allow censorship from outside, the comics industry imposed its own Comics Code Authority and for the next few years comic books deteriorated.

And then in the early 1960s, Stan Lee was responsible for creating what would become one of the most popular of all comic-book creations, the Fantastic Four. Marvel went on to create the Hulk, the Amazing Spider-Man, Iron Man, Thor, the X-Men, and many other characters, introducing a thoroughly unique universe. Lee had also allowed his characters to be less than perfect. After all, even a superhero must have a few weaknesses. And now, instead of being Atlas comics, they were known as Marvel Comics. And the self-imposed code was buried in the deep hole in which it belonged, and good comics returned like never before.

So, comic book fans of America, give credit to Stan Lee for revitalizing the superhero genre and restoring originality. And now journey with me backward through time to October 1974, when I first interviewed Lee for the San Francisco Chronicle.

Spider-Man Swings from TV Cartoons to Feature Film (at least Stan hoped so)

Spider-Man, that nemesis of the underworld who literally spins webs to snare the forces of evil, has been the luckiest of superheroes to make the transition from four-color comic-book pages to film. And the spinning all began in the brain of Stan Lee back in 1961 when he was creating a new line of characters under the Marvel Comics imprint. Spider-Man made it to television before the decade was over – a Saturday morning cartoon series with animated action that matched the bizarre comic-book plots created by Lee and his staff.

This very month "Spidey" will become – to the delight of the younger set – a recurring figure on TV's "The Electric Company," a program designed to help children fight the forces of forgetfulness as they face new studies in grammar and spelling.

Morgan Freeman and puppeteer-dancer Danny Seagren as Spidey in one of 29 "Spidey Super Stories" on the children's program "The Electric Company" between 1974 and 1977.

According to Stan Lee, Spider-Man is ready for his greatest leap of all – into his own full-length film, to be produced by Universal Studios with Lee functioning as associate producer.

"I'm here to serve as an all-around spokesman for the comic-book industry," Lee tells me as we sit down for an interview. "San Francisco is just one of the cities I'm visiting to alert the citizenry that Hollywood has made a wise decision to make Spidey the subject of a live-action-adventure film. For Marvel, this is a major breakthrough."

Lee, a tall, slender man who always seems on the verge of exploding with nervous energy, even now at the age of 51, rolls on with enthusiasm.

"As a rule, superheroes are not considered popular fodder for the screen. Superman made it in the serials, as did Captain America. Batman and Robin were a big hit on TV and in feature films, but they really were not superheroes."

Although casting has not yet been decided, Lee told me that he would like to see a "young Dustin Hoffman" in the title role. "Dustin might have been right a few years ago, but now he's a little too old. I have some other casting ideas, but don't want to reveal them until I've contacted more actors." Naturally, Lee hopes to have a hand in the shaping of the screenplay. And he has every right. He has been writing and plotting stories and creating new characters for comic books since 1939.

Life started for him not as Stan Lee but as Stanley Martin Lieber. He grew up in Manhattan and the Bronx, developing an early-in-life love for writing. By 1941 he had helped to create his first superhero character, And he proved to be the fledgling staffer at Marvel who whacked and crunched Captain America and Submariner to victory during the patriotic years of World War II.

That phase of his career was interrupted while he served in the Signal Corps. After the war he was the executive editor who produced *Astonishing Tales, Adventures into Weird Worlds* and other Atlas comics during the horror-sodden 1950s. He also worked overtime to establish a rapport between readers and artists to create a new world of fandom.

I ask Lee to give me his opinion of how he felt about the turbulent 1950s. "Comics," he replies, "were exciting until 1954, when those Senate

hearings led to the self-imposed Code within the industry. After that, comics pretty much died out. Even superheroes were out of vogue. Then, one day, we wrote something called *The Fantastic Four*. We related these new superheroes to every-day problems. What happens when you can't pay your rent? Or your costume tears and you don't have the materials to mend it?

"Well, from that first issue new ideas and characters gradually grew. And suddenly something fresh and exciting was happening. The college kids were the first to pick up on it. And we found ourselves writing on two levels. The youngsters could enjoy them for their fast pace, color and action. The older readers could enjoy them for their satire and social commentary. It was a renaissance in the comics world, and it's still going on today.

"After writing a few hundred stories," Lee tells me, "you realize your mind works like a movie camera. You see it unfold with all the various camera angles, as you might see a film unfold on the silver screen. You even begin to think after a while in terms of fast cutting. It's fantastic what the movie form can do for your imagination–and for your writing."

Lee is the only comics kingdom editor-publisher who has turned himself into a celebrity through the power of the press. For years his name adorned the splash title pages ("Startling Story by Scintillating Stan Lee") and always Lee signed his chatty, personable editorials, concluding his promise of a ton of action in the next issues with the phrase 'Nuff said.

Lee lectures at least twice a month on campuses across the nation. As publisher he no longer has time to write and edit, but he tends to such Marvel affairs as paperbacks, cartoon shows, fan clubs, games and assorted merchandising. Now he is delighted to be entering the world of movie production.

My conclusion: Stan Lee is an individual of rich paradox – while he devotes his energies to exploiting, and expounding on, his comic books (and they have been of all genres, from war to suspense to horror to love to Western), he never really wants you to take him all that seriously. For example, he begins his new book entitled "Origins of Marvel Comics" with "Greetings, culture lovers," and refuses to remove his tongue from his cheek for the rest of that book. "There's a new wave of excitement in comics today," he claims, as our interview comes to an end. "And the forthcoming Spider-Man movie should prove how it is affecting other media. You're going to be seeing a lot of innovative things now that the comic book is no longer looked upon as inferior junk."

And Lee promises (just as he does in the pages of his magazines) that "there's going to be tons of adventure and excitement when Spider-Man swings across the giant screen."

'Nuff said!

Oops, not quite 'nuff said! Not just yet. Why? 'Cause that Spider-Man movie Stan Lee dreamed of making never happened. At least not back in the 1970s. The project died the following year and Spider-Man did not make his way to the big screen for many years to come. But hold it! There was a moment of breakthrough, and it came in September of 1977 when Spider-Man escaped the web of Hollywood uncertainty and clawed his way onto the little screen. You know, TV. Not like today when you might have a giant screen stretching to 60-some inches, but back in the days when you were lucky if your TV screen made it to 25 inches.

Comic book writer Robert Napton with Stan Lee. See page 17 for more about Robert.

"The Amazing Spider-Man" would prove to be popular TV but would last for only two seasons, rumors abounding that Stan Lee was not happy with the development of the character by producer Daniel R. Goodman. It was "too juvenile" for Lee's taste. Oddly, the pilot aired in September 1977, but as a series did not begin on a weekly basis until April 1978. And that's when the star of the series, Nicholas Hammond, paid a promotional visit to San Francisco. And we sat down to talk it over.

The Web of Success
That Clings to Spider-Man

The Amazing Spider-Man first appeared in comic books in 1963 as part of a new superheroes' trend created by Stan Lee, major editor of Marvel Comics. Almost overnight the wall-climber became a four-color sensation. For the problems of Peter Parker (Spider-Man's alter ego) were the problems of reality: allergies, identity crises, shyness around pretty girls, job frustrations, etc.

Since being bitten by that radioactive spider 15 years ago, Peter Parker aka Spider-Man has grown into one of the most popular superheroes in the world. If anything, he is more widely read in foreign countries than in America. The current comic book has a readership of 70 million–and that's in 52 languages.

Now Charles Fries Productions has produced a miniseries entitled "The Amazing Spider-Man," coming in the wake of a pilot film first presented on CBS last September. (As a feature film, the pilot was a phenomenally popular Columbia foreign release, breaking box-office records in Hong Kong, Manila, Singapore and Kuala Lumpur.)

The series (which might continue if the first five episodes prove as popular as the pilot) stars Nicholas Hammond, 27, who projects enough boyish good looks and naivete to pass as the younger Parker. "I've always been aware of Spider-Man on the newsstands," says Hammond (above) during our luncheon together. "But I never followed the comics with any great zeal. Probably because I've spent most of my conscious life as an actor and just never found time for comic books. What I like most is that the stories deal 75 per cent of the time with the day-to-day problems of Peter Parker, an unremarkable young man when he isn't out fighting crime."

When Hammond does don the costume of Spider-Man, it is a simple outfit. As Hammond describes it, "It should be simple, for after all, Peter designed it himself without the aid of fashion coordinators. It consists mainly of a Spandex-isotonic material made into a huge body stocking painted red with black webbing. Spider-Man also wears a special utility belt containing a liquified latex that hardens, when it comes in contact with oxygen, into a strong synthetic cord."

That's not Nicholas Hammond! That's stuntman Fred Waugh, a former circus performer who perfected the dazzling art of climbing skyscrapers and other tall buildings.

This "web" is capable of suspending a falling body in midair or entangling attackers in a nightmarish meshing. (You can almost hear a villain saying, "This is another nice mesh you've gotten me into!")

All scenes for "The Amazing Spider-Man" are filmed on Los Angeles locations and, according to Hammond, "it's unbelievable how fast a crowd will gather once word gets out we're filming. We've had groups of 700-800 people hanging around the edges. What's amazing is, everyone knows who Spider-Man is. We were filming in a Chicano community and standing side by side were a Cal Tech lab technician and a 6-year-old boy, and both of them were in equal awe of the character. I guess you might say he's an equal opportunity fantasy hero."

One of Hammond's favorite moments came when he met Stan Lee. "Lee thinks he's Peter Parker, for he created Parker in his own fantasy image. As a Walter Mitty type who suddenly acquires phenomenal powers. He was very pleased when he saw we were doing the show according to the gospel of Stan Lee."

Part of the Stan Lee-gospel is to avoid campiness. "It worked well for Batman but there's no point in going over that old turf again. We're going another way; we want to produce a show for those who want to believe in fantasy heroes. Unlike the comic books, which are full of arch-supervillains, we're trying to deal with crime on a fairly realistic level, with good strong supporting actors, such as Theodore Bikel, Alessandro Rey and Robert Alda. I know we're based on a comic book, but realism is still the key word. We use no phony studio sets and no tricks. It's all out there for real."

Including the sequences in which Spider-Man climbs up the sides of walls? Hammond nods. "We have a former Ringling Brothers circus perform, a stunt man named Fred Waugh, who uses special harnesses and riggings. So when you see a man climbing up or down the side of a building, that's Waugh actually doing it."

Hammond identifies with Peter Parker because "he can't have any friends and maintain his secret identity as Spider-Man. He can't even have a normal sex life. He's a national hero, yet he's a recluse. He's instantly recognized by the public but he can't tell anyone who he is. He leads a life of frustrated deception." As for Hammond's own personal life, now that Spider-Man has projected him into prominence, "I realize I've been magnified yet I can't look forward to my loss of privacy. Still, I'm aware of the power of television and the recognition certainly makes me feel worthwhile."

Hammond spent most of his childhood in Paris, where his father served with NATO. His mother, Eileen Bennett, worked on the London stage and encouraged her son to follow in her footsteps. Hammond has been acting since he was nine. "I had the distinction of being the fair-haired lad who dropped a rock on Piggy in 'Lord of the Flies.'"

Before playing Peter Parker, Hammond was a member of the von Trapp family in "The Sound of Music" and Robert in "Lord of the Flies."

At the time, he was getting $10 a week. "I've never been as rich before or since. And with no parents around on that Puerto Rican island where we filmed, that was the life for me. I was the only boy out of 32 who continued to act." Of all his roles outside of Spider-Man, his most famous would-be Friedrich, one of the von Trapp children in the successful "The Sound of Music" motion picture. "So far it's been a wonderful career and life, and now with the debut of Spider-Man . . . who could ask for anything more?"

"The Amazing Spider-Man" lasted for only 13 episodes. Stan Lee later admitted he had never been happy with the series; in fact he was quoted as "hating it." Hammond continued to appear in supporting roles in TV series until he moved to Australia in the 1980s, where he continued his career in a variety of movies and TV shows, including a scene-chewing role in Quentin Tarantino's "Once Upon a Time in Hollywood." But never as another superhero.

How Comic Book Artists Can Impact Our Lives

My final meeting with Stan Lee occurs in August, 2013, when Lee comes to AT&T Park (now Oracle Park) in San Francisco for "Superheroes and Comics Night." My son Russ Stanley, Senior Vice-President of Ticket Sales for The San Francisco Giants, invites me and his mom Erica to attend. We arrive early enough that Russ takes us to meet Lee for a private moment before the late-afternoon "Question & Answer Session" begins.

I remind Lee of our 1974 meeting and rant on for a while about how big a fan I had been of his 1950s line of Atlas comic books. In fact, I am able to reveal to him for the first time that one of my favorite artists in the Atlas war and horror comics had been artist Russ Heath. Lee begins his own rant about Heath's excellent artwork, and I remind him of how memorable Heath was in handling the comic book series *Sea Devils*, among others.

I had especially been impressed, I tell Lee, with the way in which Heath wrote his name in the opening panels of his stories. The R U S S spread of letters . . . The H E A T H spread of letters. And it is at this moment that I reveal to Lee for the first time that my wife and I had named our son Russ after Russ Heath. Not Russell, just plain Russ. The way Heath had spelled it in his magnificent comic-book splash panels.

It was a true moment of revelation. Russ Heath . . . Russ Stanley, the very man who had sneaked me into the room to chat with Stan Lee.

Lee beams, shaking Russ' hand anew.

Isn't it amazing how comic books can have an ever-lasting impact on our lives?

'Nuff said!

I met Russ Heath at several comic book shows and always shared my enthusiasm for his artwork in the genres of war and fantasy.

AFTERWORDS

Stan Lee would return to AT&T Park three more times to make personal appearances. I would see him one final time at the Silicon Valley Comic Con in 2018 when he was the show's leading personality. He would die only months later at the age of 95 in Los Angeles. Behind the scenes the latter years of his life had been filled with legal issues and domestic turbulence, but he still remains one of the great Marvels of the comic-book world.

Now I can say it one final time:

'Nuff said!

December 1980:
Max the Gentle in the Presence of Ming the Merciless – Both Smiling

IT IS DECEMBER 1980 and it is a mildly chilly evening in San Francisco's Ghirardelli Square. Max Von Sydow sits quietly on a plaza bench, bemusedly watching an accordionist on roller skates as he whiplashes back and forth in a clownish fashion singing "Jingle Bells." Von Sydow–looking lean, ascetic, austere and too unobtrusive to be an internationally known movie actor–applauds politely, makes a pleasant comment about the skater's red Santa Claus cap and drops a folded piece of money into a proffered canvas bag.

Is this gentlemanly, kind soul the same man who portrays Ming the Merciless–the Grand Ruler of the planet Mongo and all its surrounding kingdoms–in Dino De Laurentiis' new space fantasy extravaganza "Flash Gordon"? The same Ming who is oozing with evil and decadence, a perverse glint forever in his hooded eyes, a satanic snarl pursing his tyrannical lips? The empiric Ming, playing God-ruler over his vast realm of extraterrestrial (and Earthly) charges?

Von Sydow, faced with the accusation, permits a gentle smile to enlighten his face and bows his head in mock shame. "Rarely," he begins, his soft, low-key voice tinged with a mixture of Swedish and mid-Atlantic English accents, "have I played characters larger than life. Oh, there was Jesus Christ in 'The Greatest Story Ever Told,' and certainly I've done my share of stage performances that required considerable energy and bravura, but I think you can say this is my first heavy-heavy villain in a strongly commercial sci-fi thriller made for, I believe, $20 million."

Max Von Sydow as Jesus Christ

And why was he persuaded to deviate so sharply into new acting spaces, after years of calmer, more soothing film roles? "Ming is really nothing more than an updated version of Faust's Mephistopheles. A demon in dictatorial robes with a bald head and an evil moustache.

"I realize it is a surprising piece of casting and I'm not at all unhappy I performed the way I did." Von Sydow did not, he admits, start out feeling so positive when De Laurentiis first approached him bearing the Lorenzo Semple Jr. screenplay, based on Michael Allen's adaptation.

"I was not impressed with the writing," he declares, nursing a glass of Dry Sack on the rocks, a sherry blending different grapes, in Ghirardelli's Mandarin Restaurant, to which he and I have moved after our outdoor adventure with the skating Santa Claus.

(As a presence von Sydow remains unobtrusive and unassuming, always answering questions quickly and directly but leaving one with the feeling that underneath is a very private individual guarding his replies with a gentleman's finesse.)

"I was not impressed with that script," he declares once again. "But they reassured me the filmed version would be funnier, more satirical. I was impressed when I met the director, Michael Hodges, who had directed 'The Terminal Man' and I was impressed with the fabulous sketches of the palace set and the imaginative costuming. Those things swayed me."

What a far cry, this supervillain, from the sensitive, enigmatic, pained characters (common to the Ingmar Bergman canon) for which he has become world-known: the errant Knight who plays chess with Death in "The Seventh Seal"; the revenge-seeking father in "The Virgin Spring"; the frightened fisherman in "Winter Light"; the garage attendant in "Wild Strawberries"; the pensive man of Kafkaesque legerdemain in "The Magician"; and the painter in "Hour of the Wolf."

In addition to our Ghirardelli Square meeting for a Sunday Chronicle piece, Max Von Sydow came to Channel 2, where we did a second interview on the "Creature Features" set.

Black-hearted Ming the Merciless may be galaxies away from these curious, penetrating character portrayals, but the dark dastard could mean new prestige and power for von Sydow in the world of movies, so effective and stylish is his performance. What a joy to behold villainy displayed with such cunning.

Ironically, Ming as a comic-strip character (created in 1934 by cartoonist Alex Raymond) was totally unknown to von Sydow when approached by De Laurentiis. Nor had he seen any of the three Universal-produced "Flash Gordon" serials starring Larry "Buster" Crabbe and Charles Middleton as Ming. (They played on Saturday afternoons, chapter by chapter, from 1936 through 1940.)

"The reason I hadn't seen them? They had never played in my native Sweden," he explains. Thus there were no conscious antecedents in preparing to play Ming. It was not until production was half over that he finally had time to sit down and review some of the serial chapters. "I was delighted to discover how well they stood up despite their period naivete and production crudities. You see, I can't Ming too seriously. He's a fantasy figure.

Charles Middleton as the original Ming the Merciless in the 1936 movie serial "Flash Gordon."

THE CAREER THAT DRIPPED WITH HORROR

"He stands for insidious, diabolical evil. Inside I react to him as Flash Gordon reacted to him. I pity him as a sick psychopathic man. And yet he's far less dangerous than, say, Adolf Hitler. There is greater danger in stupidity and indifference than in intentional evil. And Hitler, take my word, was utterly stupid. He had no connection with human emotions. That causes more harm than deviltry or pulling wings off flies."

"Flash Gordon" was produced over a difficult six-month period (from August 1979 through early 1980) at Elstree and Shepperton Studios in London. A huge airplane hangar west of London was rented for the flying hawkmen sequences. The palace scenes, he explains, took weeks to complete, they were so complicated. Von Sydow's make-up took about 90 minutes per production-day to apply.

Since completing "Flash Gordon" von Sydow has made a John Huston film, "Escape to Victory," in which he portrays sympathetic German major Karl von Steiner, who organizes a team of British POW soccer players led by Michael Caine to fight a team of German soccer champions.

Von Sydow chooses to stay away from his native Sweden during the winter months, living instead in Rome with his wife Christina (an actress he met during their stage days together in Stockholm.) "Italy," he explains, "has all the things we miss so much in Sweden: Good weather, climate and people. Nice food and wine. Beautiful countryside. Yes, the Swedish have many of those things but it takes them a while to show you."

Ingmar Bergman, says von Sydow, "is the best, the ideal director. He knows the craft of making films so thoroughly. And he knows so much about people. He has a wonderful intuition. Sometimes I feel he can read my mind. He doesn't talk much. He never analyzes the characters in his stories. He might tell you a story indirectly related to the subject and let you infer the rest. Sometimes he merely hints at the focal point of the action. I've seen changes in Bergman. In the earlier years he was obsessed with religious matters, even when not dealing with religion directly. There's been themes of fate, trust and distrust, the loss of faith. Gradually Ingmar has learned to deal with more personal relationships and his lack of communication."

Max von Sydow, an only child, was born in Lund, Sweden, in 1929. His academic father was a specialist in Scandanavian folk lore, a man of "considerable fantasy and imagination," according to von Sydow. His mother was a public-school teacher. Being close to the Denmark border, young Max saw a steady stream of refugees during World War II.

"I was a happy child but there were times when I would get lonely. I think that was the reason I took to acting in high school. I was shy, I didn't express myself well, and acting was a legitimate way of correcting that."

From 1948-51 von Sydow attended the Stockholm Royal Dramatic Theater. It was there he learned "to understand and study people, real and fictional. I came to understand myself as well. To always be true to the character based on the author's concept. I still have my deficits. I still work slowly; I need much time for preparation. I'm still weak at improvisation."

After several years of low pay on Sweden's municipal stages, and making Swedish films (none of which were exported), he was "discovered" by Bergman. "Seventh Seal" (1957) came two years later, followed by a string of Bergman films that became internationally popular among the "art film" crowd. In 1962 George Stevens brought von Sydow to America to play Jesus Christ. Everyone warned him it would be the birth/death of an American career, but despite the film's sluggish pacing–on the screen and at the box office–he stayed to make another turkey, a 1965 action film called "The Reward," which had limited play dates. "It was a strange, impossible part for me," recalls von Sydow. "The director fought with the producer and decided to cut out most of the dialogue. But I loved co-starring with Yvette Mimieux." That didn't finish off von Sydow, either. He stayed to thrive in "Hawaii," "The Kremlin Letter," "Night Visitor" and "Three Days of the Condor," occasionally returning to Sweden if Bergman needed him.

His role as Father Merrin in "The Exorcist" (see below), later repeated in "Exorcist II: The Heretic," brought him more exposure and recognition than all his other American films together. "It was an entertaining picture but the negativism and destruction scared me more than the Demon or Beelzebub. I think something happened to me between reading the script and seeing the finished film. I was disturbed by the fact that so many people went to see what happened to the little girl and got carried away with the special effects. Is it a scary symptom of something that's happening throughout the world? Have we grown to hate children?"

Theater and movies, he adds, "still can increase universality between individuals, dealing with problems that are common to us all. The only danger are producers who abuse their privilege." Although Ming the Merciless meets an horrendous-albeit-fitting demise on screen in the last few minutes of the film, there are hints that he or his spirit lives on, and a question mark coming after "The End" intimates a sequel. Would von Sydow consider a sequel? "I always base my final decision on the screenplay and the people involved. Given those factors, yes. I would play Ming again."

AFTERWORDS

Although there would be no sequel to replay Ming the Merciless, Von Sydow's career in motion pictures and TV series continued nonstop. In the wake of Ming, he portrayed King Osric opposite Arnold Schwarzenegger in "Conan the Barbarian." He would also appear in "The Tudors" (2002) and "Star Wars Episode VII: The Force Awakens" (2015). Playing the Three-Eyed Raven in "Game of Thrones" (2016) would earn him a Primetime Emmy Award nomination. He was living in France when he died in March 2020 at the age of 90.

FLASH!!!
IN THE NEXT EXCITING CHAPTER
YOU'LL MEET THE ORIGINAL MR. GORDON!

A FLASH-Y FELLOW FROM SERIALS PAST STILL HAS DASH IN THE 20TH CENTURY

"HEY JOHN, JUST CALL ME BUSTER"

Yeah, that's me interviewing Larry "Buster" Crabbe, famous for playing Flash Gordon, on my "Creature Features" set in 1980. Unfortunately, a tape of the interview was never saved and it is lost for all eternity. However, before that in November, 1976, I had met Crabbe for the first time for a San Francisco Chronicle interview, which did survive in my story files. And here it is.

THE MAN who opens the door is familiar in some ways, unfamiliar in others. The eyeglasses and mustache are new accoutrements, but the curly blond hair and affable smile are immutable after 40 years. Once the mind's eye has spanned those four decades, taking into account natural physical aging and the fact no make-up is involved, there is no mistaking that the man before me is Flash Gordon himself, Larry "Buster" Crabbe.

Buster, as he has been professionally known since entering the film world in 1932, leads the way into an unpretentious hotel room which barely has enough space for a bed, let alone two human beings. He slides his 6'1" frame into a chair near a window looking west over San Francisco and pours out two glasses of red wine.

Rays of late afternoon light spill across Crabbe, drawing attention to his remarkable physical condition at 68. He's still about 180 pounds. He's well-tanned and solid around the middle.

He looks relaxed and is dressed relaxed in a sports shirt adorned with blossoming roses. Crabbe, although officially retired and living comfortably in Scottsdale, Ariz., is far from being forgotten.

Crabbe posing with a co-star from 1933's "King of the Jungle," in which he portrayed Kaspa the Lion Man.

Jean Rogers portrayed Dale Arden in two of the "Flash Gordon" serials. "It was a great training ground," she said, and went on to work at three Hollywood studios.

He has just written a new book for Playboy Press, "Energistics," an exercising and dieting program for older men and women, and he is still cheered and cherished wherever they play reruns of the old "Flash Gordon" serials.

Crabbe, it quickly becomes apparent, is an incessant talker and recalls every phase of his career in minutest detail–names, places, dates–as vividly as yesterday. He starts at the beginning, quickly recounting his birth in Oakland, his upbringing in Hawaii where he grew to love sports, swimming the most. While studying law at USC, he qualified for the 1932 Olympics. "Paramount was preparing 'King of the Jungle' and loaded about 20 of us into a bus and took us to the studio for screen tests. Who would end up playing Kaspa the Lion Man? We threw javelins, pitched rocks and stood around beefcaking it up in loin cloths. I went on to win an Olympic Gold Medal in the 400-meter freestyle by one-tenth of a second. That fraction changed my life. Paramount cast me in the film, which was a ripoff of Tarzan."

Later Crabbe was to portray the apeman in "Tarzan the Fearless." "It was awful," he recalls. "No production values at all, compared to the MGM series that starred Johnny Weissmuller. Funny how today everyone remembers it. For me it was embarrassing."

Not so "Flash Gordon," the first in a trilogy of serials released in 1936. "I thought it was fine as a comic strip but I doubted the public would accept it as a film. Fortunately, I was wrong. We made the serial quickly, doing as many as 85 set-ups a day. But Universal was pumping a lot of money into the project and it looked really good."

It was the studio's second biggest money-maker that year, Deanna Durbin's "Three Smart Girls" being the first. "Universal didn't make a 'Flash Gordon' sequel right away, because it just kept repeating the original in theaters, making plenty of money. We finally did a second version in 1938 ["Flash Gordon's Trip to Mars"] and a third ["Flash Gordon Conquers the Universe"] in 1940. By then they were looking shoddy and interest was waning." Crabbe also did the 1939 multi-chaptered "Buck Rogers," which was never well-received.

Crabbe was never on the grab by other studios for A-rated movies. He remained in the B-league in the 1940s, making 42

In "Tarzan the Fearless" Buster Crabbe co-starred with Julie Bishop, who portrayed the daughter of a historian studying African tribes who has been kidnapped by a worshipper of evil.

"Billy the Kid" Western programmers for PRC, one of the cheapest production companies of the era. By the last year (1946) the producer was turning them out in only four days. Crabbe couldn't take it any longer and decided to hit the saddle and ride away.

THE CAREER THAT DRIPPED WITH HORROR

Crabbe portrayed Billy "the Kid" Carson in 42 low-budget oaters with Al "Fuzzy" St. John (left) as his comic sidekick. The movies were cranked out by the Poverty Row studio PRC from 1941 through 1946.

"Out of all those oaters," he estimates, "I think the first ones under producer Sig Newfield were 'not bad.' But the rest . . ."

In the late 1940s, with low-budget feature films jeopardized by the coming of television, Crabbe formed his own Aquacade and went to Europe with a troupe of 75 aquatic specialists, many of them in the skimpiest costumes Buster could dare to have designed. The show had its moments, and Crabbe returned to New York in 1951, realizing new possibilities in TV.

"For three years I did a live TV show, re-running my old Western movies and talking to the youngsters half-an-hour each night." Always willing to risk new enterprises, Crabbe opened Camp Meenahga on Zaraneck Lake in the Adirondack Mountains. "We had 127 acres, 16 buildings, sailing, scuba diving, water sports, camp-outs." He maintained his interest in the camp until 1969.

In 1954 Crabbe made one more return to acting in "Captain Gallant," a French Foreign Legion action series co-starring his son Cuffy which was produced on location in Morocco and France. The series ran for several years and is still shown in some syndicated markets. Today Crabbe (below with Charles Middleton) operates Cascade Industries (manufacturers of the Buster Crabbe Swimming Pool) and he often speaks to college students about the good old days he had in Hollywood, interspersing his comments with "Flash Gordon" film clips.

Crabbe appeared as Brigadier Gordon with Gil Gerard in a 1979 episode of "Buck Rogers in the 25th Century."

Crabbe still swims daily and he works out at least once a week. "I don't go in much for bodybuilding–just toning up the muscles and keeping them from atrophying."

Leaping from his chair, Crabbe reaches for his suitcase as though Emperor Ming was leveling his paralyzer ray at him. "Excuse me. I've got to meet my daughter for dinner. Then I've got to catch a plane back to L.A. Or should I take a rocketship?" It's obvious that even at the age of 68 Crabbe is a man who loves to get into the swim of things.

AFTERWORDS

Yeah, that's me with Buster Crabbe in 1980, right after our now-lost "Creature Features" interview. We were doing a special show held in San Jose and I had the pleasure of introducing him to a large audience and afterward we shared a table selling our stuff. Buster Crabbe did very little acting after our meeting. He played a lawman in the Fred Olen Ray zombie film "The Alien Dead." His last film was "The Comeback Trail" in 1982.

A year later he died in Scottsdale, Ariz., of a heart attack at the age of 85. He summed up his career with the following: "If you're lucky, you bring a little excitement to the world. If you're really lucky, you lend your fame to worthwhile causes -- as I was recently privileged to do by raising money for the Olympics, or promoting healthy activities. Apart from that, you're just another human being, trying to make a living."

Crabbe clad as the star of the TV series "Captain Gallant of the Foreign Legion," which presented 48 episodes from 1955-1957.

THE CAREER THAT DRIPPED WITH HORROR

It's fascinating to me that one writer has accomplished so much in the categories of horror, fantasy and science-fiction. Yet Stephen King keeps producing new books nonstop. I'm also fascinated when I travel back through time to a day four decades ago when I met King and he unloaded on me all his feelings about the art of writing novels. It belonged in a time and place all its own. How he would feel today, having accomplished so many projects, would probably be totally different. So, jump into the time machine with me and let's whirl backward through time to September 1979 when King was . . . but wait, here he comes now. Now as in Eternal Now.

MEET THE HEIR APPARENT TO RAY BRADBURY AND THE WRITER THAT HIS READERS LOVE -- AS LONG AS HE SCARES THE HELL INTO THEM

EVERYTHING he writes in the horror genre, it seems, becomes instant first-class fodder for the movies. In 1974 when he sold his first novel, "Carrie," it quickly sold over two million copies, was translated into seven languages and was adapted into a superb fright film by director Brian de Palma, with Sissy Spacek in the titular role as a teenager who unleashes her telekinetic talents at her senior prom. For weeks, everyone was talking about the "bucket of blood" scene, the Crucifixion moment and the "hand-from-the-grave" sequence.

From the moment the viewers began leaping from their seats and screaming their lungs out, Stephen King was a writer in vogue. A novelist in demand. He wrote his second book, "Salem's Lot," a nifty variation on the Dracula theme, and sold it as a miniseries to TV with Tobe Hooper ("The Texas Chainsaw Massacre") directing and James Mason starring. Not too shabby for a young kid from Bangor, Maine.

"Here's Johnny!"

King wrote his third book, "The Shining," the story of a haunted hotel in the Colorado Mountains and a child gifted with precognition, and it was gobbled up by Stanley Kubrick, who is now in post-production in Europe and expects to have the film with Jack Nicholson (right) on the market by next summer.

(Stand fast! Next up after this piece you will meet the haunted hotel's bartender, Joe Turkel. He will pour you a drink of movie history you will never forget.)

With "Night Shift," an anthology of King's early stories from *Cavalier, Penthouse* and other male-oriented magazines, King did something totally startling, maybe even shocking!

THE CAREER THAT DRIPPED WITH HORROR

STARTLING MYSTERY STORIES

ACME   Fall No. 6

UNUSUAL - EERIE - STRANGE   50¢

MY LADY
OF THE
TUNNEL
by
ARTHUR J. BURKS
•
Jules de Grandin
in
THE
DRUID'S
SHADOW
by
SEABURY QUINN
•
DEATH
FROM
WITHIN
by
STERLING S. CRAMER
•
BEVERLY HAAF
ANNA HUNGER

The Glass
Floor

by Stephen King

This is the digest-sized magazine (1967) that I took to our meeting. King signed it, explaining it was the first piece of fiction he ever sold. The rest is history.

He sold the book not once but twice–two separate sets of short stories to two different producers. He further negotiated himself into one of the deals by writing a trilogy script for NBC.

Hold it! Wait! Who is this Stephen King and why are they saying all those great things about him? What is there about King that makes greenhorn novelists, even hardened professionals, drool with envy? Why have critics called him the heir apparent to Ray Bradbury? John McDonald, in his unrestrained introduction to "Night Shift," wrote: "Insofar as story is concerned, and pleasure is concerned, there are not enough Stephen Kings to go around."

For one thing, King knows his characters and how to make them suffer. The pages of his books drip with pain and passion and a sense of real people despite the surrounding horrors. For another, he's studied all the classics and knows suspense, terror and tempo. King deals with images and horrors that we're all familiar with from our exposure to movies and TV, but he twists the cliches to make them work in fresh, shocking, and unique ways.

King's book, "Dead Zone," is another blood-and-sweat tale about a young man (symbolizing Everyman, since he is named Johnny Smith) who possesses the talent of precognition, and who realizes the U.S. government may topple if a certain political candidate takes office.

Does Smith have the right to become a Lee Harvey Oswald? A provocative theme that makes "Dead Zone" the most significant–if not the scariest–of King's books.

"Dead Zone" is already on the best-selling list when the young author (32 years to be exact) arrives in San Francisco as part of a nationwide promotional tour. Just a year ago a massive science-fiction novel by King, "The Stand," was issued at 823 pages, so I ask King how he manages to be so prolific, turning out one epic novel per year. He shrugs in his disarming, boyish fashion and looks about as frightened as a tranquilized poodle dog. "I write only two hours a day, but I guess the secret is that I write every day, the only exceptions being Christmas and my birthday, September 21."

I point out that many of his books deal with young people possessed of strange, eerie talents and I wonder aloud if this was a reflection back on his own childhood. "I had a happy childhood," King responds, "or at least that's the way I look back on it. I was never voted the most likely to succeed in my class but neither was I the outcast that Carrie was. There's something you see as a student, a kind of sociological stratum that goes down, especially in high school, which is the last place where young people are open enough in their emotions to really let go and do a number on someone who doesn't fit in.

"There're always two or three who're picked on, who're driven away. I've known Carries from both sides of the desk. I knew her as a student and I saw the same kind of girl when I taught at high school in Hampden, Maine.

"I used parapsychology as a means to an end, a tool for fiction. I first read a piece in *Life Magazine* about a house in upstate New York where crucifixes, crosses and pictures of Jesus flew through the air and bottles of holy water exploded–but only when a young girl was in the house. I carried that idea in my mind five or six years and decided psychokinesis, the ability to move objects mentally, would be a good talent to give a girl being picked on. 'Carrie' is the-worm-turns kind of story and if the worm turns, you must give her some kind of power.

"I admit that I deal a lot with children in my books," continues King. "It's a sappy, romantic idea but I think that children are good; they make a perfect foil for evil. Children are innately powerful. The function of growing older is really a function of developing tunnel-vision until you see your life only on a certain track. Whereas kids see everything and feel everything across a wide range.

"That's one of the reasons so few of us remember what childhood was actually like, because this tunnel-vision closes in. If you and I saw a drunk in the gutter, we'd walk right past because we're busy and too caught up in our lives to care. But to a child, that drunk in the gutter would fascinate him. It would become the focal point of his life. To use a child is to open up that tunnel-vision. Sensations and fears become part of the character, and are conveyed to the reader."

One portion of "Dead Zone" has Johnny Smith solving a series of murders with his strange talent, and King admits that this was inspired by Peter Hurkos, the psychic detective. "Actually, it's another tool, just like psychokinesis for Carrie. I had known about Hurkos' career, and I'd followed the new stories of his triumphs and failures. The idea that this man could possess some strange talent . . . to be able to touch objects and clothing and become a sort of human bloodhound or to know the future. The possibilities seemed limitless.

"Suppose you or I could see the future. Most people think they would go to the racetrack and make a fortune and spend the rest of their lives being very rich and happy. But what if you shook someone's hand and saw he was going to die in 24 hours? The more I worked with the idea, the more I saw that the man would become a freak. People would be afraid to touch him. He would lose contact with humanity. No matter how good the results for the rest of the world, they would be dreadful for Johnny."

I ask King about the inspiration behind "Salem's Lot." "I wrote my first vampire story, 'Night Doth Come,' when I was nine years old. Then I read 'Dracula' when I was 11 and for years, I carried the idea of the vampire against the modern world. Later, when I was teaching a horror course in high school, I asked myself, what would happen if Dracula came to New York City? Would he be run down by a taxi? Would he drink blood in the Bronx?

"Then I decided to have all the triumphant forces in Stoker's book–rationalism, science, light–defeated by a modern vampire."

King was born in Portland, Maine, and was raised by his mother Nellie Ruth after his father, a merchant seaman, deserted the family. An odd thing happened when he was a child. He was walking with a school friend when his friend was struck down by a train. He would later claim to have no memory of the incident, which may have had some effect years later on his writing.

Eventually he graduated in 1970 from the University of Maine with a B.A. Degree in English. He discovered the E.C. horror comics published by William Gaines and became a devoted fan of fantasy writer H. P. Lovecraft as published by Arkham House books under the editorship of August Derleth (see right). "Once I found Lovecraft," King tells me, "I knew I wanted to write."

But lean years were ahead as he married and had three children. He finally took that teaching job. After selling short stories to magazines, he continued to write stories which began selling to higher paying markets. "I sold 'Carrie' thinking I would earn enough to buy a new car, unaware that something greater was about to happen."

After "Carrie" sold like crazy he gave up teaching to write full-time. He maintains his prolific output by sometimes working on two projects simultaneously.

Today King still lives in the Bangor area of Maine with his wife and three children. And what of his involvement with Stanley Kubrick's film version of "The Shining?"

"Originally the book was owned by Producers Circle, part of Lew Grade's organization. I did a first screenplay which they were fairly happy with, then Kubrick got in touch with Warner Brothers and said he wanted the property. No, he demanded it. And Warner secured the rights. Kubrick was perfectly up front about wanting to write, produce and direct. "So," says King, "I stepped back, but that was perfectly all right with me. I like doing screenplays but only as a hobby. I'm sure Kubrick will do a fine job. I've heard there's a life-size head of Jack Nicholson that breaks open at the end and releases a ghastly flood of worms."

And of course, there's another novel being created every day of the week. Anything else cooking, Stephen? King grins that boyish grin again. "I guarantee that whatever I do, I will be trying to stir your blood and scare the living daylights out of you."

AFTERWORDS

King has lived up to his promise, producing book after book. His two sons Owen and Joseph have also become writers with published books. He has confessed that he became an alcoholic and pill addict during the 1980s but has since cured himself. He underwent an accident in 1999 while walking roadside in Lovell, Maine. He was severely injured but soon recovered and resumed his life as usual. Producing book after book. Very much alive, very much breathing, and very much continuing to scare the pants off America.

That's Stephen King atop a 1958 Plymouth Fury, one of 25 models used in the making of his thriller "Christine." Step on the gas and shift your eyeballs into high gear. And swing 'em to the right!

IN THE BEGINNING, Detroit created the car in just seven days, and the Chrysler Corporation stood back from the assembly line and said, "It was good."

But "it" was not good. For this 1958 Plymouth Fury had been forged in metallic malevolence. Its parts were criminal chrome . . .

Homicidal headlights . . . And tires of squealing, mangling death.

And now this . . . this automobile had a life of her own.
This car called Christine.

Isn't it too bad about what happened to John Stanley in the loading dock.
I wonder who will be doing "Creature Features" from now on.
Well, Stanley did say he wanted to live life in the fast lane, and meet life head on.

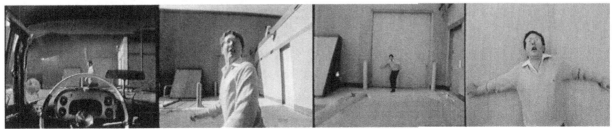

MANGLING, CRUNCHING WHEELS OF SQUEALING DEATH

A Meeting With the Producer of "Christine"
AKA "The Killer Car From the Year 1958"
. . . Jesus Chrysler, a "Killer Car" ?????

It was in early December 1983 when Richard Kobritz, the producer of the horror film "Christine," drove a 1958 Plymouth Fury onto my "Creature Features" set to serve as the background as we sat down to discuss how he had handled the adaptation of Stephen King's popular novel.

Stanley: Before making "Christine" you produced the Stephen King TV miniseries "Salem's Lot" about vampires taking over a New England town. You must be a big fan of King.

Korbitz: Stephen's books are very special to me. When I make a film I always look for something I know will be entertaining, and some of King's books have been pure fun and pure success at the box office.

Stanley: And "Christine" . . . what was the turning point for you?

Korbitz: First of all, John Carpenter had been picked to direct and I knew that he was perfect for bringing King's theme to life. John had already proven himself making "Assault on Precinct 13" and "Halloween II."

Stanley: And King's book?

Korbitz: I knew immediately that "Christine" would be a unique experience. King probed into the depth of our love affair with American-made automobiles. He took that appreciation, which you can call love, and twisted it into how three young teenagers wrap their lives around the automobiles they drive, and how they measure their success by the kind of car they display as they speed through a neighborhood or down a four-lane freeway.

THE CAREER THAT DRIPPED WITH HORROR

Korbitz: Of course, it has something to do with their sexuality, and how the right kind of car could attract a beautiful woman. That's a major part of King's theme.

Stanley: You had a very experienced special effects man on the scene, Roy Arbogast. Didn't he do the mechanical effects for "Close Encounters of the Third Kind"?

Korbitz: Absolutely. And before that he was in charge of the shark in "Jaws."

Stanley: And "Star Wars: Return of the Jedi," right?

Korbitz: Correct. We were given 25 Plymouth Fury models, all 25 years of age. And Arbogast took each one and rebuilt it to fit the needs of the plot. Well, he used up 17 of them anyway. Each car was regenerated. One to be set on fire. One to be christened "Pristine Christine." I'm glad we had some left over so I could bring one with me today.

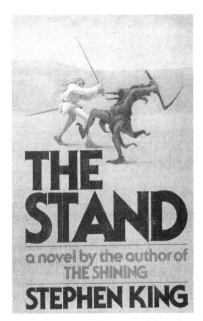

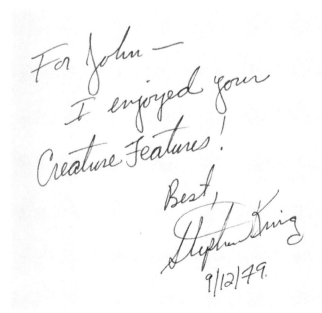

Top: "Christine" producer Richard Kobritz and the killer '58 Fury on the set of "Creature Features." Middle right: Director John Carpenter lining up a shot. Bottom: Stephen King's best-seller "The Stand," which he autographed to me in 1979 at a Bay Area fantasy show.

Kenn Davis, the artist whose wonderful work is spread across pages 138-144, called me in 1985 to tell me that actor Joseph Turkel, a personal friend of his through his brother-screenwriter Zekial Marko (author of the 1965 noir thriller "Once a Thief"), was in town and would make a good interview. Turkel ended up driving to my home in Pacifica and we spent an evening talking for several hours. Here are the results.

What a Character . . . Actor
Joe Turkel, One of the Best of Movieland's Bad Guys

I HAVE NEVER quite met a character actor who turned out to be a real-life character all his own as much as Joseph Turkel. He is the backbone of show business who remains in the shadows of better-known actors and actresses–unappreciated and seldom recognized beyond a vague "I've seen that face somewhere in movies before."

Unlike stars who tend to rise and fall, the supporting player goes on forever–willing to settle for secondary roles but, in the process, building an impressive body of work. And the variety of parts often permits him to hone his acting craft to a point of perfection.

I will never forget his performance in "Paths of Glory," one of three Stanley Kubrick films in which he was featured. He portrays a World War I French soldier, Pvt. Pierre Arnaud, who is chosen at random as one of three battle-weary troopers sentenced to be shot to death because their officer (Kirk Douglas) did not carry out an attack on German troops. The execution sequence and Turkel's performance are among cinema's most unforgettable moments of death. I will always remember his line of dialogue: "I'm not afraid of dying tomorrow, only of getting killed."

Above: Joe Turkel's dying soldier in Kubrick's 1957 war movie "Paths of Glory" Below: Joe as the Overlook Hotel bartender serving smiling Jack Nicholson in "The Shining" (1980).

Turkel is also a stand-out in "The Shining" (1980, directed by Kubrick) as creepy bartender Lloyd, who serves Jack Nicholson at a moment when he couldn't be crazier in the dining room of the Overlook Hotel. And Turkel will be fondly remembered for his role as Dr. Eldon Tyrell in "Blade Runner" (1982).

Joseph Turkel, in a career that has spanned four decades, looks upon each of his roles as something unique–a one-time challenge that deserved to be polished into a gem. Turkel has appeared in an estimated 200 motion pictures and approximately 300 TV episodes. And he claims to be the only actor who can say he's been in three of Stanley Kubrick's motion pictures.

But the reason we met in Pacifica was about an upcoming episode of "Tales From the Darkside," a low-budget anthology horror series in the vein of "The Twilight Zone."

"I was in bed with a temperature of 101," Turkel tells me, "when I got a call from Tommy Castronova. Tommy used to be an actor – in fact, we were together in 'The St. Valentine's Day Massacre' – but now he's producing 'Tales from the Darkside.' He insisted I do this episode, 'Leviathan,' I could barely get out of bed. I had bronchitis and walking pneumonia–but I did the episode and I'm glad I did."

Turkel portrays a magician who is facing hard times, performing in a cheap circus sideshow. "A professional magician came in and rehearsed me on the three-ring trick, the vanishing flowers routine and the rope-cutting bit. Then he trained me in the performing of my character's masterpiece: levitating a human body."

"Tales From the Darkside" was originated by George Romero, director of "Night of the Living Dead" and "Creepshow." It has no Rod Serling as on-camera narrator, but it does have pithy shocker tales of the supernatural with O. Henry endings, made on what Turkel calls

Turkel on the set of "The Shining" as Stanley Kubrick sets up the next shot. This was his third film working with Kubrick.

"well-meant money–carefully spent dollars that show in production values and good story."

Turkel calls himself "a blithe spirit. I've always felt young and my lifestyle has always reflected charging out the door to perform a new character. Sometimes I didn't care what the part was. I just wanted to stay in front of that camera. Acting became the most important thing in my world. It's a business about illusions, flickering illusions. Me dressed up in costumes and playing cowboys, Cavalry officers, Indians, Nazis, Italian prisoners, GIs, sailors, Marines, test pilots, gangsters. I can't remember what all."

Joe loved to autograph photos, which is why he brought four to my home.

Usually, those characters he played were heavies, which never bothered him a bit. "The heavy or bad guy is an attention getter, an action part, a great edge to make you a big character player. A heavy can't lose: If the picture is a hit, you made it a hit. And if it flops, well, the star screwed it up.

"Those bad guys were killed by every conceivable means: shooting, garroting, fire, poison, speeding automobiles, firing squads, hand grenades. I enjoyed each and every death."

Among movies he appeared in was Vittorio Gassman's "The Glass Wall" and "Man Crazy," a cheap Neville Brand picture. It was this quickie that Stanley Kubrick saw. "When Stanley called me, it was all very casual and I didn't think much about it."

Kubrick wanted him for "The Killing," to play Vince Edwards' sadistic gunsel. The 1956 film was destined to become a classic caper flick, a true film noir, and Turkel stood out as never before.

Just as he had in the other two Kubrick films which he helped to keep alive for decades.

His characters, he tells me, "have appeared in more shows than anyone could remember. I've done 'Boston Blackie,' 'Racket Squad,' 'Highway Patrol,' 'The Untouchables,' 'One Step Beyond,' 'Bonanza.' It never stops."

AFTERWORDS

But his non-stop acting career would slow down and finally come to a stop after our meeting when Turkel decided to become a screenwriter. And in 1998, at the age of 71, he decided to retire from it all. In the meantime, remember his advice to would-be actors: "Never buy anything you can't hock. And my advice to the rest of the world in general is from sports writer Grantland Rice: 'Don't worry, don't hurry and don't forget to smell the flowers along the way.'"

Left: Joe Turkel (left) as a circus magician in "Levitation," an episode of the anthology horror series "Tales From the Darkside." Right: That's Joe seated to the right of Rutger Hauer in a scene from Ridley Scott's classic thriller "Blade Runner," considered one of the best science-fiction films of its time. Hauer portrayed Ray Batty, a humanoid robot (called a "replicant") and Turkel was Dr. Eldon Tyrell, owner of the company that produced the replicants.

COMING UP NEXT...

VAN WILLIAMS AS THE GREEN HORNET
BRUCE LEE AS KATO

HORNET, KATO, KUNG-FU:
ALL ENEMIES OF THE UNDERWORLD

THE GREEN HORNET shifts nervously in the backseat of the Black Beauty. His eyes–two glowing orbs centered within the slits of his face mask and spiraling downward, almost to the tip of his nose–blaze out toward the camera and crew that litter the Desilu Studio sound stage. It is September 1966 and seated in the front seat is the driver, Kato, without whom the Hornet would have a hard time getting around the metropolis in which they dwell and often race-like-hell through to put an end to evil.

Some technician, it seems, has picked up the wrong reel of film for a rear projection shot required to give the effect of the Black Beauty cruising along a nocturnal city street. For instead of a quiet boulevard passing in the rear window, police cars with twirling red lights speed toward the Beauty as if to slam into it. This is a burst of action the script clearly does not call for. Meanwhile, the Green Hornet (actually Britt Reid, newspaper publisher of the Daily Sentinel) yawns once, thrusting a gloved hand against his cheek.

"Hey, bud, get with it back there," demands the impatient director. "Let's get this street shot zooming." The inappropriate footage is rewound, the correct roll substituted in its place. Now the crew is ready for another take. The camera rolls and the Hornet buzzes into action: "Run fast, dark and silent, Kato. We've only got . . . Hey, how does that next line go?"

Kato knows the line and immediately delivers it to the Hornet. Meanwhile, the camera has stopped rolling after a scream of "Cut!" The director adds: "Okay, let's try it again." He begins to pace nervously back and forth behind the camera team.

On the second take The Hornet tries to deliver his line of dialogue again, and fails again.

Once again, without a second's hesitation, Kato recites the dialogue to the Green Hornet. Rewind, relight, retake. Now, on the third attempt, the Masked Marauder triumphs in his fight against the forces of forgetfulness. He blurts out the remainder of his dialogue, forewarning of a mysterious rendezvous in the dead of night and other plot complexities.

Everyone seems satisfied with the third take, including Van Williams, who removes his one-piece face mask, green felt hat with black band and green overcoat as he climbs out of the mock-up interior of the Black Beauty. Parked nearby on the same set is a sleek-looking 1966 Chrysler Imperial, which has been redesigned for an estimated $50,000 to take on all the characteristics needed for the Black Beauty. Among its features: a magnesium grill, a built-in TV camera, an exhaust that can spread ice onto the highway or street to cause pursuing vehicles to spin out of control, and special brushes near the rear wheels designed to sweep away any tire tracks being left by the Black Beauty. (See page 194 for a full image)

Kato, I've been told, is an unknown, up-and-coming actor, whose name is Bruce Lee. He appeared in four episodes of Adam West's "Batman" series before being selected to play Kato. And he's a martial arts expert. He turns to face me after he slams the driver's door. "You are from San Francisco," he says. "I was born in your city but grew up in Hong Kong because my father sang in Cantonese opera. After I was attacked by street marauders when I was a teenager, I took up martial arts and developed a love for defending my body."

"And knocking over bodies," remarks Williams, patting Lee on the back.

"A love of my life," says Lee. "Well, after that I came back to San Francisco, where I worked at a Chinatown restaurant for a while. Then I moved up north to attend Seattle University, where eventually I opened a kung fu school, teaching karate and tae kwon do. I love action. I love moving my body."

"And knocking over other bodies," repeats Williams.

Lee laughs and begins swinging his arms through the air vigorously.

Williams pats Lee on the back again. "Thanks, Bruce, for remembering my line. Damn it, I thought I had it down pat. And suddenly, nothing up here." He points to his forehead.

"I learn all the dialogue in each script," says Lee, and Williams nods. Lee pats Williams on the back again and continues. "It's important to know every word that will be said. It helps me to remember when I must speak. I spend many hours with each script. Always know what others are doing. In kung-fu you follow the same rule in order to face your enemies as they attack."

Someone waves at Lee and he shuffles away while adjusting Kato's cap. Williams sighs. "Bruce is good to have around. I think he'll be going places, especially with his skills with martial arts. He really knows how to fly through the sky, feet first. Or head first."

At the age of 32, Williams had already achieved some success by appearing in 69 episodes of "Surfside Six" and 36 episodes of "Bourbon Street Beat." The roles came and went without any opportunity to propel himself upward into films.

Williams, who seems more bland than suave, and more boyish than handsome, is aware of his youthfulness but merely shrugs when it's pointed out to him . . . in a friendly way, of course. "I'm what they wanted for the part," he tells me, "so here I am. But it isn't the first time my

The Green Hornet and Kato appeared in a popular crossover episode of "Batman" with Adam West and Burt Ward in 1967 called "Piece of the Action." Both shows were produced for ABC by William Dozier.

looks have been questioned. I did a TV pilot, 'Pursue and Destroy,' but it was never bought because everyone considered me too young to be a submarine captain. Turns out, though, there actually were some World War II commanders younger than me."

Williams was raised in Fort Worth, Texas, by a father who was a cattle baron. By the 1950s he was running a skin-diving school in the Hawaiian Islands when he met producer Mike Todd and his wife Elizabeth Taylor. Todd suggested that Williams' good looks might open doors to Hollywood and on that recommendation alone Williams came to live in Los Angeles and began landing small roles, such as "Radio Man" in "The Day The Earth Stood Still."

Williams and Diane McBain co-starred in the private detective series "Surfside 6." He lived on a houseboat next to McBain's yacht.

Williams explains that this version of "The Green Hornet," originally a beloved radio series that ran from 1936 through 1952, is the work of producer William Dozier, who had sprung into prominence six months earlier with "Batman," a series that spoofed the comic-book characters and starred Adam West (as Batman) and Burt Ward (as Robin the Boy Wonder).

Williams admits with a shake of his head that he dislikes "Batman" because "it's a spoof of a spoof," but agrees with Dozier that his Hornet is a straightforward, stylish action series, with emphasis on plot, gimmicks and stunts, with little time spent on deep character development. "There's none of the campy comedy that has predominated on 'Batman,'" he promised me.

Perhaps not, but the fact remains that the Black Beauty (actually a chromeless four-door Imperial with magnesium grill and a sleek, ugly look to it) comes equipped with brooms "to brush away the tire tracks." Other features of the Black Beauty not mentioned above: an infra-red shield that hides the auto from undesired eyes; an ultrasonic sound gun capable of tearing down walls and doors (and presumably human beings); and built-in rockets and missiles controlled by a super panel of buttons installed in the back seat.

The Hornet himself, still considered by honest citizens to be a denizen of the underworld, will continue to pack his traditional gas gun ("Here, friends, have a whiff of this!"), the butt of which now leaves the impression of a bee when smashed against soft human flesh.

"What's really interesting about the Hornet," says Williams, "is how he came to be created. George Trendle [right, with Clayton Moore] had first dreamed up 'The Lone Ranger' and was quite successful with that Western hero on radio. Then he decided to duplicate the formula and plunked it down in midtown Manhattan. The updating turned the Lone Ranger into the Hornet, Tonto into Kato, great horse Silver into the Black Beauty. Thus, Trendle had two successful radio shows with practically the same plots working for him." (Trendle, an incredibly active man, also created "Sergeant Preston of the Yukon" for radio and TV fans.)

Action films, continues Williams, have always been his favorite form of entertainment. "And this series will depend heavily on robust acrobatics and physical exertion. We have something extra unusual with our hand-to-hand fighting because Bruce, as Britt Reid's faithful houseboy, is an expert in the art of kung fu.

"This is an ancient Chinese form of self-defense, which is older than karate. It combines elements of karate and jiujutsu and will be demonstrated in a most rugged style."

Does he feel the show has an above-average chance for success? "Positively," he declares. "There has never before been a better period for a costumed hero. Of course, we'll nab the kids, who love this sort of thing anyway. And we should have a strong adult audience which remembers the radio series and will be curious to see how we're treating the new adventures."

Van Williams' dreams of a long-running masked hero with a gas gun to defeat lawbreakers were not to be fulfilled. The series was cancelled after just 26 episodes and Williams landed only one-shot roles in many series until 1975, when he starred in "Westwind." He finally gave up acting in 1993. He lived to be 82, passing away in 2016.

Bruce Lee fared much better, going on to play a recurring role in the 1971 TV series "Longstreet." A visit to Hong Kong opened the door to the production of three martial arts motion pictures: "The Big Boss" (aka "Fists of Fury"), "Way of the Dragon" and "Enter the Dragon." In the next piece I will tell you more about what led to his sudden death at the age of 32 while making "Enter the Dragon."

But first I want to introduce you to his son, Brandon Lee. I met him in August 1992 as he was following in his father's footprints, and my moments telling Brandon about his father making "The Green Hornet" became very significant.

THE CAREER THAT DRIPPED WITH HORROR

FATHER AND SON:

BRUCE LEE

BRANDON LEE

Son of a Gun . . . No! Son of a Kung-Fu Star . . . Brandon Lee

YOU COULD SAY it's in his blood. What could be more transfusional than the son of Bruce Lee turning out to be a martial-arts motion-picture actor? Following in the footsteps of one's father is a time-honored tradition, but in the case of Brandon Lee, he would prefer that you put more stress on actor than on martial arts.

That is not to say he isn't enjoying his current reputation as an up-and-coming star in the action genre. If this is the way for him to become a movie actor, and subsequently make "a body of work" from comedies to dramas, so be it. Lee, 27, first hit it big in the Hong Kong market in the box-office action hit "Legacy of Rage" (1986), but it was a while before that reputation caught up with him in America and he was given the chance to star in the 1991 actioner "Showdown in Little Tokyo."

Lee's newest adventure, "Rapid Fire," opening in 1,500 theaters nationwide, is a classy showpiece for Lee. It's brimming with well-choreographed hand-to-hand battles intermingled with blazing machine guns, rifles, pistols and knives swishing through the atmosphere. The fights and their split-second timing are nothing short of spectacular, embellished by cliff-hanger escapes reminiscent of the Saturday matinee serials of the 1940s.

In "Rapid Fire," Lee portrays Jake Lo, a soft-spoken college student who reluctantly is drawn into a three-way war between the Chicago Mafioso, a gang led by a Golden Triangle drug lord, and a band of crusading Windy City cops (bossed by Powers Booth) who want to destroy both evil gangs.

The film is set up so that Brandon is at odds with all three elements who are using him for their own

Brandon Lee faces off against Powers Booth in the crime thriller "Rapid Fire."

ends, and hence you can't help but root for him as he escapes from one breathless, cliff-hanging situation after another. Those who recall the brilliant if brief career of Bruce Lee–a Chinese-American who played Kato on TV's "The Green Hornet" in 1966 and flamed briefly in the early 1970s as the world's best-known martial-arts film star in a series of "chop socky" actioners–will not see his son attempting to duplicate his father's techniques, which no other movie actor has ever matched anyway. Brandon achieves a less individualistic style, perhaps, but holds his own as an able actor and ferocious fighter.

What the young Lee exhibits best is a sense of vulnerability that's unusual in a martial-arts star. He's also showcased as a likeable guy, the antithesis of the Steven Seagal image. He doesn't quite have the self-effacing sense of humor of Jean-Claude Van Damme, but he does have the wholesome appeal that earmarked the early years of Chuck Norris' career.

In person, the handsome Lee is warm and soft-spoken, pausing to choose his words with care and presenting a well-mannered image without rough edges. "If there's any kind of modern action film that I admire the most," he begins, eager to discuss his attitude toward martial-arts movies, "it's Jackie Chan's work in the Hong Kong industry. His pieces are unparalleled. His energy is boundless."

He continues that "most American action films don't compare. I think that too many of them are edited so much that you lose the geography of the fight and all you have are blurred close-up images which keep cutting back and forth. A good example of bad work is the climactic fight between Gary Busey and Mel Gibson in the first 'Lethal Weapon' film. It's made up of quick cuts that only give you an impression of what's happening without really showing you the entire tableau of action."

Lee believes that the most important element in an action movie is what the main character has at stake. "If the viewer cares whether he wins or loses, then all the action means something.

Chuck Norris in his film debut fought it out with Bruce Lee in a legendary action sequence in "The Way of the Dragon" (1972).

But if it's uninteresting, if his cause is weak, the greatest battles in the world aren't going to save the picture from box office disaster."

Brandon Lee was born in Oakland. His mother Linda Lee Caldwell, a diving beauty from Scandinavia, first met Bruce in San Francisco when he was still struggling to make a film career for himself. When Brandon was three months old the family moved to Hong Kong and stayed for eight years. Bruce Lee was teaching martial arts to son Brandon by the time he could walk. "I have very vivid memories of a father-son relationship," he says, "but we never really talked much about him being a star or his attitudes about film making. I do remember him working very hard and coming home beat and tired. He totally threw himself into each of his movie projects."

Bruce Lee would star in a small number of pictures – including "Enter the Dragon," "Way of the Dragon" and "The Big Boss" (aka "Fist of Fury") – that turned him into an international rage almost overnight. But in the summer of 1973, just as he was making "Enter the Dragon," he collapsed and died at the age of 32. His death has been attributed to a swelling of the brain, what is called cerebral edema. Suffering from headaches, he had taken an anti-pain pill called Equagesic given to him by an actress friend. Within hours he was found dead. After his death, Brandon's mother moved him and his sister Shannon to Los Angeles.

At home with the Lee family: Brandon (left), mom Linda Lee Caldwell, and Bruce.

"I've studied all of Dad's movies over and over again," Lee tells me. "I can quote each line of dialogue. What I like most about Dad, aside from his personal raw talent and drive, is that he could show so much energy on the screen. And he could act. He understood how to underplay his characters, and he was great at bringing personal moments to life on the screen."

At this point I have to interrupt Brandon and tell him about my time on the set of "The Green Hornet" in 1966 and how his father had remembered the dialogue that Van Williams couldn't remember while "driving" the Black Beauty.

Immediately Brandon leaps up and wants to know every detail I can remember about seeing his father on the "Green Hornet" set at Desilu Studios. He listens intently, slapping his knee. "By God, my father did teach me things, whether I knew it or not at the time. I haven't forgotten any of his movie dialogue. I'm so pleased you told me, because I don't think he told me much about playing Kato. It was a start, but I don't think he had fond memories about it."

Brandon slaps his knee again. "As for Dad's fight choreography, he had a level of sophistication that's missing from today's movies. His style was the best ever executed up to that time. He knew how to put beats into a fight. Like playing music.

"These were comedic and dramatic pauses that allowed the audience to catch its breath, and which allowed Dad to manipulate the audience. Dad always expressed his character during a fight. In contrast, nowadays 90 bodies fall to the ground, but the hero standing at the center of the melee has no expression of character, or a sign of victory."

Lee says his father "also knew how to use those strange sounds he made to best advantage. They weren't meaningless grunts and groans that were caused by exertion. They were a calculated part of his style. They were forms of punctuation: to signal, to scare, to taunt, to ridicule, to warn. And sometimes merely to amuse."

While Brandon studied acting at Emerson College in Massachusetts, and later took courses from the Lee Stransberg Academy and drama coaches Eric Morse and Lynette Katselas, Hong Kong producers constantly assailed him with scripts that he promptly rejected. "For one reason," he explains, "the stories were lowbrow and beneath doing. For another, the only reason they wanted me was to exploit my father's name. I wanted to have nothing to do with that crap."

Instead, he joined the Los Angeles theater group Legal Aliens and acted in stage productions, hoping he could improve his dramatic range. "All the while," he admits, "I was hoping to break into American films, but only when I felt I was ready." He landed a small part as Chung Lang in "Kung Fu: The Movie," but it was really an offer to make "Legacy of Rage" (also 1986) in Hong Kong that brought him popularity. But, because the film was in Cantonese, that popularity was confined to the Far East.

Brandon returned to Los Angeles, but found that he was still considered an unknown in Hollywood. It was "Showdown in Little Tokyo" that introduced him to American audiences in 1991. In an interesting twist brought to the film by director Mark L. Lester, Lee played an L. A. policeman who knew nothing about Asian culture, while his Caucasian partner Dolph Lundgren was an expert on the Orient.

Brandon Lee's 1992 Hollywood breakthrough "Rapid Fire," choreographed by his friend Jeff Imada.

Brandon seems none too eager to discuss "Showdown," perhaps because he had no control over the way the action was choreographed. And when I mention "Laser Mission" (a 1989 actioner set in Africa) he says nothing at all, perhaps for the same reason.

He points out that when Fox offered him "Rapid Fire," the initial project of a nonexclusive contract with the studio, the first thing he insisted on was choreographing his own battles with a friend of 18 years, Jeff Imada, an experienced fight coordinator in Hollywood. "This time I went in overprepared," admits Lee. "I knew every move backward and forward. I insisted that we build the sets according to what was needed for the fights, so that we could collapse and destroy things the way we wanted."

Now he talks about how an action film has to walk a thin line between "reality and theatrically–by that I mean going for a larger-than-life feeling but still making the action conform to a heightened sense of reality. You have to account for every bullet hit and an actor has to respond to a kick or sock on the jaw and not just keep going.

"I really get angry when 20 men with machine guns are firing at Arnold Schwarzenegger and he just stands there shooting back, killing them all and never getting hit himself. I think you even have to be fair to the bad guy. It's not right to make him look weak or foolish. The more threatening in a real way, the better an adversary he makes."

To prove his desire to branch out as an actor, Lee already has his next picture planned, and it's not a martial-arts actioner. He describes "The Crow" as a supernatural thriller. "I portray a rock-and-roll musician who returns from the dead. It'll have some martial-arts action, but mainly it'll allow me to stretch as an actor."

Lee compares his career with what Dad once called "broken rhythm." "That's a combat principal in which you fight in a rhythmic style. Punch . . . punch . . . punch. This lulls the opponent into a rhythm of his own. And then you break the rhythm and surprise your enemy with a sneak punch out of synch. That's how I hope my career goes. A different punch every now and then, the way Clint Eastwood does it. What I want is a body of work and not just work for the body."

They used to call Bruce Lee by the nickname of Siu-loong, or "Super Dragon." If his son covets a title of his own, it would have to be "Super Actor."

AFTERWORDS

Bruce Lee's son dies after movie mishap

WILMINGTON, N.C. (AP) — Actor Brandon Lee, son of martial arts movie legend Bruce Lee who died at age 32, was killed Wednesday by a projectile believed to have come from a gun on the set of the movie he was starring in.

Lee, 28, was struck in the abdomen when a gun rigged to shoot blanks fired. He died at New Hanover Regional Medical Center, where he had undergone surgery, said center spokeswoman Cathy Painter. Lee died nearly 12 hours after being brought to the emergency ward, she said.

Dr. Warren W. McMurry, the surgeon, said the intestinal injuries and major vascular injuries were consistent with a bullet wound. "I

Please see LEE/2A

Brandon Lee

Less than a year after my meeting with Brandon Lee–March 1993–I am catching a plane to San Diego at the Oakland Airport when I stop to buy a newspaper. I am shocked to discover that Brandon Lee is dead at the age of 28. Shot to death on the set of the very film he had told me about, "The Crow," while it was being made in Wilmington, North Carolina.

Shot to death making a movie?

One of Brandon's costars, Michael Massee, had been given a .44 magnum pistol loaded with blanks. What no one realized was that the barrel contained part of a fragment of a bullet. When Massee pulled the trigger, the blank (which contained a live primer) went off and forced the bullet fragment directly into Brandon's abdomen.

He would die in a medical center twelve hours later.

Ironically, he had been asked to portray his dad in "Dragon: The Bruce Lee Story," but turned it down in order to make "The Crow," which was finally finished and released in May, 1994.

ANOTHER TRAGIC POSTSCRIPT: Twenty-eight years later on October 21, 2021, a similar tragedy occurred in Santa Fe, New Mexico, on the set of Alec Baldwin's western "Rust." Baldwin was practicing drawing his pistol when the firearm discharged, killing rising cinematographer Halyna Hutchens and wounding director Joel Souza.

MEETING AT MORNINGSIDE CEMETERY

SUDDENLY I received a phone call from the unknown. A voice I couldn't recognize told me that because I was a TV horror host, I might want to hurry to Morningside Cemetery in Colma to meet an important horror film producer from Hollywood, who was about to catch a plane out of San Francisco Airport. The producer and his leading man would be at the Mausoleum, but I had to get there fast if I expected to do a quick interview. Feeling I had nothing to lose, I jumped into my car and headed for Morningside Cemetery. And was standing in front of the mausoleum in just a matter of minutes. And suddenly . . .

Stanley: Oh, you scared the Phantasm right out of me! Hey, I know you! You're Angus Scrimm. You play the Tall Man in "Phantasm." They tell me you're very gregarious and outgoing and friendly and ... charming and ... talkative and … chatty.

(SCRIMM GRABS STANLEY AND THROWS HIM INTO A WAITING HEARSE!)

Stanley: What's the idea of bringing me out here? Say, who are you, anyway?

Coscarelli: I'm Don Coscarelli, I'm writer and director of "Phantasm." We just thought we'd get you in the right mood for the picture so you can take it back to your "Creature Features" audience and tell them all about it. Didn't we, Angus?

Angus: I wanted to entertain you in a setting in which I feel most at home. I promise you every comfort.

THE CAREER THAT DRIPPED WITH HORROR

Angus Scrimm (The Tall Man) and "Phantasm" writer-director Don Coscarelli out on a joy ride with yours truly.

Stanley: Well, you certainly believe in atmosphere and realistic settings. This graveyard is just like a scene in "Phantasm." Where did you get the inspiration to make such a terrifying film?

Coscarelli: Well, as a matter of fact, I've always loved graveyards and I'd always loved horror pictures. In fact, we have a "Creature Features" type show in Los Angeles that I always used to watch when I was a young boy. It used to scare the heck out of me. At any rate, I always wanted to make a horror film and "Phantasm" was it.

Stanley: The film is certainly unrelenting. Horror after horror, like a nightmare. Would you say that it's representative of your own personal nightmares, Don?

Coscarelli: It definitely is. In fact, one of the best scenes is about our little weapon that the Tall Man uses in his mausoleum. It's called the Silver Sphere. What it does is, it flies around through the hallways at any intruder and seeks them out and kills them, right?

Stanley: That's the ball that has a knife on it.

Coscarelli: Yes. It sticks into their heads, bores into their brains and sucks all the blood out of their heads.

Stanley: Don, you'd made two previous films, neither of which had a horror film theme to it. What made you decide to do a horror film on your third time out as a producer-director?

Coscarelli: Well, horror pictures have always had good box office and that's what I initially wanted to do, a horror picture. But the great thing about a horror picture, you can get an audience to scream. Angus and I go to the

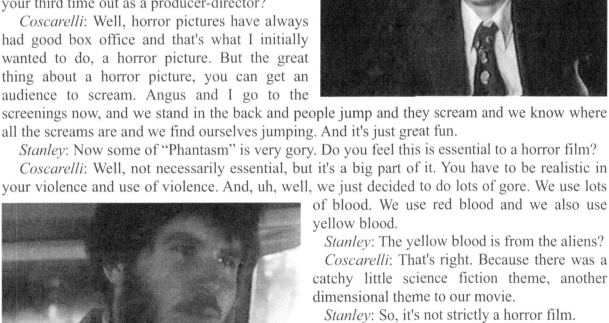

screenings now, and we stand in the back and people jump and they scream and we know where all the screams are and we find ourselves jumping. And it's just great fun.

Stanley: Now some of "Phantasm" is very gory. Do you feel this is essential to a horror film?

Coscarelli: Well, not necessarily essential, but it's a big part of it. You have to be realistic in your violence and use of violence. And, uh, well, we just decided to do lots of gore. We use lots

of blood. We use red blood and we also use yellow blood.

Stanley: The yellow blood is from the aliens?

Coscarelli: That's right. Because there was a catchy little science fiction theme, another dimensional theme to our movie.

Stanley: So, it's not strictly a horror film.

Coscarelli: We like to think of it as a bizarre science fiction-horror-fantasy because it embraces all of those genres.

Stanley: Angus Scrimm. How would you, in your own unforgettable words, describe "Phantasm"?

Scrimm: It's about some of the most lovable characters you'd ever want to meet. There's a lady in lavender who lures a lover out to the cemetery and then plunges a butcher knife into him. And that's fairly convenient for me because it saves me the trouble of going out to gather up the last remains. Then there's a driver of an ice cream truck who carries pieces of dead bodies in his freezer. We call them corpse-sicles. Then there's a little demon that lives in people's hair and drills into their brains. And then there's a caretaker who has his fingers chopped off and he goes wandering

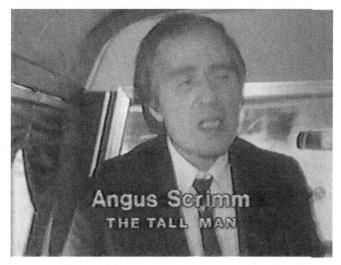

about the countryside, choking. That's our crowd. And I'm proud to say that not one of them has ever done anything that wasn't utterly depraved.

Stanley: Is it true that your name really isn't Angus Scrimm? That you're trying to conceal your true identity because you used to be a Shakespearean actor?

Scrimm: I don't want to talk about that. Most of those productions and songs, those actors … they all died out of town.

Stanley: Is it true, Angus. that you've made such films as "Sweet Kill," "Scream Bloody Murder" and "The Severed Arm?"

Scrimm: I helped the set director on those. I supplied some of the inanimate objects.

Stanley: You look like a man who could, uh, provide those things. Yes. Tell me, after working with Don in "Phantasm" as the Tall Man, would you consider making another film with him?

Scrimm: Under no circumstances. In fact, I have plans for him in my next plot.

Coscarelli: Okay, John, I think you got all the information you need to take back to your "Creature Features" audience and tell them about "Phantasm." Driver, stop here. Get rid of Stanley and get us to the airport as fast as possible. We're late already!

Scrimm: I hope you have a most entertaining afternoon at Morningside Cemetery.

(STANLEY GETS THROWN OUT OF THE HEARSE)

THE CAREER THAT DRIPPED WITH HORROR

The Fright Before Christmas

Twas the night before Christmas

And all throughout the dungeon,

Not a Creature was stirring,

Not even a Curmudgeon.

The stockings were hung

by the coffin with care,

The presents were wrapped to delight and to scare.

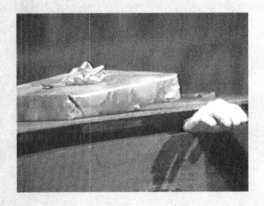

The corpse was all nestled

in a mahogany casing,

After living a life that had

been utterly debasing

Over by the guillotine, an item of dread.

I couldn't help but notice

a severed head.

When out in the cemetery

there arose such a clatter

I could hear drops of blood

as they started to splatter.

Suddenly I heard knocking
and had to pause

It wasn't Satan at the door.
It was Santa Claus!

His coloring was all scarlet
from his head to his toe
As he scrambled like
the Red Death
from a story by Poe.

I suddenly realized
I had eyesight trouble
Two Santa Clauses?
I was seeing double!

THE CAREER THAT DRIPPED WITH HORROR

He had a round face
and a round fat belly.
Too much beer while
watching the telly?

Now he spoke not a word
with nary a sign
As he turned to the monster
called Frankenstein.

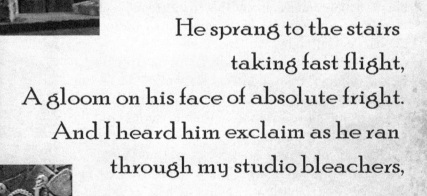

He sprang to the stairs
taking fast flight,
A gloom on his face of absolute fright.
And I heard him exclaim as he ran
through my studio bleachers,

"Never again
will I come to this show,
'Creature Features'."

I Say! Here Comes Mr. Essex, a Bloke Who Wants to ZILCH You To Death!

MR. WINSTON ESSEX is no schlock story-teller. He has none of the ghoulish poor taste of Raymond, the host of radio's "Inner Sanctum" series which dominated on radio during the 1940s with that creaking door in the background as he spun horror yarns with countless puns. Nor does this fellow Essex indulge in the alliterative, pseudo-philosophy of "Night Gallery" host Rod Serling.

Rather, Mr. Essex is a gentle raconteur, delivering his narratives straight from the shoulder and tinging them with British aplomb and gentility. And he chooses not a slime-covered crypt or a vault of horror but a stately mansion for his background setting. Upper crust horror, old chap, upper crust horror. For the intellectual, right? Well, not quite.

Who is this Mr. Essex, really? Truly a British-born fellow, hailing from London, known in the acting business as Sebastian Cabot who intellectually lends subtlety to an otherwise unsubtle series of the supernatural, "Ghost Story."

"I am there," says Cabot, when we meet in 1972, "as a kind of gimmick for William Castle, my producer. To establish a certain tone and introduce a

During our meeting Sebastian Cabot signed this photo: "Dear John: Bloody good luck, chap." Indeed, it was a bloody good moment for a TV horror host, meeting this British gent.

note of fear; to condition the audience. Then, hopefully, our tale will zilch them to death." Castle is no stranger to the business of producing horror stories for the masses, having established a reputation for "gimmicks" to help scare the pants off of millions of movie goers. He started his gimmicks with "Macabre" (1958), making a deal with Lloyds of London so each attendee was covered for $1,000. All the viewer had to do to collect was die while watching the film.

That was Castle's first gimmick, followed in 1959 by a skeleton that slid across the ceiling of the theater just when the audience least expected it watching "The House on Haunted Hill." For "Thirteen Ghosts" (1960) a pair of colored glasses enabled viewers to see supernatural beings.

But put Mr. Castle aside and let's get back to Mr. Essex. Cabot, though time was running out, has asked me to meet him in his suite at the Jack Tar Hotel in San Francisco. When I arrive at the giant hotel complex, I see that his suitcase is almost packed. He has an airplane to catch but there is time for breakfast. Relax, old chap, relax. He rubs his rotund stomach appreciatively and decides to call room service. Something that has to do, he remarks, with a 225-pound gentleman who needs to eat to stay alive. "Call it my tummybucket," he says jokingly. He strikes it with his hand. "You heard nothing. That means it's totally empty."

Cabot finishes stuffing clothing into his suitcase and plops on his rumpled bed, scratching at his well-trimmed beard. He is dressed in tweed trousers and a reddish shirt which is augmented by a red scarf knotted around his neck. Very neat, very natty. As I stare at him, I am reminded of his five seasons on the comedy series "Family Affair," in which he portrayed the staid, oft-stereotyped British butler Giles French. The utter essence of an Englishman. "There's been more to my life than stuffy Englishmen. You may recall all those TV series I guested on back in the 1950s and '60s. Mystery shows, Westerns, comedies. I've done so much zilching around Hollywood."

Here is Cabot (top) posing as butler Giles French in "Family Affair." Below him are (middle) Jonathan Whitaker, Brian Keith, (bottom) Kathy Garver and Anissa Jones.

"Zilch it all," he replies, once I begin to ask my newspaperman questions. "This Mr. Essex, he bloody well represents how people think of me. As an elegant, well-dressed, suave Briton. Stiff upper lip and all that. Like Giles the butler, but without the foolish remarks and all those 'Will that be all, sir?' Zilch. What they forget is this: I've played skid row derelicts, rummies, heavies, lightweights and everything between since my days on the London stage. That started when I

Sebastian Cabot, host of "Ghost Story," a short-lived series that was renamed "Circle of Fear," but he no longer introduced the tales. And away he went.

was just 27. The year was 1945 and the play was 'A Bell for Adano.' But to get back to 'Ghost Story.' Essex and that chap I played on 'Family Affair,' they really are not me. I consider myself an actor of far greater range."

Breakfast arrives. What, no toast? . . . Hmm, well, what about the hot water? Hmm . . . it's lukewarm. Cabot retires into the bathroom where he heats up his own hot water on a special warming device while the waiter leaves to begin a search for the elusive toast. Plopping down again, Cabot starts to peel a large grapefruit, which comprises the remainder of his breakfast and at least fills part of his empty tummybucket. "Trying to get down to 210 pounds, don't you know. That's where I feel the most comfortable. Damn the bubbly, I wish I didn't have this urge. Now, let's get back to that 'Ghost Story' business, shall we?" He tells me, "Certainly I've always enjoyed a good horror story, though I'm not a hound by any means. England, that's where I was born."

Kathy Garver is one terrific and beautiful lady who has written an autobiography, "Surviving Cissy," which she signed for me in 2015.

"London, you know, has a rich history of supernatural literature. Being fog-bound most of the time, and those bloody bogs and all that. And please don't forget about Jack. The Ripper, that is. He turned London into an infamous hole of death. But as for this life after death business, which we seem to be stressing in a fictional fashion in 'Ghost Story.' I'm no believer. However, I do believe we generate a psychic current, and when we die that energy is discharged into the atmosphere. It bounces around and is captured by others receptive to it. Hence, psychic phenomena. But as for corpses rising up from graves, well, if I ever saw that happening, I'd start to look for the special effects man responsible."

Cabot dumps several teabags into his pot of "piping hot" water and waits for a "strong brew" to develop. At that moment the waiter returns with that missing plate of toast. What, no jelly? Cabot affects a German accent, pounding the service table with his fist. "Ach, in my country we would have had you shot for this. We make lampshades out of men like you."

Cabot winks at the flustered waiter as he scurries from the room. "I forewarned you I was a character actor." He walks to the bed and presses the weight of his bulky knee against the bulging suitcase. A soup commercial is on "The Dinah Shore Show" and this reminds him about his cup of tea.

Finally, Cabot is pleased with the strong brew, mixing in milk in large quantities. He pushes away the peelings of his grapefruit, which he has disposed of with considerable relish. "Something else few people realize about me. I do a lot of lecture/reading tours. It's my love affair with the English language. Edward Lear, Walter Mitty, Oscar Wilde, Winnie the Pooh. A singular mixture for colleges and women's clubs. I travel a great deal, you see. My summers are spent at a home I have in Vancouver. This 'Ghost Story' business is just a small part of my life. I do a number of the introductions and closings back-to-back, then I'm free and on the road again. Zilching from here to there."

Finally, it's time to zilch off to the San Francisco Airport. Cabot picks up his suitcase and gives the TV screen a final glance (Dinah Shore is selling ladies' undies) before shutting the set off. As he heads for the door, he gives me one final glance: the look of Mr. Essex. Gentility still lives in Sebastian Cabot, character actor or not. Thank God he did not give me the Zilch look.

AFTERWORDS

"Ghost Story" would only last for 14 episodes and then be retitled "Circle of Fear," presenting stories not necessarily of the supernatural. And there was no longer Mr. Essex to introduce the yarns. Sebastian Cabot was zilching, free to roam the world at will or go to work as a character actor. Though he had five more years of life after our encounter, he did very little on-camera acting. In "The Miracle of 34th Avenue" he did portray Santa Claus but he preferred to continue his voice-over work in Winnie the Pooh shorts and spending most of his time in Victoria, British Columbia. Following two strokes, he died in 1977 in a Victoria hospital at the age of 77. His ashes were shipped to America and were placed in the Westwood Memorial Park Cemetery.

MUSIC FOR A BLOOD-SUCKING SUCCULENT
THE WIZARD OF MUPPETS, FRANK OZ,
DIRECTS A SONG-AND-DANCE VERSION
OF A HORROR CLASSIC

PRODUCER-DIRECTOR Roger Corman had no idea what he was creating in 1959 when he saw a standing storeroom set at one of the Hollywood studios and decided to use it before it was broken down. He hired Charles B. Griffith to write a screenplay around the set, and that script was finished within a week. Immediately the exploitation king of quickies rounded up a cast and directed the storeroom scenes in just two days and one night.

Cut to the result: What emerged from that hurry-up job was to become one of the most enduring low-budget horror features ever to come out of Hollywood, and the picture that Corman says best established him as an "underground legend" and made him "more fans and friends" than his more-expensive exploits in film. (And don't forget, this became the fourth motion picture to feature Jack Nicholson. Although his role as Wilbur Force was small and short, nothing more than a cameo, it was memorably funny. More about that later.)

It was – hold your breath – "Little Shop of Horrors" (American-International, 1960), and it didn't just come and go in a few weeks. While so-called serious critics ignored it or panned it, more insightful types prophetically saw something special in the dark humor surrounding the film's characters. *Castle of Frankenstein*, an intelligent science fiction and horror genre magazine, ecstatically reported it was "very inventive, resourceful and a darn funny self-parody spoof . . . yeah, a little kinky, but full of in-jokes."

"Little Shop" was a black-comedy original, depicting a nerdy clerk named Seymour Krelborn working in Mushnik's Flower Shop who fed human body parts to a ravenous, man-eating plant that kept crying "Feed Me!" And which kept burping.

"I'M FOZZIE, WITH MISS PIGGY, BUT NEITHER OF US ARE IN THIS STORY ABOUT OUR FRANK OZ!"

THE MODERN WIZARDRY OF OZ: HOW HE CREATED A NEW "HOUSE OF HORRORS" NOT SO LITTLE

I took these photos of Roger Corman in his New Horizons office in Los Angeles in 1991.

The film stayed alive through repeated showings on TV's "Creature Features" and a cult following built over the years. The imagery of the man-eater especially stuck with playwright Howard Ashman and musician/lyricist Alan Menken, who teamed in 1982 to write an off-Broadway musical-comedy version that instantly captured audiences. The plant, named Audrey II, grew larger and larger in each act until it had eaten all the characters and completely engulfed the stage, its tendrils wriggling out into the aisles.

This choreographed "Little Shop" (featuring such songs as "Something Green," "Skid Row" and an ever-present singing trio that wryly commented on the proceedings) caught on and remained a favorite for years at the Westwood Theater in Los Angeles and the Orpheum in Greenwich Village. It seemed only a matter of time before it would become a film again, this time in the big-budget league.

On the surface it seems to follow the stage version, but there are some subtle changes in tone that make the film crueler and more brutal. And, there's a completely different ending. The man who directed the new film, responsible for the subtle changes in tone that make it a less charming experience than the play, is Frank Oz, who will always be remembered as the Muppets' manipulator and the voice of Miss Piggy, Fozzie Bear and the Cookie Monster. He's also the wizard who created Yoda in "The Empire Strikes Back."

It's as if Oz, after many years of helping Muppet creator Jim Henson to stage G-rated TV shows for children, wanted to crash out into the adult market (the new version is rated PG-13) and demonstrate another side to his talents. Oz's previous assignments (co-directing "Dark Crystal" with Henson and directing "The Muppets Take Manhattan" alone) hardly hinted at the inventiveness and style that Oz has brought to his film, whatever one may think of its harsher overtones.

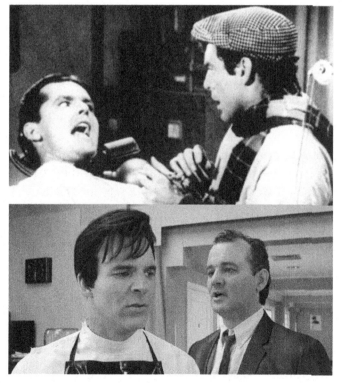

THE YANKS ARE COMING! Jack Nicholson made a cameo appearance in 1960's "Little Shop of Horrors" but it became a turning point in his early days in Hollywood. In the 1986 version, Bill Murray took over Nicholson's role as Arthur Denton, the guy who loves pain, with Steve Martin as the drill instructor aka the dentist aka Dr. Orin Scrivello.

THE CAREER THAT DRIPPED WITH HORROR

It was December of 1986. The new version of "Little Shop" was opening across America and Oz was on his way to the Hawaiian Islands with his wife Robin and 10-month-old son when he stopped over in the Bay Area for one day to visit his mother and father, who live in Oakland, the very place where Frank Richard Oznowicz was raised after being brought to America from Hereford, England, his place of birth on May 25, 1944.

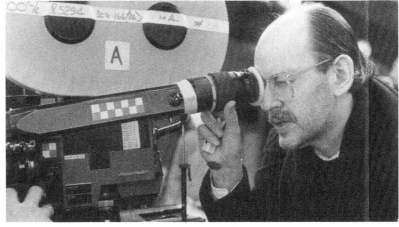

Frank Oz, the puppeteer famous for "The Muppet Show" and "Sesame Street," has directed several feature films, including "Dirty Rotten Scoundrels," "Bowfinger," "The Dark Crystal," and "What About Bob."

While having dinner at the Claremont Hotel, the 41-year-old artisan reflected on how "Little Shop of Horrors" came to dominate two years of his life. "It started when David Geffen, the producer and record executive, asked if I'd like to take a shot at directing 'Little Shop.' Martin Scorsese and John Landis had been involved, even Steven Spielberg's name had popped up, so I knew this project was a biggie.

"But my original feeling was to say no. The weight of doing 14 songs and dances and handling a special effects plant difficult to manipulate, it all sounded overwhelming. And everyone always says a movie isn't as good as the play or the book. A no-win situation."

But Oz thought it over a while longer "and I got excited about the three singers who appear throughout the play like a Greek Chorus: Crystal, Ronette and Chiffon. For me they were the key to a film version. They'd allow me to do something stylish, they'd give me a freedom of range. They were the statement. So I changed my mind and accepted."

Crystal, Ronette and Chiffon, the song-and-dance team that appeared in the 1986 remake of "Little Shop of Horrors."

The time frame for "Little Shop" became the year of the first film's release, 1960, with '55 Chevies lined up outside the shop. "I wanted to capture a sense of American innocence – the innocence we all lost a part of when President John F. Kennedy was assassinated in 1963." For Oz the important subtext was its Faustian theme – "a full meal as opposed to a half-empty plate of food. Seymour Krelborn sells his soul to a man-eating plant so he can stay close to Audrey, the woman he loves, and eventually escape skid row."

A year and a half ago the pound was strong so Oz decided to film at Pinewood Studios outside London, using the huge soundstage where many of the spectacular James Bond films have been produced. Also, Oz knew many special effects artists living nearby, having made "Dark Crystal" and six years of Muppet TV shows in England. This facilitated putting together a massive crew that was needed to bring Audrey II (right) to life.

Ellen Greene stood out as Audrey in the "Little Shop" remake and was nominated for Funniest Actress in a Motion Picture at the American Comedy Awards. She was previously nominated for a Tony for the same role in the 1983 stage version.

Oz spent an unusually long period, seven months, to film "Little Shop," primarily because of the difficulties of animatronics, the articulation of the plant creature. "There are no miniatures, no blue screens, no matte paintings, no stop-motion scenes," he stressed. "When you see the plant, you're seeing the real full-scale monster. For the tougher shots, it took as many as 50 to 60 stage hands to manipulate Audrey via hydraulics, remote-control cables and other devices. I think there were like 11 miles of cables involved. I'd spend a whole day getting three or four takes, and consider myself lucky."

The toughest part was getting Audrey's lips to move in syncopation with the singing performers for the musical numbers. And for the scene where Audrey opens a cash register, takes out a dime and makes a phone call. Oz had to direct 83 takes to get it just right.

Animatronics, he explained, "is a new term to describe the manipulation of film creatures. Yoda in 'Empire,' the mini-monsters in 'Gremlins' or the characters in 'Dark Crystal.' It's to differentiate from the other special effects people who move spaceships, explode cars, and all that." One of the famous scenes from the 1960 version depicted Jack Nicholson as a masochistic patient who urges his dentist to drill without novocaine because he loves pain.

In this new version, that cameo role is filled by Bill Murray, with Steve Martin as the malevolent, laughing gas-happy dentist, Dr. Orin Scrivello.

Oz allowed the comedians to ad lib some of their lines and this is where the comedy becomes mean and (no pun intended) senseless, demonstrating, more than any other scene, the "hard edge" and "toughness" Oz was trying to bring to the material. "I wanted to fall somewhere between 'Mame' and 'Rocky Horror Picture Show,' but I didn't want to go overboard. The original script was full of blood but I took all that out. It was repulsive. It's one thing to see slapstick, but another when you see the painful results of the slap."

Even so, Oz still admitted that "I did not make this film for pre-teenagers. I was really putting my a– on the line." Although Oz vowed that "I'll continue working with the Muppets until I keel over," and announced he would work with Henson on the next Muppet feature, he emphasized that "I want to do more human being stuff."

But for the moment, he was anticipating a long rest in Hawaii for the next month. "I don't want to be in L.A. or New York when the film opens," he confessed. "I don't want to get condescending phone calls if it's bad, and I don't want to have to believe my own publicity if the picture's a smash. To paraphrase Ernest Hemingway, when you're a celebrity the birds fly down and pick at you. Right now I just want to lay in the sun and do my own laundry."

Here we see Frank Oz (left) directing "Dark Crystal" with Jim Henson at his side.

AFTERWORDS

"Little Shop of Horrors" performed okay at the box office, raking in a little over $38 million (but costing around $25 million to get produced). Oz never stopped working and continued with "Sesame Street" doing such voices as Bert, Grover and Cookie Monster through 2014. He has been busy doing the voice of Yoda in "Star Wars: The Last Jedi" (2017), "Star Wars: The Rise of Skywalker" (2019) and "Star Wars: Jedi Temple Challenge" (2020). For this wonderful talent, it may never end. He is, indeed, the modern Wizard of Oz.

HOW RODDY McDOWELL WENT APE: HIS LEGACY OF MONKEY BUSINESS

RODDY McDOWELL, who died from lung cancer in 1998 at the age of 70, will always be remembered as a child star who went from the London stage to Hollywood features of many genres. In film he scored big as the chimpanzee Cornelius in "Planet of the Apes" (1968) and the three sequels that followed.

I have the joy of meeting McDowell at 20th Century Fox in November 1974, when he is starring in the TV version of "Planet of the Apes," this time as a chimp named Galen. He was the only actor from the films that made a transition to television, though as a different character. "I've never starred in a series before," he tells me, "But I thought it would be a challenge to portray Galen. He has a sense of fun, curiosity, adventure. He's the kind of character an actor can enjoy working with. He's a combination of my Cornelius but with greater understanding and compassion and humanity – pardon the expression."

He adds: "This is my work. This is my life. Any professional endeavor is predicated on hard work, progress and growth. This is a workaday business. It can be tiring, mentally and physically. By 3 p.m. there's no oxygen left on the set and by 4 p.m. you've got cotton wool in your brain. Acting is creative, and it is also tough."

As Roddy speaks, his face is covered with the ape-mask of Galen. The only natural part of him discernible are brown, inquisitive eyes peering through the rubber foam and his real teeth

deep within the mouth housing unit. The actor smokes Marlboro cigarettes incessantly through a lengthy holder. Between scenes he slips in and out of a comfortable blue bathrobe. There is a no-nonsense feeling he generates.

Before the rolling camera he demonstrates his love for Galen with character touches. In one scene, he falls into the arms of an astronaut friend, whimpering sadly and nestling in search of sympathetic love.

In another sequence, his forehead enwrapped in a blood-soaked bandage, he utters short simian sounds that make you want to embrace him and comfort his pain.

Shortly after our meeting Roddy was forced to shed his ape-mask when CBS-TV announced it was cancelling "Planet of the Apes" because the complexity of the feature films had been abandoned or simplified too much for TV viewing.

The TV version of "Planet of the Apes" lasted only 14 episodes, but McDowell kept on taking roles of a rich variety up to the year of his death. "This is my work" proved to be an utterly true motto.

THE CAREER THAT DRIPPED WITH HORROR

How to Make a "Nightmare" In Five Easy Years, er . . . Steps!

Dan Caldwell (above left), who portrayed Professor Seabrook, did only a handful of roles before his death at the age of 80 from Alzheimer's. Leading lady Barrie Youngfellow (above right) went on to star in 120 episodes of "It's a Living" (1980-89). Behind her is The Avenger, played by Irving Israel. John Cochran (below left) was a Bay Area actor who played Scotty, a Sherlock Holmes-style character. What happened to him after "Nightmare" . . . we don't know. Drew Eshelmen (below right) portrayed Gary Arlington, seen at bottom in his real-life San Francisco comic book store.

"NIGHTMARE IN BLOOD," a horror thriller that opened in theaters across America in September 1978, was designed by me and my writing-producing partner Kenn Davis to be a chilly "vampire flick" and a bow to fandom, which had begun growing across America with the help of "Star Trek" events and other fan-related conventions. While I was director, Kenn was director of cinematography and assistant film editor.

The main characters comprise a staff putting on a horror-movie convention. Although it was said to be held in San Francisco the footage was actually shot at the Fox Theater in downtown Oakland, CA. The staff consists of mystery writer Seabrook (Dan Caldwell), a lovely fashion designer (Barrie Youngfellow), a Sherlock Holmes-like sleuth named Scotty (John Cochran) and a comic-book store owner (Drew Eshelman) patterned after real-life Gary Arlington.

Gary had been a close friend since 1966, when he opened San Francisco's first comic-book store in the Mission District and went on to create Underground Comix. He helped us construct a comic-book store set, one of the more important settings for our theme. We treated our screen Arlington like a religious figure: He wore a priest-like robe and spoke in a Biblical style.

This group has invited a Hollywood actor named Malakai (Jerry Walter), a star famed for portraying the same bloodsucker in a series of hit vampire films.

Jerry Walter was a wonderful portrayer of a vampire but his acting career was very limited to a handful of films, mainly 1978's "Invasion of the Body Snatchers" plus San Francisco-made TV episodes. Ironically, he died four months after "Nightmare in Blood" was released to theaters.

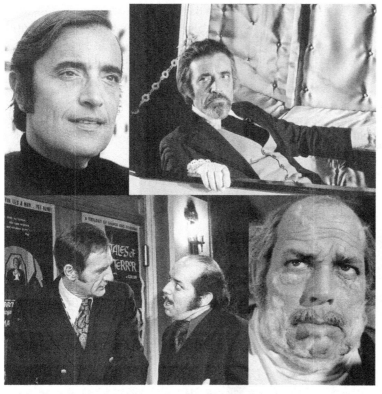

Above: Malakai's PR team consisted of San Francisco comedian Ray K. Goman and Hy Pyke. Pyke was superb at portraying crazed, maniacal characters, including tavern owner Lewis in "Blade Runner." Below: Malaki and his henchmen in their secret laboratory.

Accompanying Malakai are two public relations men (stand-up comedian Ray K. Goman and Hy Pyke). What nobody is aware of: Malakai is really a centuries-old vampire and his PR guys are the original Burke and Hare killers who committed murders in 1828 in Edinburgh, Scotland. The three intend to murder as many modern characters as possible.

Guest starring in a cameo role that opened the film was Kerwin Mathews, star of such Ray Harryhausen action fantasies as "The 7th Voyage of Sinbad" and "The Three Worlds of Gulliver." Playing other important roles were Morgan Upton as the host of "Fright Flicks" (the set of Bob Wilkins' "Creature Features" was used) and Dr. Unworth (Justin Bishop), an unlikeable fellow patterned after real-life Dr. Fredric Wertham. Unworth's new book, "Rape of the Young Mind," has declared that comic books cause juvenile delinquency. Unworth and Malakai will have a verbal showdown during an episode on "Fright Flicks."

Hidden away in the attending crowd is The Avenger (Irving Israel), who has been in pursuit of Malakai since his involvement with Hitler's concentration camps during World War II. He plans to use a stake and the Star of David to destroy the actor/vampire.

Gradually Professor Seabrook and Scotty uncover the truth about Malakai and his henchmen and the film climaxes on the Fox Theater stage as characters become interwoven and the final showdown between Malakai and The Avenger occurs next to Malakai's coffin, which had been designed and constructed by my father Myron Stanley.

THE CAREER THAT DRIPPED WITH HORROR

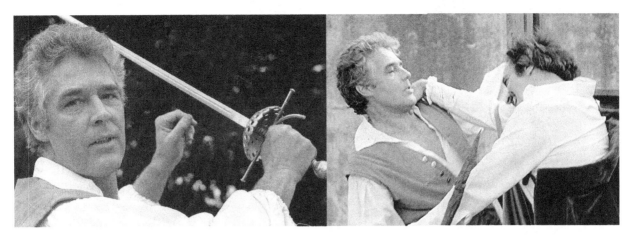

We discovered Kerwin Mathews working in a San Francisco store and he agreed
to spend one day with us to portray a swordsman in our opening segment.
We filmed his guillotine sequence just a few hundred feet away from the toll plaza
of the Golden Gate Bridge, in an old military gun emplacement.

Above left: Irving Israel (aka Mark Anger) was at his best portraying our revenge-driven
hero The Avenger. He also appeared in "American Graffiti" and "Tucker: The Man
and His Dream." Above right: Justin Bishop was superb at portraying an anti-comic book
socialist you loved to hate, but he has no other movie or TV credits. Below: Highlights
of the final battle on the Fox Theater stage between Malakai and The Avenger.

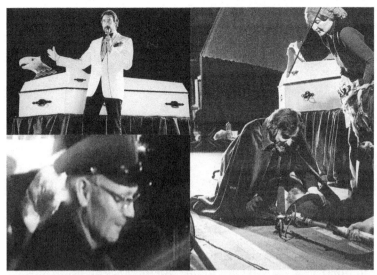

Clockwise: In his speech, Professor Seabrook warns the audience that "Creatures of the undead do exist. Beware the monster, he walks among us." ... A shot of the production crew during the Malakai-Avenger battle ... My father Myron Stanley acting as the doorman to the movie theater.

Top row: publicity photos showcasing my wife Erica in the arms of Jerry Walter aka Malakai. Second row left: Onstage at Paris' Le Grand Rex Theater, where "Nightmare in Blood" premiered in 1977. To the right of me is Italian horror director Dario Argento. Right: that's Bob Wilkins' "Creature Features" set with Morgan Upton as host George Wilson. Below: the 1984 VHS release, unauthorized British version, and the final remastered Techniscope version, released on DVD in 2006.

The very final sequence has Professor Seabrook up on stage, addressing an audience of fans about the dangers of vampirism and murderous spirits that spring up from the past to haunt us. As you enjoy life, he warns the audience, beware. Watch for pure evil which always threatens us.

During production my wife Erica volunteered to pose with Jerry Walter for some provocative vampire stills. Meanwhile, Kenn and I would spend the next year editing the film. We finally got a deal and shot some new footage. Finished by 1977, we submitted a print to the Sixth International Fantasy Festival and were accepted to show "Nightmare in Blood" at Le Grand Rex (the largest theater in Paris) in March 1977. I was invited to appear on the stage with Italian filmmaker Dario Argento, famed for horror films of the *Giallo* genre. The film was well-received and Erica and I had a wonderful week viewing Paris' fabulous sites.

In 1984, a VHS version was finally released by Video City Productions, a company located in the Bay Area. While the film had been shot in Techniscope, a wide-screen format, the quality of the VHS tape was not all that good. Then, suddenly there was an unauthorized British VHS release, which was a complete steal but we were not able to stop it. Finally in 2006, an excellent DVD copy was made and released by Image Entertainment that captured the full Techniscope frame. Kenn and I did an audio commentary that was included in the final release.

So, we had worked for five years to complete "Nightmare in Blood." Yeah, it had its rough-and-tumble moments. But in the end, it was worth the bloody effort.

Above: Bob Wilkins meeting Morgan Upton the night we photographed the
"Fright Flicks" sequence on Bob's set, and Bob's cameo as a horror enthusiast
standing next to Justin Bishop outside the Fox Theater.
Below: Another fan outside the Fox (in an ape costume) was future film director Fred Dekker.

Below: Make-up man James Catania placing the Star of
David on Jerry Walter's forehead, and a local exhibition
poster for the movie's 1978 theatrical release.

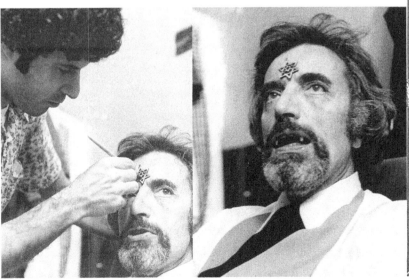

HORROR FANS OF AMERICA!
AT LAST!
A HORROR FILM ABOUT
HORROR FILMS!

FOR 200
YEARS HE
CAPTIVATED
AUDIENCES-
1767...
TRANSYLVANIA
1822...
EDINBURGH
1936...
BERLIN
1947...
HOLLYWOOD
200 YEARS
OF
TERROR!...
UNTIL
NOW!

NIGHTMARE IN BLOOD
JULY 26
SEE IT! AT A LOCAL THEATER!

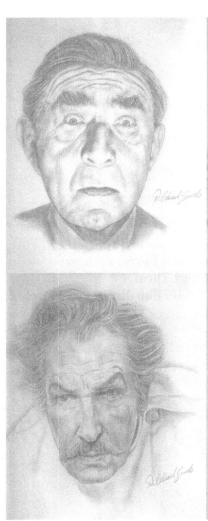

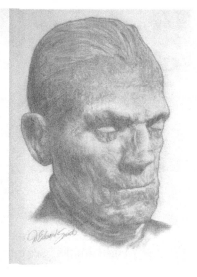

The Art of David Edward Smith: (L-R Top) Bela Lugosi famed for "Dracula" and Ygor in "Son of Frankenstein"; Lon Chaney Jr. remembered as "The Wolf Man,"; Boris Karloff, the greatest Frankenstein of all time. (L-R Bottom) Vincent Price, star of many Hammer horror classics; and Lon Chaney Sr. in his iconic "Phantom of the Opera" role.

Horror Art by a Creature Features Fan

THE SKETCHES you see on this page were accomplished by David Edward Smith, and I felt I needed to bring him to your attention because of his love of "Creature Features," dating as far back as Bob Wilkins' Sacramento shows and even including my years as host in the Bay Area. Smith, today a resident of Vacaville, heard I was editing this book and submitted all five icons.

"I was very impressed with the films you and Bob played," he told me. "The style of black-and-white photography, the use of light and shadows, it had a heavy influence on my future as a commercial artist.

"Ultimately I decided to do art to please myself. I'd tune in the news and it seemed at times like the world was moving in a frightening direction. This inspired me to return to my roots: the classic horror stars of days past, which had started as a result of watching Boris Karloff in 'Frankenstein.' In reality, they are not as scary as some things we observe in real life. They are like old friends. Not so menacing anymore, but reminders of a golden age of cinema."

Thank you, David, for submitting your work, just in time as we wrap things up.

Artist David Edward Smith sketching Vampirella

THE CAREER THAT DRIPPED WITH HORROR

Memories Are Made of These:
QUIET MOMENTS

THERE IS only one second of time.
It is called the Eternal Now.
It passes in an instant. We keep moving ahead into the next Eternal Now and eventually it is a lifetime of Eternal Nows. Some moments we forget, but some we remember vividly. They are like slaps on the face. And they become unforgettable. These moments often return to us at a particular moment. What I call quiet moments when we can focus on that Eternal Now that left us so long ago.

As "Creature Features" host and as newspaperman I have enjoyed many quiet moments. And I now want to share them with you. Highlights of a life that have come and gone. But thanks to photography we are able to see them vividly again and relive them in our imaginations. Make sure you are surrounded by silence, a necessary element of quiet moments.

And so now here they are . . .

Of all my photos, this one always leaps out at me for it captured one of those rare moments when I looked shocked about something as I sat with Bob Wilkins.

HORROR HOSTS

Top Left: Vampira was TV's very first horror hostess, who set new standards on LA TV in the 1950s. She also is the woman in "Plan Nine From Outer Space," and is obviously the inspiration for the Elvira persona.

Top Right: I was an annual guest on "Creepy KOFY Movie Time," which played horror/sci-fi films on Saturday nights for a decade. There were always a few babes in scanty costumes. How sweet it was!

Left Center: It was a tingling moment when I met Kevin Scarpino, oops . . . I mean Son of Ghoul. Following in the footsteps of Cleveland's legendary '60s horror host, Ghoulardi, The Son of Ghoul is the longest running costumed horror host in the nation!

Left Bottom: It was always a pleasure to appear with Miss Misery (Reyna Young), the Bay Area's Queen of Horror. She gave me a cameo role in her feature "Monster of the Golden Gate" and even had me highlighted on the cover of her "Miss Misery's Movie Massacre."

SON OF GHOUL

To John
Your Great

Sorry
Ghoul

MISS MISERY'S MOVIE MASSACRE

Special Guest
John Stanley

Dear John
you are an
dear friend
Baba
Darling
SF

Merry Christmas to all and to all a good fright!

To John & Erica ~
Yours Cruelly...
Elvira

Elvira, Mistress of the Dark, never failed to send me and my wife Erica a signed Christmas card with at least one photo of her on the card.

Top and Center Left: The new "Creature Features" cast featuring 6'7" manservant Livingston, pantomime champion Tangella and host Vincent Van Dahl. They've done hundreds of shows on the Bay Area station KOFY with Tom Wyrsch as director and his son Jeffrey as camera operator.

Top Right: Horror host Mr. Lobo (Erik Lobo to the IRS) became a close friend from the day Bob Wilkins and I began to appear together, and he and his wife Dixie Dellamorto are still busy churning out episodes of "Cinema Insomnia," many of which air on OSI-74, a web television service available on Roku.

Bottom: Miss Misery (Reyna Young, right) and Lord Blood Rah (Frank Wallace-Ailsworth) appeared with me on "Creepy KOFY Movie Time" in October 2011.

LEARNING CURVES

Top Left: My first appearance on Bob Wilkins' "Creature Features," when he played my short horror film "Homecoming: A Fable," gave me the opportunity to meet Miss Horror Film, but I never learned her true identity. But does it matter?

Top Right: I only met Julie Newmar for one afternoon at a Hollywood convention, but who needs excuses to give this photo more than one glance.

Left Center and below: Pepper Alexandria was a belly dancer who often brought her wiggling ladies onto the "Creature Features" set. Years later, I hosted the costume contests staged at her annual "Carnival of Stars" in various Bay Area locations. She remains a most intellectual dancing star and horror fan. She is certainly hip to the cause.

THE CAREER THAT DRIPPED WITH HORROR

Left Center: All I remember is that I fell asleep in my "Creature Features" chair and when I awoke a bikini-clad beauty was stretched out on the coffin next to me, normally used to seat a guest. It became a surprise ending to one of my comedy sketches, the content of which I cannot remember. Except her content.

Right Center: I only met June Wilkinson for a few moments at a Bay Area film convention but it was memorable, as she ranked third behind Mamie Van Doren and Jayne Mansfield in portraying the blonde bombshell.

Bottom Left: Angelique Pettyjohn will always be remembered for portraying Shahna in the "Star Trek" episode "The Gamesters of Triskelion." And for her to wear Shahna's costume when she guested on "Creature Features" . . . I couldn't thank her enough. Unfortunately, Angelique died of cancer in 1992 at the age of 48.

Bottom Right: I had dinner in North Beach with Carol Doda in 2012. She made international news by becoming the first public topless dancer in the early 1960s. She died in 2015 at 78.

LISA TODD AND STANLEY ON THE "HEE HAW" SET IN NASHVILLE (1979)

UP CLOSE & PERSONAL

Top Left: One of the best monster make-up fans is Steven Kirk, who is one of the co-hosts on "Soundwaves TV."

Middle Left to Right: A fan who always participated as if he were part of the family was Danny Wyrsch, brother of Tom Wyrsch. ... Perpetual guest Don Bishop is utterly creative at make-up and costumes, as this photo of him as Bele, a character from the "Star Trek" episode "Let That Be Your Last Battlefield," reveals. ... Promoter Bob Johnson produced many of the shows Bob Wilkins and I attended during the 2000s and I will always consider him one of the best. I have fond memories of his Castro Theater programs and for bringing Judy O'Dea to the Giants ballpark. I interviewed her on the pitcher's mound.

Bottom Left to Right: Eric Yee, shown here with one of his robot props, almost always came to our events wearing a Japanese monster costume. He was also one of Tom Wyrsch's cameramen for "Watch Horror Films, Keep America Strong." ... Tom McClusky, a close friend of Don Bishop's. The two of them usually arrived at the event sites together.

Top Left: An attendee at many of our early WonderCons was Charlie Jennings (above with Bob Wilkins), son of the late Captain Adrian Jennings, a long-time friend of the family. Today, out of San Francisco's Pier 39, Charlie runs Bay Voyager, which features a 12-passenger vessel that takes you to major sites including Alcatraz, the Golden Gate Bridge, and the Bay Bridge.

Top Right: "Sci-Fi Bob" Ekman, film archivist for the Pyschotronix Film Festival, which was held annually at Foothill College. a tradition for more than 25 years, showing 16mm monster movie trailers and retro cartoons. Paul Etcheverry and Scott Moon are co-curators of the event.

Middle Right: Bob Anthony specialized in character make-up that often helped me carry out some of my sketches. He was present nearly all the time when I was doing "Creature Features," and he and his mother will always remain vividly etched in my imagination.

Bottom Left: Me with Will "The Thrill" Viharo and the "Lost In Space" robot. This was taken in 2014 right before he and his wife Monica (the "Tiki Goddess") moved to Seattle, Washington.

Bottom Right: I'm standing with Randy Richards from Grand Forks, North Dakota, who works in the office of U.S. Senator Kevin Cramer (Republican). Randy is a long-time "Creature Features" fan who often has breakfast with me.

THE CAREER THAT DRIPPED WITH HORROR   *PAGE 231*

Signed & Sealed

Top Left: Legendary entertainer Bob Hope signed this when I interviewed him at his Toluca Lake home on the eve of his 90th birthday. For me, it was time spent with the funniest man in radio, TV and movies. He lived to be 100.

Top Middle: That's Clint Walker of "Cheyenne" fame, a Warner Bros. TV classic that lasted from 1955 to 1963. I saw almost every episode when I was growing up in Napa Valley.

Top Right: Jon Provost, who portrayed Timmy on "Lassie" (1954-1964) and again in "The New Lassie" (1989-1992), became a good friend when he appeared at some of our shows to sell his autobiography "Timmy's in the Well."

Bottom Left: Jim Warren, known for publishing *Famous Monsters of Filmland* as well as the comic book magazines *Eerie, Vampirella*, and *Blazing Combat*. Another unforgettable moment, as I had collected most of his comics.

Bottom Right: Independent film director Henry Jaglom, whom I respect for his unusual approach to cinema, signed this photo when he was in San Francisco promoting "Venice/Venice."

Upper Left: Harrison Ford signed this Indiana Jones photo to my son Russ; and below is a double shot signed by "Patriot Games" director Phillip Noyce and star Ford who portrayed CIA analyst Jack Ryan. ... Lower Left: Hawaiian wrestler Professor Toru Tanaka signed this still from "An Eye For An Eye," in which he co-starred with Chuck Norris, when he was my guest on "Creature Features" in 1984.

Upper Right: Fess Parker was a hero of the 1950s, portraying Davy Crockett in Walt Disney TV movies. He was portraying TV's Daniel Boone (1964-1970) when he signed this for me in 1966.

Lower Right: Thank God I asked Clint Eastwood to sign this "Unforgiven" photo to my son Russ. That 1992 Western won Clint two Oscars for acting and directing. Eastwood was once the mayor of Carmel, and rescued the landmark Mission Ranch from condo developers and renovated the property. That is where I met the filmmaking legend for lunch, just days before "Unforgiven" opened.

MORE FAMOUS PEOPLE!

Upper Left: Cloris Leachman, promoting her new film "Herbie Goes Bananas," was among the funniest guests I enjoyed on "Creature Features." She also did a sketch with me during which she said "Let me give you a hand up the stairs" as she gave me a severed hand. I was very saddened when she passed away in January 2021.

Upper Right: That's me locked in a cage at the San Francisco Zoo and those dames are Carol Kane and Lee Grant promoting their film "The Mafu Cage." They tried to find the key to unlock my cage but couldn't, and they wandered away to further their careers in Hollywood. Me, I just kept screaming for help. I guess I really made a monkey of myself. Speaking of monkeys...

Above: It wasn't often I interviewed a chimpanzee. It happened when "Tarzan the Ape Man" opened in the summer of 1981 and a chimp and trainer came to my "Creature Features" set to talk about the movie which starred Bo Derek and was directed by her husband John Derek. My camera crew went absolutely ape.

Right: Film noir expert Eddie Muller, now a regular on Turner Classic Movies, agreed to let me do a documentary in 2010 about his success putting on film noir festivals in several cities around the country. Wayne Hess was my cameraman and editor on "The Czar Of Noir." I first met Eddie when he and his father, the boxing writer-editor for the San Francisco Examiner, came to visit me in the editorial office of the San Francisco Chronicle and thank me for writing several articles about film noir.

THE CAREER THAT DRIPPED WITH HORROR

ON THE
SET

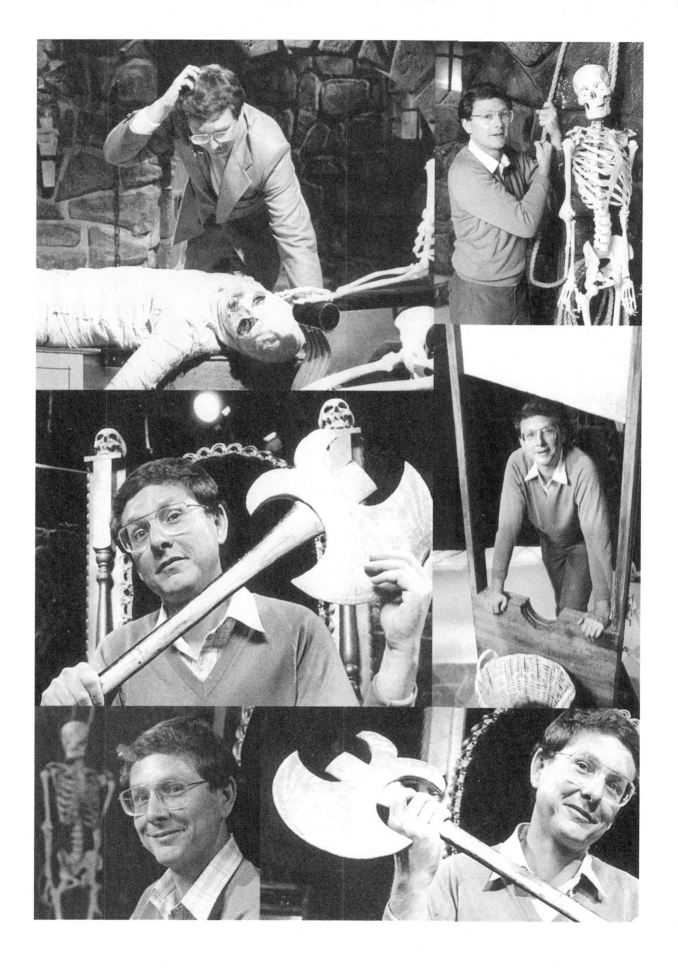

THE CAREER THAT DRIPPED WITH HORROR

Caricatures by famed cartoonist Jim Hummel

SPX Master at KTVU

Jim Minton (pictured below, left and center) became my master of special effects at KTVU by creating multiple images of me for my weekly 30-second promotions for upcoming shows. My favorites: sinking in the bog, two hosts for the price of one, six John Stanleys on cameras at once, or … how about the time I was sawed in half? The caricature (far right) is of Bob Wilkins, as Minton thought he might look in his later years.

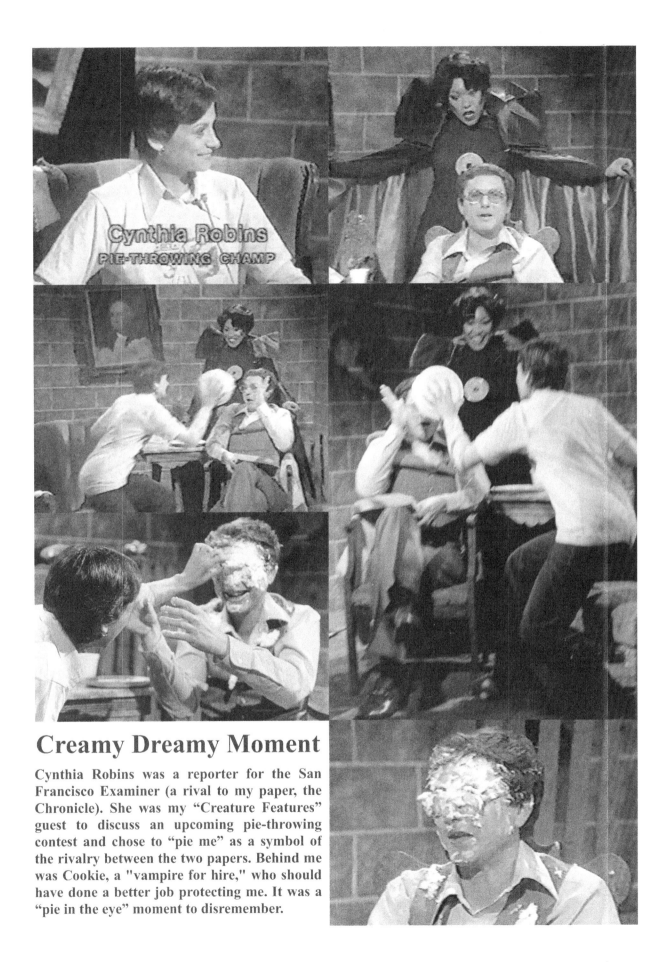

Creamy Dreamy Moment

Cynthia Robins was a reporter for the San Francisco Examiner (a rival to my paper, the Chronicle). She was my "Creature Features" guest to discuss an upcoming pie-throwing contest and chose to "pie me" as a symbol of the rivalry between the two papers. Behind me was Cookie, a "vampire for hire," who should have done a better job protecting me. It was a "pie in the eye" moment to disremember.

A FEW MORE BEFORE WE GO

Left: I was invited to host a film event at the Sahara Tahoe hotel in South Lake Tahoe in 1981.

Right: Carlos Tabarez, brother-in-law to my DVD partner Wayne Hess, portrayed Jack the Ripper in our 2011 DVD set "John Stanley Meets Jack the Ripper." Sad to report that in January 2020, Carlos died of Lou Gehrig's Disease. He was only 67.

Bottom Right: Peter Marino, who worked decades in the record business in Hollywood, resettled in San Francisco and served as a publicist for many years. He became one of my best friends during the 1970-80s and would regularly attend my KTVU "Creature Features" Christmas lunches.

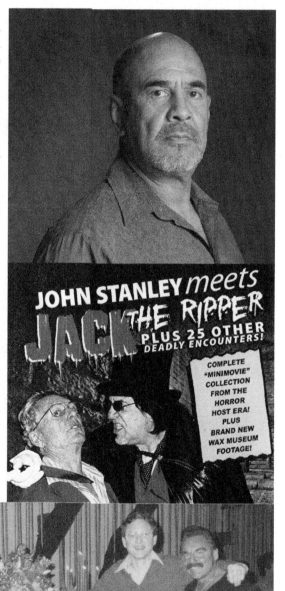

THE CAREER THAT DRIPPED WITH HORROR

Malcolm Whyte remains one of my closest friends and one of the most creative. In 1966, we co-authored "The Great Comic Game Book" for Price/Stern/Sloan and in 1974 co-authored "Monster Movie Game," (right) which Bob Wilkins promoted through an on-air quiz (pictured on page 132). Mal is the creator of San Francisco's Comic Art Museum as well as Troubador Press, which specialized in publishing coloring books for adults as well as educational books for children. Of his 200 books, he authored or co-wrote 45 of them. He also created Word Play Publications, which offers limited, signed illustrated books. He and wife Karen (also a writer) are truly amazing.

Bobby Cannon (left) helped me assemble two sets of "Creature Features" double bill DVDs, and performs with the symphonic metal band Something Wicked.

Frannie Baxter (right), or Francie as friends call her, was once part of a "Star Wars" fan club and came dressed as Princess Leia on the morning I conducted an interview with Christopher Lee (below left) in 1979. She now works for See's Candies and every Christmas brings me a box of chocolates. At no charge, of course.

Below left: That's me with Christopher Lee, who almost walked out as my guest but changed his mind when he saw my filmed interview with Ray Bradbury. Right: My KTVU film editor Bill Longen asks Lee for an autograph that same morning.

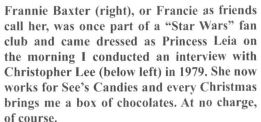

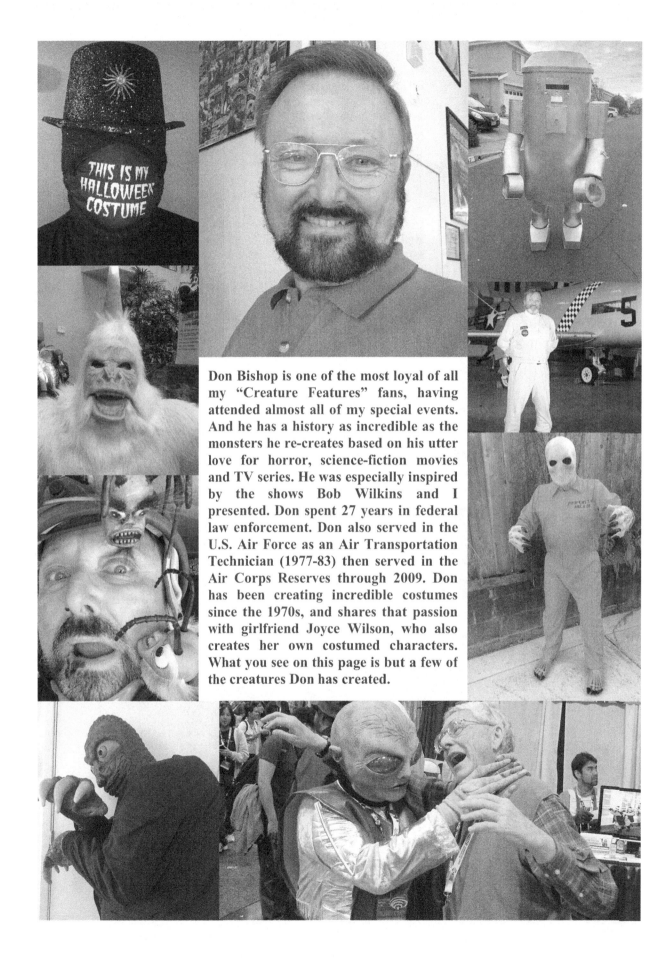

Don Bishop is one of the most loyal of all my "Creature Features" fans, having attended almost all of my special events. And he has a history as incredible as the monsters he re-creates based on his utter love for horror, science-fiction movies and TV series. He was especially inspired by the shows Bob Wilkins and I presented. Don spent 27 years in federal law enforcement. Don also served in the U.S. Air Force as an Air Transportation Technician (1977-83) then served in the Air Corps Reserves through 2009. Don has been creating incredible costumes since the 1970s, and shares that passion with girlfriend Joyce Wilson, who also creates her own costumed characters. What you see on this page is but a few of the creatures Don has created.

THE CAREER THAT DRIPPED WITH HORROR

Bill Longen (upper left), originally my first film editor at KTVU from 1979-80, by sheer coincidence, was the Castro Theater's technical director, whom I worked with during the Bob Johnson shows. Bill also helped me and Wayne Hess produce "I Was a TV Horror Host" by allowing us to shoot scenes at the Castro.

Steve L. Wyatt (upper middle) is one of California's busiest comic-book show producers. A resident of Bakersfield, he created the "Big WOW Comic Festival" set in San Jose and that featured "live on stage Creature Features host John Stanley." In 2016 he sold "The Big WOW" to Apple, after which it became The Silicon Valley Comic Con. After working with Apple co-founder Steve Wozniak, he decided to return to independently producing his own shows in various California cities. Steve has an eBay store, Moonball's Magical Comic Cavalcade (ebay.com/str/Moonball-Comics). He's truly an amazing comic-book lover turned businessman.

Judith Morgan Jennings (below right) was my publicity lady during my "Creature Features" years and will forever be one of the most important members of the KTVU staff. She also saw to it that I got to do many station-related interviews with Hollywood stars for the San Francisco Chronicle. And one time in 1986, I drove with her and her husband, Dean Jennings, to Carmel Valley to interview Jimmy Doolittle, the Air Corps general who led the raid on Tokyo in 1942.

Steve Brown (below left) has done everything from spinning records on the radio to working with the Grateful Dead, but I met him while he was filming Tom Wyrsch's documentaries (see page 18). Whatever job he chooses, his bottom line is "to have the most fun I can."

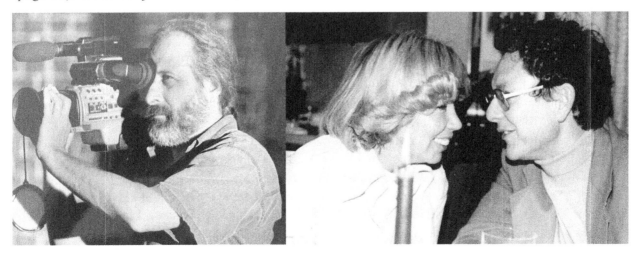

"It's a Wrap!"

AND SO, it's time to lean back a couple of feet, take a deep breath and give thanks to all those who served during the years Bob Wilkins and I made a comeback before the public. I've attempted to display all those major personalities who participated in the WonderCons, CreatureCons and Bob Johnson's Bay Area programs with photographs that thankfully were stored away and have survived the passage of two decades.

It's truly amazing how Bob Wilkins created a cult following. It began in Sacramento where he started out as an advertising executive at an NBC affiliate station, KCRA-TV. He was asked to introduce one horror film, as if the whole thing was going to be a joke, and ended up serving for several years as a Saturday night horror host, relying mainly on his sense of humor, without costume or character make-up. Just plain old Bob in suit and tie, portraying himself. And almost always putting down the upcoming film as he sat in a yellow rocking chair, surrounded by a human skull with a candle stuck into its top and the sign on the wall that became famous: "Watch Horror Films, Keep America Strong."

Because I needed cable TV where I lived, I discovered one night that we were receiving that Sacramento station and I began watching Bob, even writing him letters of encouragement. He responded to those letters and we became friends, even though we never met. When I heard he was moving to KTVU, a station I was very familiar with, often covering its personalities and special movies for the Chronicle, I arranged to interview him a couple of weeks before his debut, scheduled for January 9, 1971.

So it was that the Sunday before the

Bob Wilkins sketch by David Edward Smith

Saturday night he premiered my story appeared in the San Francisco Chronicle, and Bob was off to incredible ratings success for the next few years. We stayed in touch and soon he invited me to guest on his show the night he ran my 16 mm horror short, "Homecoming: A Fable."

We remained great friends and I occasionally was a guest. Meanwhile, Bob also did a Saturday night horror show in Sacramento at KTXL (Channel 40) and was one busy guy, especially when he became a KTVU weatherman for a year or so and then, in 1977, assumed the character of Captain Cosmic, the host of an afternoon series that included serials ("Flash Gordon") and Japanese sci-fi. He continued through January 1980. His weekly show on KTXL would continue into 1981 before his complete retirement from being a horror-host celebrity.

THE CAREER THAT DRIPPED WITH HORROR

When I learned he was leaving his Saturday night show in November 1978, I called him, thinking it would be a great story for the Chronicle. Surprisingly, Bob recommended that I replace him, as I seemed to know more about fantasy films than anyone else. At first, I laughed it off, then realized he was serious, and a few days later agreed to audition for the role in December. A phone call on Christmas Eve from Judith Morgan Jennings, the station's public relations gal, informed me off the record I had been selected to replace Bob. There's never been another Christmas Eve like it.

It was a wonderful five-and-a-half years working at KTVU. I didn't completely follow in the footsteps of Bob as I would spend much time talking about the cast and the history of the films I was hosting. I also got out of the studio with my cameraman to make what I called "minimovies" in Bay Area locations, such as the Chinese Wax Museum at Fisherman's Wharf ("Nightmare in the Chamber of Horrors") and a hotel which had a Sherlock Holmes Museum ("Adventure of the Persian Slipper"). One of my favorites was a face-off with martial arts star Chuck Norris ("Good TV Hosts Wear Black") followed two years later with the two-part "Return of the Channel 2 Dragon" when I met Norris and Richard Roundtree making "An Eye For An Eye" in the foothills of Orinda. Another personal favorite was "Attack of the Incredible Killer Scarecrow." I would also do 30-second "Creature Features" promotions with famous stars such as Buddy Ebsen, Leonard Nimoy, Cloris Leachman, Rodney Dangerfield, Edy Williams, Misty Rowe and countless others.

John Stanley sketch by David Edward Smith

Because of my Hollywood contacts I was able to convince the Walt Disney studio to bring the star of a new movie to my set on a Friday so I could do an interview and have it on air around the same time the film was premiering. Then that same Friday wife Erica and I would meet that star at Ernie's Restaurant, one of San Francisco's finest, where I would conduct an interview for the Chronicle. (One of the most memorable moments was meeting Ray Bradbury a week before the opening of Disney's "Something Wicked This Way Comes.")

After leaving Channel 2 I had never dreamed that the "Creature Features" franchise would come to life again. Yeah, I continued covering entertainment celebrities for the San Francisco Chronicle and I kept writing and publishing my movie guides but nowhere was there a clue about Bob and I rejoining ranks. Until that fate-filled meeting in 1999 with Tom Wyrsch.

Ironically, Tom became a "Creature Features" producer in the fall of 2016 and has at press time directed more than 300 shows hosted by Jeff Bodean (aka Vincent Van Dahl) with Livingston and Tangella as supporting players. Life does have its ironic twists and turns, and I thank Bob Wilkins and all the others who were there year after year, giving their support. Doing all they could to keep the fandom alive.

It was great, and I will never forget any of you and what all of you stood for, and how you all came to symbolize a major highlight of my life. – **John Stanley**

A Celebration Of Life

Bob Wilkins

1932 – 2009

ANOTHER JOHN STANLEY CLASSIC!

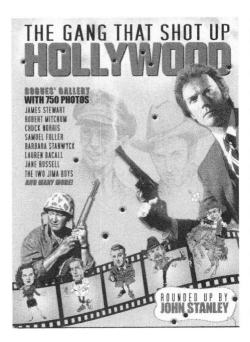

A collection of his one-on-one interviews with some of Hollywood's most popular stars:

* CLINT EASTWOOD: After a surprise meeting on the set of "Rawhide," enjoy four encounters covering "Dirty Harry," "Unforgiven" (at Clint's Mission Ranch Inn in Carmel), "Flags of Our Fathers" and "Letters from Iwo Jima."

* JAMES STEWART: Enter Jimmy's Beverly Hills home and meet dogs Beau and Simba as Mr. Stewart describes highlights of his film career, including the making of "It's a Wonderful Life" and a steady stream of classic Westerns. During a second visit Stanley covers Jimmy's films made with Alfred Hitchcock, including "Vertigo" and "Rope." Also learn details about Jimmy's World War II standing tall as a B-24 bomber pilot.

* ROBERT MITCHUM: The truth, told for the first time, why and how Bob was arrested during a drug orgy back in 1948. Strictly private details.

FEMME FATALES GALORE, ALL INTERVIEWED IN PRIVATE:

JANE RUSSELL: The sexy history of making "The Outlaw" with Howard Hughes (below)

COLEEN GRAY: Behind the scenes making "Kiss of Death" with Richard Widmark

MARIE WINDSOR: She had more than a leg to stand on, and a "Narrow Margin" on film

IDA LUPINO: The memorable "High Sierra" femme, and one of the first hit female directors

EVELYN KEYES: How she went from cheesecake to a queen of leading ladies

LAUREN BACALL: To have or have not? Humphrey Bogart decided to have . . .

BARBARA STANWYCK: When she was starring in TV's "The Big Valley"

CARROLL BAKER: How she came to be the star of "Baby Doll"

OTHER MALE MOVIE MEN COVERED IN DEPTH:

KARL MALDEN, on Alcatraz Island yet, making "Streets of San Francisco"

EDDIE MULLER and how he became a savior of noir motion pictures

MICHAEL DOUGLAS, on the edge of making "One Flew Over the Cuckoo's Nest"

ORIGINALLY SOLD FOR $21.99 . . . TODAY YOU CAN ORDER IT FOR JUST $10 PLUS $5 FOR SHIPPING AND HANDLING

JUST GO TO stanleybooks.net . . where you can order via PayPal or you can send check or money order to 1082 Grand Teton Drive, Pacifica, CA 94044

ROBERT BLOCH FANTASIES

This is John Stanley's 1987 trade paperback featuring short stories by Robert Bloch that originally ran in the pulp magazine *Fantastic Adventures* back in the 1940s. Lefty Feep was a racetrack tout who was forever falling into fantasy worlds occupied by dancing mice, bowling dwarfs, invisible clothing, flying carpets and a chicken laying a Golden Age.

In addition to seven reprinted short stories and one brand-new thrown into the mix by Bloch, there is also a lengthy introduction by horror novelist Chelsea Quinn Yarbro, as well

as a detailed second intro by John Stanley, detailing how he first encountered Bloch while free-lancing for Forrest J. Ackerman's *Castle of Frankenstein* magazine. Stanley also details how he traveled to Bloch's home and pitched the idea of reprinting the Lefty Feep short stories. There are eight sketches (one for each short story) by Kenn Davis, who had co-produced the 1977 horror film thriller "Nightmare in Blood" and who had co-written with Stanley the historic "Bogart '48" paperback novel released in 1980.

ORDER THIS HISTORIC TRADE PAPERBACK FROM CREATURES AT LARGE PRESS FOR ONLY $15 PLUS $5 FOR SHIPPING AND HANDLING.

You can order via PayPal through the website **stanleybooks.net** or pay by check or money order to John Stanley, 1082 Grand Teton Drive, Pacifica CA 94044. Tell Stanley to whom you would like the book to be signed.

"I WAS A TV HORROR HOST": THE JOHN STANLEY STORY ON A 2-DVD SET

Disc #1: A History of the San Francisco-Bay Area TV Horror Specialist plus comedy promotions with Chuck Norris, Leonard Nimoy, Buddy Ebsen, plus the comedy game show "Monster Movie Quiz," which originally ran on Bob Wilkins' TV series.

Disc #2: Lengthy meetings with Leonard Nimoy, Christopher Lee, Ray Harryhausen, Ray Bradbury, Anthony Perkins, Joe Dante, Karl Malden, Rodney Dangerfield, Arnold Schwarzenegger, Max Von Sydow, Robert Bloch, Rick Baker and the great Bob Wilkins

$25 plus $5 for shipping and handling . . . Order through PayPal at stanleybooks.net or send check or money order to John Stanley, 1082 Grand Teton Drive, Pacifica CA 94044.

THE CAREER THAT DRIPPED WITH HORROR

Made in the USA
Monee, IL
27 December 2022

23712437R00142